W9-BFE-364

VANCOUVER'S GLORY YEARS

VANCOUVER'S GLORY YEARS

PUBLIC TRANSIT
1890–1915

HEATHER CONN and **HENRY EWERT**
FOREWORD BY MAYOR LARRY CAMPBELL

whitecap

Visit our web site at www.whitecap.ca

Edited by Elaine Jones
Proofread by Marial Shea
Cover design by Jacqui Thomas
Front cover credits, clockwise from upper left: CVA TRANS. P. 115 N.70 (see p. 97);
    George E. Timms Photo, VPL 19782 (see p. 22); CVA SGN 881 (see p. 83);
    CVA L9N 1189.3 (see p. 190)
Back cover credit: George E. Timms Photo, VPL 8395 (see p. 202)
Interior design by Margaret Lee / bamboosilk.com

Printed and bound in Canada

National Library of Canada Cataloguing in Publication Data
Conn, Heather
    Vancouver's glory years : public transit, 1890-1915 / Heather Conn,
        Henry Ewert.

Includes bibliographical references and index.
ISBN 1-55285-517-1

    1. Street-railroads--British Columbia--Vancouver--History. 2. Local
transit--British Columbia--Vancouver--History. 3. Vancouver (B.C.)--History.
I. Ewert, Henry, 1937- II. Title.

HE4509.V35C66 2003   388.4'6'0971133   C2003-905951-0

The publisher acknowledges the support of the Canada Council for the Arts and the Cultural Services Branch of
the Government of British Columbia for our publishing program. We acknowledge the financial support of the
Government of Canada through the Book Publishing Industry Development Program for our publishing activities.

To the memory of Ted Gardner,
who understood the beauty of streetcars and interurbans

Acknowledgements

This book would never have happened without the support and enthusiasm of two key people: Henry Ewert, who recognized the untapped merit of many of the photos, lauded the project's vision and scope, and provided many decades' worth of expertise; and David Stumpo, former president of Coast Mountain Bus Company, whose passion for transit history and belief in its ability to enrich our lives fuelled this journey.

Many thanks to all the archivists who provided research assistance, particularly Pat Crawford, Information Specialist for BC Hydro's Information Services in Burnaby. Daien Ide in Collections at the Japanese Canadian National Museum in Burnaby keenly offered book sources and gave much-appreciated feedback on portions of the manuscript.

It was a delight to hear the personal stories of early transit-related life told by the late Ted Gardner and Vancouver retiree Ralph Shaw. Their willingness to share lively memories is greatly appreciated. Similarly, Jim Wong-Chu of the Asian Canadian Writers' Workshop provided valuable insights and suggestions for further reading regarding the treatment of Asians in Vancouver's formative years.

I hope that this book will add new pieces to the jigsaw puzzle of Vancouver's transit and human history, yet it owes much to those who already created many of the pieces and painstakingly defined their borders. One who stands out in this regard is Patricia Roy of the history department at the University of Victoria, who published the first ground-breaking research on transit history in the Vancouver region and who kindly reviewed major portions of this manuscript. Jean Barman, Professor of Educational Studies at the University of B.C., shared primary research and other assistance while her own Vancouver history books served as welcome reference.

Additional thanks go to researcher and transit enthusiast Brian Elder, who volunteered his patience and extensive knowledge to read the manuscript and offered helpful background research, and to Robert McCullough, Robin Rivers and Leanne McDonald at Whitecap Books for their overwhelming support and encouragement. Editor Elaine Jones's thorough treatment of, and thoughtful comments regarding, the manuscript were much appreciated.

Lastly, a huge thank you to my parents, Marian and Al Conn, whose ceaseless curiosity, intellectual depth and lifelong fascination with, and appreciation of, history, combined with avid reading and international travel, provided a blueprint for my life, my academic studies, and this book.

Authors' Note

Although this book focuses on Vancouver's early transit past, it seeks to highlight the subject within the broader historical significance of the period. Hence, some photo captions mention important landmarks and pertinent dates and events unrelated to transit.

For those who seek an exhaustive account of public transportation only during this time, we recommend Henry Ewert's book *The Story of the B.C. Electric Railway Company*.

The inclusion of individual photos of early transit employees is based solely on the availability and relevance of these images and their related subject matter. The selection does not imply a slight to the hundreds whose names do not appear here; instead, we hope that these photos will serve to symbolize and acknowledge the contributions of all transit employees during this period.

The reader might appreciate a reminder that cameras were indeed rare during this time, limited almost exclusively to professional photographers and well-heeled corporations.

Throughout the book, the modern term "public transit" is used synonymously with street railways, even though only the latter phrase was in use during this period. In some cases, we have rounded off numbers relating to distance or length of transit lines.

Please note that the informal term "trams" is used in reference only to interurbans, not streetcars. This was how the term was used in the Vancouver region, in contrast to the British Isles, where "tram" referred to a streetcar. (To confuse the issue, local media at the time sometimes referred to streetcars as trams.)

Contents

Foreword

Vancouver's Glory Years: Public Transit 1890–1915 is a marvellous review of Vancouver's turn-of-the-century boom period. Its focus is the streetcar and the interurban – the earliest forms of public transit in Vancouver. It tells the story – with photographs, archival tales and personal anecdotes – of how public transit wove together the city's urban form, created its streets and neighbourhoods and helped shape the emerging social character of its citizens.

Little more than a century ago, in 1881, early Vancouver was staked out by engineers of the Canadian Pacific Railway. The town settlement of a few hundred people was then known as Granville or Gastown. Within two decades of its incorporation Vancouver became British Columbia's largest city. Population growth was astonishingly swift — 20 per cent a year in those early decades. By 1890 – just three years after C.P.R.'s first passenger train arrived from Montreal – the city of Vancouver welcomed a new type of rail service: the electric streetcar. With the opening of its first 10 kilometres of track, the new street railways brought other "modernizing" technologies to Vancouver – electricity and street lighting.

That wasn't all. As Vancouver's Glory Years amply illustrates, the streetcar and interurban lines carved out new corridors of residential housing, retail districts and commercial trade across the city and region, eventually all the way to Chilliwack. Many of Vancouver's present-day neighbourhoods – Fairview, Kitsilano, Mt. Pleasant, Kerrisdale and Grandview – grew up and prospered around the streetcar right of ways. Our key shopping streets – in Kerrisdale, along 4th Avenue, Main Street, Dunbar, Cambie, Commercial Drive and much of downtown – emerged during the streetcar era. These streets remain thriving retail centres today largely because of the concentrated storefronts and commercial activity spurred by the popular use of public transit over 100 years ago.

The basic pattern of those street railways was further established and extended by the Bartholomew Plan in the late 1920s – a network that today continues to shape and mould city planning, development and travel patterns. Today, a similar interplay between transit demand, land-use patterns and commercial activity is clearly evident; it remains a central factor in how City Hall and the citizens it represents decide on how and where to build, expand and use public transit in Greater Vancouver.

We can see now how transit's impact was as much social as structural. Public transit became one of the great levellers of modern urban life, breaking down personal and cultural barriers between people as they shared the physical space and novelty of the street railways. The streetcar system extended mobility for women, one factor among many in their growing independence. For people of every background, public transit made the city more accessible and expanded their horizons of civic interaction.

Today, our daily transit trips remain a container of social and civic life. As Mayor, I often take the Broadway trolley bus or B-Line bus as I commute between my home and City Hall. Every day I delight in the many faces, new and familiar, who journey on the bus. Our trolleys and buses still serve as a kind of city crossroads, a mobile meeting-place of students, tourists, office workers, business people, seniors: citizens of all stripes and sensibilities, of varying colours, classes and ages.

By the 1950s, the electric trolley bus system took over from the street railway system, while still providing efficient, quiet and pollution-free travel along Vancouver's main corridors. Indeed, most of those Vancouver trolleys travel along the old streetcar routes of yesteryear. Trolley buses are the workhorse of the entire region's public transit system, serving up to 40 per cent of all daily transit users. Happily, TransLink, the region's transportation authority, plans to fully replace the existing fleet with new trolleys by 2006.

Meanwhile, the Expo SkyTrain line, built in 1986, follows the east-west corridor of a planned, but never built, interurban route. More recently, the region has started the West Coast Express and the new Millennium Line. In Vancouver we've begun a modest revival of the heritage streetcar along the south shore of False Creek, with plans afoot to roll streetcar service into the downtown. So sometimes everything old is new again.

Streetcars may now hold minor status in a multi-functional transportation system of pedestrians and cyclists, motor vehicles and roads, shuttles and handyDARTs, tourist buses and trolleys, SkyTrains and SeaBuses, commuter rail and air travel. Yet Vancouver's transit system continues as a crucial public service and amenity, a central element of civic infrastructure. It remains the site of social interaction and the subject of ongoing political debate and public passions – just as streetcars and interurban trains were in the early days of the Lower Mainland.

Vancouver's Glory Years: Public Transit 1890–1915 is a delightful and engaging tour of Vancouver's transit history. Authors Heather Conn and Henry Ewert have provided all of us with an insightful reminder of how deep an imprint the streetcars and interurbans left on Vancouver and the surrounding region. Congratulations to them for their tremendous efforts.

Enjoy the read, and happy commuting.

Larry Campbell
Mayor, Vancouver, British Columbia

A Glimpse of Glory

On June 27, 1890, an event occurred in the little boom town of Vancouver that altered its destiny forever. Two parallel rails, little more than three miles (5 kilometres) long, wound past Burrard Inlet's squatters and wooden shacks, past tree stumps and plank roads, and beyond West End mansions. Mere strips of steel, they passed seven lumber mills, dozens of hotels and three chartered banks, and ran almost up to the original wooden Granville Street Bridge. The first car to run on these rail lines introduced a remarkable service that this port town had never seen – one only newly available even in New York City – public transit.

Six state-of-the-art streetcars began regular service that day. Until then, Vancouver had never moved people en masse in public vehicles, let alone powered machines by electricity. Widespread use of electrical power was still an untried, dubious prospect at the time, but visionaries opted for it over horse-drawn streetcars, the city's original choice. This decision determined the course of Vancouver's progress over the next 25 years; public transit, known then as street railways, launched a glorious period of unparalleled growth and development that helped to define the city well into the 1960s and beyond.

Vancouver's early "people's vehicles" with affordable fares were an exciting innovation for a city of 10,000 residents, who otherwise had only their feet, a bicycle or a costly horse-and-carriage ride for transportation through muddy urban streets.

Around the turn of the century, no dream seemed unreachable. Vancouver's entrepreneurs and power-brokers dreamed of replacing swamp and stumps with Edwardian elegance. A fever of construction, fuelled by Canadian Pacific Railway (C.P.R.) dollars, brought real estate developments, a glitzy opera house, expensive bridges and opulent homes to the forested landscape.

The city's newly mobile pioneers developed routines of daily commuting. They chatted up the streetcar conductor, who collected (besides fares) mail and parcels and produce from merchants along the way to deliver en route to at-home mothers. For early Vancouverites, public transit was a mechanical magic carpet, whooshing them away to shop, visit, run errands and reach ever-expanding leisure activities, such as sporting events and entertainment facilities.

1893

Vancouver Electric Railway & Light Co. Ltd.

TIME TABLE

CARS GOING WEST

(MT. PLEASANT)	From 6:15 a.m. to 12 noon and from 7:30 to 10:30 p.m. Minutes past each hour				Between the hours of 12 noon and 7 p.m. Minutes past each hour				
Leave 9th Ave	00	15	30	45	00	12	24	36	48
Market Hall	09	24	39	54	09	21	33	45	57
Carrall St	12	27	42	57	12	24	36	48	00
Post Office	15	30	45	00	15	27	39	51	03
Hotel Vancouver	19	34	49	04	19	31	43	55	07
Arr. Drake St.	23	38	53	08	22	34	46	58	10

CARS GOING EAST

(COLONIAL HOTEL)									
Leave Drake St	08	23	38	53	02	14	26	38	50
Hotel Vancouver	12	27	42	57	06	18	30	42	54
Post Office	15	30	45	00	09	21	33	45	57
Carrall St	18	33	48	03	12	24	36	48	00
Market Hall	21	36	51	06	16	28	40	52	04
Arr. 9th Ave	30	45	00	15	24	36	48	00	12

First car leaves 9th Ave .... 6:15 a.m. | First car leaves Drake St ..... 6:23 a.m.
Last   "   "   " .... 10:30 p.m. | Last   "   "   " ..... 10:53 p.m.

SUNDAY SERVICE from 9:15 a.m. to 9:30 p.m. Time the same as morning service week days. Last car leaves Mt. Pleasant for West End at 9:30 p.m. Last car leaves West End for Mt. Pleasant at 9:53 p.m.

C. F. HUTCHINGS,
Superintendent.

1530

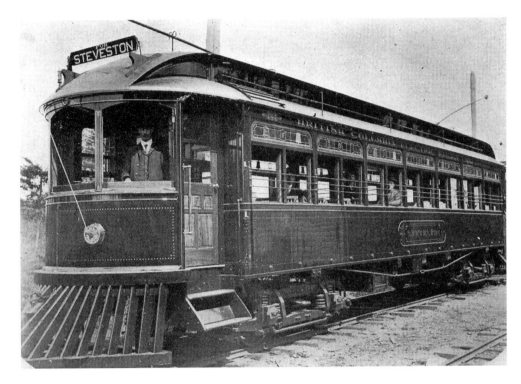

A LONG LIFE — The "Steveston," destined for Steveston from Vancouver, was a home-built, state-of-the-art interurban in 1905. Rebuilt in 1912 and numbered 1207, it operates today, restored, on Vancouver's Downtown Historical Railway.

PHOTO SOURCE: HE COLLECTION

This public-ride concept, so familiar today, had no precedent in pre-1900 Vancouver. Transit news, however minor, made the city's front-page headlines for years. Many people boarded an open-air vehicle just for the pleasure of the trip, with no destination in mind. (This pastime was honed as a commercial venture in 1909, when the city's first roofless observation car provided daily sightseeing trips with colourful entertainment to tourists and locals alike.) Some doctors claimed that a simple streetcar ride could aid relaxation and cure insomnia.

Public transit transformed daily life for the majority of Vancouverites in the late 1890s. For the first time, people of every race, religion and nationality could sit, stand or jostle under the same roof for the same fare, whether an east-end housewife, transient logger, Chinese restaurateur, downtown lawyer, or cannery worker of First Nations or Japanese descent. (Although they all rode in the same cars in Vancouver's early days, passengers of native or Asian ancestry on other transit modes, such as stagecoaches, had to sit in the back seat.)

Shrewd realtors soon cashed in on public transit. Through newspaper advertisements and billboard-like signs, they used transit service as a primary selling tool to woo settlers and developers to vast, uncleared tracts of land. Some realtors, such as the C.P.R., even helped to finance the construction of transit lines; they were well aware that a new transit extension would prompt a fat increase in land values. Population growth followed the direction of streetcar lines, creating communities that remain today, such as Cedar Cottage, Point Grey, Grandview and Shaughnessy. Streetcar service enabled Vancouver's exploding population to spread over a wide area and create

INTERURBAN BEAUTY — Gleaming in jade green, a race track special train, led by interurban 1501, and trailed by 1307, 1600, and 1308, waits for its passengers in the loop at Richmond's Minoru Park race track in the summer of 1914.

PHOTO SOURCE: HE COLLECTION

suburbs. Low-income employees could live in pleasant, family neighbourhoods and commute to work without the need to live in congested areas closer to their workplace.

Soon after public transit began in Vancouver, city residents saw the service as a new *right* of passage. Settlers and retailers wrote strongly worded petitions demanding streetcar operations in their community. They repeatedly requested more vehicles, more frequent service and longer hours. In response to ever-increasing demand, road crews laid so many new streetcar tracks and expanded existing transit lines so furiously that a special streetcar delivered paycheques directly to track workers on site. An ever-widening array of tracks and lines created a phenomenal infrastructure, which laid the foundation for the city's bus routes many decades later. A number of the city's streetcar lines remained almost unchanged until they were shut down in the mid-1950s.

Local businessmen joined forces with British investors in 1897 to ensure transit's presence in Vancouver under the new B.C. Electric Railway Company. The company built a deluxe, six-storey head office and depot downtown, which still remains today at the corner of Carrall and Hastings streets. The imposing brick structure surpassed any of the city's pillared banks or official buildings of the day. Dozens and dozens of interurbans left on daily schedules from its premises while hundreds of employees, from track greasers and service crews to inspectors and building teams, found stable, permanent work with good benefits with the well-respected company. Such guaranteed income was rare at a time of resource-based seasonal labour. For many, economic prosperity had arrived.

Confidence ran high at B.C. Electric when orders for new vehicles proved too large to meet. The upstart company made a daring move and decided to no longer depend on U.S. and eastern Canadian manufacturers. Instead, it proudly announced that it would build its own manufacturing plant in neighbouring New Westminster. At these shops, highly skilled tradesmen built the first-ever, made-in-B.C. interurban cars in 1903; the vehicles' sleek craftsmanship brought widespread admiration and awards, earning them distinction as "the handsomest and best equipped electric cars in America," according to *The British Columbian*. The shops produced top transit vehicles for more than a decade. The luxurious cars reflected the period's Edwardian finery; they offered spacious rattan seats with head rests, toilets, a water cooler and a smoking section.

The interurban served as a significant catalyst for expansion and settlement. Canada's longest interurban railway line, 64 miles (102.7 kilometres) from New Westminster to Chilliwack, opened in 1910 and proved revolutionary to the future of the Fraser Valley. It brought rail freight and passenger service to Vancouver's outlying areas for the first time; Vancouverites, in turn, enjoyed daily delivery of fresh milk and produce from the valley's farmers, along with express packages, mail and other freight. This spelled the end of steamboat business on the Fraser River; settlers could now access land and goods directly. Public transit had proven it could outplay the competition.

These glory years of Vancouver's population boom, commercial success and transit expansion spawned a new dilemma: obsolescence. The city changed and grew so quickly by 1900 that many transit features, from depots and car barns to the first streetcars, were outdated in less than a decade. The transit system had already outgrown itself, swallowed by its own success, but it continued to reflect the eager optimism of its origins, adding trend-setting vehicles, such as the "stepless, " or hobble skirt, car in 1913. For the first time, a public vehicle was tailor made to meet a cultural requirement – women who wore constricting hobble skirts could step easily onto the streetcar because the floor was only a few inches above street level.

In just over two decades, Vancouver transit had shifted from simple, utilitarian roots to fashionable innovation, change that paralleled the city's own evolution from stumbling adolescent to confident sophisticate. No other period in Vancouver's history is defined by such overwhelming duckling-to-swan transformation as the high-flying years from 1890 to 1915. Such a heady transition did not come easily; during these years, the city and its street railways endured a deep recession, bankruptcies, the start of the First World War, and the rising popularity of another transportation trend, which would drastically threaten, and ultimately overtake, the hegemony of the public transit vehicle: the automobile.

In today's Vancouver, these once-disparate modes, the car and public transit, now meet on the same streets, sharing the path that streetcars began so distinctly more than a century ago. At the start of the last century, buoyed by hopeful dreams, no one could guess where those first simple tracks would ultimately lead. The city of the 1890s had eyes only for new beginnings, not to foresee distant endings. Electricity lit the way into 25 years of glory.

CHAPTER ONE

Survival & Revival
1890 – 1897

IN THE BEGINNING – Vancouver had six streetcars on site when regular transit service began on June 27, 1890. Car 12, one of the flagship originals built by John Stephenson Company in New York City, is shown here on Powell Street in 1890, its Stephenson advertising still visible. Canadian Pacific rail cars stand in the background.

At the time, the notion of electric streetcars was only four years old, the same age as the city of Vancouver. There was no finer streetcar on the continent than the one in this photo: little Vancouver stood in the vanguard of public transportation.

The Phoenix Rises

The completion of our street car and electric light system will be hailed with delight by all our citizens. It marks a new era in the history of Vancouver . . . Not only to the business man who, in the heart of the city, thinks it necessary to go at full speed in order to keep up with his work, but more especially to the residents in the suburbs, this electric tramway [streetcar] will be indeed a blessing.

The Daily World, **June 26, 1890**

Two trial streetcars "as full as it was possible for them to be"
A modern observer might call it baby-snatching, but in 1890 Vancouver, it was a move to make history. When the city's first streetcar, number 14, rattled along Westminster Avenue (now Main Street) to Hastings Street for a trial run on June 26, a Mr. Snyder grabbed a neighbour's baby and ran off with him to catch the novelty vehicle. Mr. Snyder jumped on board in the middle of the block, the infant locked in his arms, and called back to the anxious mother: "He's going to be the first baby in Vancouver to ride on a streetcar," reported the June 28, 1935, issue of the transit newsletter *The Buzzer*. The child's image-conscious mother replied: "But his face is dirty." She needn't have worried. The two passengers disembarked after a short ride, and her tiny son, James Edward Smith, earned an historic distinction from that day on, dirty face and all.

On that special Friday, all schoolchildren got time off to watch the strange machine that ran without horses. Astonished boys ran along the tracks as adults applauded this work of wonder on its 3.35-mile (5.6-kilometre) route. Even more than a half-century later, New Westminster resident W.B. Wellwood remembered: "The streetcars were a real event in those days, and we used to stop our games to watch one go by."[1]

1890

It was a matter of amazement that horses were not startled by this innovation [streetcar service].

The B.C. Electric Employees' Magazine, November 1924

- Besides public transit, telephones and electric light, Vancouver has 2,700 buildings, including five schools, a city hall, seven lumber mills, 55 hotels, two iron foundries, a sugar refinery, the provincial government building and courthouse and three chartered banks.[8]

Vancouver's first streetcar, which appeared well before the turn of the century, rose like a phoenix from the city's ashes; the Great Fire had wiped out Vancouver entirely, except for one hotel, four years earlier. The street railway system was introduced with pride and symbolized the Terminal City's optimism. This west-coast port of hardy pioneers, hopeful immigrants, ambitious businessmen and itinerant workers would rebuild a city of enviable proportions. *The Daily World* shared its praise with the city's readers on June 26, 1890:

The [streetcar] line is a splendid one, equipped with all the most modern machinery, and is probably unexcelled by any on the continent. No expense has been spared in ensuring perfection, every detail being carefully arranged ere a trial trip was made, and the company and its officials must indeed be congratulated on the success achieved.

Only five years earlier, the hammering of the last spike on the Canadian Pacific Railway had linked the Pacific coast to eastern Canada for the first time. Now, this former transient town was a bona fide city – with its own streetcar service! The *Vancouver Daily News-Advertiser* wrote of the test run:

The trial was as satisfactory as could be desired. . . . [A] number of shareholders and scores of citizens [took] advantage of the opportunity to test the comfort of a mode of locomotion now possible for the first time in Vancouver. There are probably many persons in the city who have not before seen an electric railway in operation. But whether they had or not, all those who yesterday witnessed the initial trips made by the car of the Vancouver Electric Railway and Lighting [sic] company had before them a service as complete as that offered in any city on this continent . . . [T]he manner in which the car swung around the sharp curves last evening showed that both the road and its designer are "all right."[2]

This vanguard vehicle proved that the dream of electricity as a viable new source of power could come true, when most machinery still ran on steam or coal. On the day of the streetcar's trial run – June 26, 1890 – Vancouver's *Daily World* reported with anticipation: "The long distances one is obliged to travel is going to [have] . . . rendered rapid locomotion necessary, and this could only be obtained by means of electric power, which is now fast taking the lead all the world over." The streetcar put Vancouver on the map both literally and figuratively; the city kept pace with both Toronto and New York City in the transit race for technical innovation. The technology was scarcely four years old.

On Vancouver's test runs, conductor Dugald Carmichael saw his role as history-in-the-making. He kept the first fare, a five-cent piece dated 1886, as a souvenir, which he hung from his gold watch and chain. (He received it from passenger Lillian Parkes, later

Mrs. F. R. Lyne.) Carmichael apparently liked to show off his memorable fare in subsequent years, reported the August 9, 1935, issue of *The Buzzer*, but he always made it clear that he didn't take it from the company; he had deposited his own nickel in return.

The Vancouver Daily News-Advertiser reported that although the test cars ran all day, they did not carry passengers until after 6 o'clock, when "from that time two cars were running until ten o'clock, and were all the time as full as it was possible for them to be. No accident occurred, even a runaway, the horses surprising people by the way they took to them!" The Vancouver *Daily World* declared triumphantly on June 26:

> *The practical completion of this work marks another epoch in the history of Vancouver. This is an era of rapid movements, and the operation of our street railway will prove to be of incalculable advantage to the citizens generally. Those residing in the suburbs will be brought within a few minutes' time of the heart or business centre of the city. New sections of the city will be rendered accessible to the business man, who after the hurry of the day is over, desires to retire to a quiet, secluded portion of the city. In brief, the Vancouver Electric Street Railway [sic] fills a long-felt want, an aching void, which will be appreciated by every one who has to travel any great distance.*

Two days after the grand occasion of the streetcar's trial runs, Mayor David Oppenheimer, who had invested heavily in street railways, and other dignitaries rode the first of four streetcars that launched the city's official transit service. As the inaugural vehicle came along Westminster Avenue, the mayor called out to Annie Parkes, who was walking on the sidewalk: "Come on board, Mrs. Parkes, and be the first lady to ride on the electric car in Vancouver."[3] So she did, and as the first paying passenger, set a precedent for female passengers to follow.

Electric power a "new fangled notion"

The choice to power Vancouver's streetcars with electricity was indeed radical for its time. Electrical power was still in its infancy and many deemed it risky. "There is no doubt that the electric light wire is dangerous – that it has killed a great many people," warned the *Vancouver Daily World* on January 14, 1890. Vancouver's own street lights, described

A jaunt with jolts: Don't carry your watch in your shoe

The perceived threat of a lightning strike or electric shock while riding a streetcar had some early Vancouverites more than a little nervous. Wouldn't that high trolley wire attract angry energy from the sky?

The Daily World tried to pacify its readers about such concerns. Before regular streetcar service even began, a June 26, 1890 article explained: "There is practically no danger from lightning to a passenger on an electric road. It is safer by far, to be in an electric car in a storm than in any other conveyance, as paths are supplied which will at least conduct the lightning down under the car."

The article gave a technical breakdown of the car's equipment, noting that each vehicle had a lightning arrester that would allow the bolt to bypass the motors and "escape to the earth." It added that the chances of receiving an electric shock as a streetcar passenger were minimal:

> *The sparking sometimes seen when an electric car starts is due to the wheels getting on to the dirt and the jumping of the electricity from the wheels to the rails. This, however, is done away with by recent inventions. . . . Expert electrical engineers say there is absolutely no danger of a shock while on or about a car. Employees often receive slight shocks while operating the cars, but thus far there have been no ill effects. Watches are not magnetized, so a well proportioned railway motor has any perceptible magnetic field over two feet from it, and unless one carries his watch in his shoe it would never be in the slightest affected.*

as "mere glow-worms," hardly gave a strong endorsement for full-bodied power; each carbon globe or bulb, installed on August 8, 1887, gave the equivalent light of 32 candles.[4] In fact, alderman Humphreys had pooh-poohed a proposal to use electric lights at city hall; he opposed the use of "any new fangled notions" like electricity. Despite his protests, city council contracted to light city hall with electric lights, each one the equivalent of 16 candles.[5]

Indeed, city council's lobbying, combined with pressure from the public and the city's power brokers, swayed the decision to opt for electricity to run Vancouver's streetcars. The original plan was to use horse-drawn cars; contractors had already bought horses and built a large, steepled stable.

The Vancouver Daily World reversed its position on June 26, 1890, only five months after it had branded electricity a dangerous risk: "Of one thing the public is convinced, and that is, the horse car must go." The newspaper added that the fast rise in electric street railways elsewhere provided conclusive evidence that electricity had passed the experimental stage.

Of course, electrical equipment manufacturers and public directors of the Vancouver Electric Railway and Light Company hoped to cash in on this trend. (This transit company had formed on May 21, 1890, replacing its predecessor Vancouver Street Railways Company, created on April 6, 1889.) With transit service launched in the middle of a recession, these private groups undoubtedly saw the profit potential of electric-powered streetcars.

The Vancouver Street Railways Company confirmed its decision to use electric power, rather than horses, on August 9, 1889 – only six days before all the track work was completed. This change in plans resulted in a 10-month delay of streetcar service. The decision drew on U.S. sources; the company ordered the electrical equipment from Hartford, Connecticut, and the streetcars from John Stephenson Company in New York. The electricity required to run the system was generated locally, at a steam power house on Barnard (Union Street), next to the car barn.

A year in Vancouver's pre-transit era (1886)

- The City of Vancouver incorporates as the new "Terminal City."
- Vancouver Street Railways Company begins to lay track down Granville Street for the city's first streetcar route.
- Rudyard Kipling buys land in Vancouver. He writes of the city: "[A] great sleepiness lies upon Vancouver as compared to an American town; men don't fly up and down the streets telling lies and the spittoons in the delightfully comfortable hotels are unused; the baths are free and the doors unlocked."[7]
- The Great Fire of June 13 destroys the entire city.
- The city anticipates the arrival of the first Canadian Pacific Railway transcontinental train (it will arrive in Vancouver on May 23, 1887).

Once streetcar service began, four vehicles trundled through what was then Vancouver's early commercial district, an influential hub that focused on Powell (later home of "Little Tokyo" and Japanese immigrants), and Alexander and Cordova (then Oppenheimer) streets. This area also housed a range of residents from the city's business elite to civic officials and the skilled working class. These citizens were among the first in the city to receive not only streetcar service, but electricity, water and sewage pipes.

The streetcar linked the perimeters of the city's east- and west-end residential districts, which previously stood isolated by forest. It cost only five cents, the price of a newspaper, to take a ride along Westminster Avenue and Powell Street and westward to Granville; the

AN UNSTABLE FUTURE – This ample stable was built in July 1889 at the southwest corner of Westminster Avenue (Main Street) and Front Street (First Avenue) to house the horses that would pull Vancouver's streetcars.

When Vancouver Street Railways decided, a month later, to use electric power rather then horses, the company sold the stable and horses to Guerney Cab Company.

Later occupied by Garvin Ice & Fuel, this building remained a Vancouver landmark until the late 1930s. Notice the streetcar tracks in the foreground heading to the left up Main Street to Broadway. (Ninth Avenue officially became Broadway on August 29, 1909, although locals had called it Broadway all along.)

PHOTO SOURCE: CVA: BU P. 180

streetcars then turned up Granville and ended at Drake Street. At Westminster Avenue, a line ran past the car barns on Barnard (Union) to Second Avenue. At rush hour, six cars operated across the system.

The successful operation of Vancouver's streetcars depended on respectful relations between the city and the transit company; this symbiotic relationship would deteriorate markedly in years to come. But at the outset, the operating company agreed to a speed limit of six miles per hour (9.6 kilometres per hour) in return for the use of certain streets – even though the streetcars could reach a whopping 20 miles per hour (32 kilometres per hour) if desired. Vancouver Electric Railway also gave the city an option to buy the streetcar system after 30 years.

As if to prove its electrical prowess to the city, the company gave an extra flourish to its streetcar launch: it unveiled the city's first arc lights only days after transit service began. This new source of power for both its streetcar and street lighting systems gave Vancouver enviable status – it could compete with, or surpass, any Canadian city back east. (Vancouver also emerged with the second incandescent electric light station in Canada, Victoria the first.)

By this time, local media had grown rhapsodic over the introduction of electric light to Vancouver; the June 26, 1890, edition of *The Daily World* likened it to an almost-Biblical force of goodness and morality that would triumph over any seeming evils:

SERVICE START-UP – One of Vancouver's first six streetcars, number 15, runs eastbound on Cordova Street in 1890, about to turn north onto Carrall Street. Built in New York City by John Stephenson Company, cars 10, 11, 12, 13, 14, and 15 were the finest vehicles of their type.

By this time, Vancouver already has the look of an established city, even though it is only four years old.

PHOTO SOURCE: CVA: STR. P. 343 N. 303

The electric light will . . . [send] its brilliant beams into the dark places, the midnight becoming as bright as the noon-day. Vancouver will, when everything is in working order and the lamps are all placed in position, be the best lighted city on the coast. The old times of dark, wet nights, and falling off high sidewalks, will now be forgotten in the radiance which will permeate every part of the city . . . The people of Vancouver love the light better than the darkness, since their deeds are not evil.

For they are engaged in the work of building up here by the Pacific, upon solid and sure foundations, the metropolis of the trade of three continents, a stately city throbbing with busy life and pushing steadily on to the goal of its high destiny.

But despite such visions of grandeur and the transit company's own grandiose plans, the latter could not make money. Many budget-conscious residents still chose to walk to stores, schools and work rather than help finance a corporation. Why pay a fare when you can get there for free?

Future brightness fades

By 1892, little had changed in the nature of streetcar service. Vancouver Electric Railway and Light Company was still losing money and could not sell a single share, nor could the company find someone to float a bond. The public voiced strong opposition to purchasing the troubled company and city council did nothing. Before the end of the year, the transit organization was losing close to $1,300 a month on its street railway and light operations combined.[6]

By February the following year, the company went into liquidation. The trustees who took it over hoped that if the streetcar system could close some of its lines, it might eke out a slight profit. The Broadway section of the Fairview line, a desolate, almost uninhabited stretch of 1.7 miles (2.7 kilometres), was closed, along with service east of Westminster Avenue (Main Street) on Powell Street. Service in Mount Pleasant fell from hourly all day to two-hourly in the mornings and evenings. These cutbacks, although not permanent, left residents furious.

Trustees were able to borrow money to pay for a project that had been in the works before the liquidation: laying double tracks from Main and Hastings to Hastings and Granville. This job was completed in 1895. That year, Vancouver's street railway system added new lines and double-tracked a number of existing routes across the city. This trend continued for several years. Streetcars were now a growing and established part of the city and required greater infrastructure. People had grown accustomed to these handy vehicles and demanded up-to-date service. In fact, by 1897, several influential citizens who lived along Pender Street, west of Granville, wanted to pick up their mail by streetcar on their way to the office. Therefore, a new line was built on this street to cater to their wishes and provide a more direct route to the post office.

That same year, a new London-based company, B.C. Electric Railway Company, took over Vancouver's street railway operations. The city's residents, most of British ancestry, saw no reason to protest foreign ownership of the region's main utility company. They didn't try to make their street railway system a public utility because it would require higher taxes to subsidize it. At the same time, the promoters of the region's street railways didn't want money tied up in the capital-intensive projects of a public company – they wanted quick returns on their investment. Some of the company's original investors obviously favoured private ownership because they wanted to increase the value of their real estate, which surrounded transit lines. Thus, a British-run, private company gained control of Vancouver's transit system and a major transportation

Vancouver Transit Start-Up: A chronology

1889 April 6 – Vancouver Street Railways Company incorporates; Vancouver city council grants a charter for construction of a street railway.

1890 May 21 – Vancouver Electric Railway & Light Company Ltd. forms.

1891 April 20 – The interurban operating company, Westminster and Vancouver Tramway Company, forms by amalgamating with the Westminster Street Railway Company, New Westminster's streetcar operating company.

1892 April 13 – South Vancouver incorporates as a municipality.

1893 Vancouver's streetcars offer service every 12 minutes on weekdays between noon and 7 p.m., and every 15 minutes at other times and on Sundays. A book of 120 streetcar tickets costs four dollars.

1894 The Consolidated Railway and Light Company takes over street railway and lighting systems in Vancouver, North Vancouver and New Westminster. This company results from the reorganization of the Vancouver and New Westminster street railway systems.

1895 The Railway Amalgamation Syndicate of London takes over the Consolidated Railway and Light Company.

1896 October 13 – Consolidated Railway Company (shortened from Consolidated Railway and Light Company) goes into receivership.

1897 A new entity based in London, England, B.C. Electric Railway Company Ltd., incorporates on April 3 and takes over the Consolidated Railway Company on April 15.

1891

It wasn't until 1891 that streetcars went up the Main Street hill, but when they did, it was with a flourish as they hung a sign on the cars saying, "All passengers will be carried up the hill without extra charge" (to the delight of thrill-seeking passengers who would pay five cents to ride up then pay five cents to ride down and on and on). The motormen, when coasting down, would dance a one-footed jig on the floor bell-pedal to clear the way.

Claude Douglas[9]

- Vancouver has 13,000 residents; six years earlier, it had only 400.
- By February, Vancouver's six streetcars have carried almost 340,000 passengers and earned an average of $76.14 per day.
- New Westminster turns on the city's new electric lights on January 2.
- E.H. Wall of New York demonstrates the Edison gramophone for the first time in Vancouver at Manor House.
- The first telephone line in Richmond is installed in a Steveston store. While the caller waits, store messengers are sent to find the person to whom the call was made.

network. This upstart organization ultimately maintained long-running power, both literally and figuratively, as it aimed to reinvent the role of transit in the region.

Vancouver to New Westminster: a new link between two cities

Before Vancouver even existed as a city, New Westminster had established itself as a commercial hub. Founded on the Fraser River, its informal farmer's market and Royal Agricultural Exhibition made it a thriving focus for trade. Named by Queen Victoria and dubbed "the Royal City," its downtown streets wore a genteel air, with rows of tall brick buildings and upscale stores. But New Westminster lacked an important feature that would increase its prominence – a street railway system.

It took New Westminster a year to catch up with Vancouver and launch its own streetcar service in early October 1891, under the Westminster and Vancouver Tramway Company. Meanwhile, Vancouver's greater population and C.P.R. presence, combined with its transit system, accelerated a shift in power between the two cities that would define their futures. At the time, both urban centres still remained relatively isolated, surrounded by thick virgin forest and impassable terrain. The cities had train service, but it was a long, roundabout route with infrequent schedules. The idea of creating a new interurban service, with the greatest technology available on a direct route, seemed preposterous, especially through swampy wilderness. Such a service existed nowhere else in Canada. Could it be done? Would it work?

If introduced, such a service would change the fate of both Vancouver and New Westminster forever. And indeed it did. It helped to redirect influence out of New Westminster and into Vancouver; transit growth in the latter city created infrastructure and ever-increasing streetcar lines that far outweighed New Westminster's offerings. After all, it was far easier to build new lines in Vancouver; New Westminster's steep terrain demanded switches and sand pits for safety. Despite these differences, these two cities have remained linked by public transportation ever since Canada's first interurban (tram) line became a reality.

From the outset, Vancouver's second mayor, David Oppenheimer, was a major investor in street railways and directly involved in the birth of New Westminster's public transit system. He and his brother owned a great deal of land through their Vancouver Improvement Company. He saw the value in an electric rail line between the two cities, a proposal that would cut the distance of existing travel by train between the two cities in half. Oppenheimer joined wealthy business partners Henry V. Edmonds, John A. Webster and Benjamin Douglas to create the Westminster and Vancouver Tramway Company on April 20, 1891. (They amalgamated with New Westminster's existing streetcar company, Westminster Street Railway Company.)

That year, work began on what would later become the Central Park line, part of Canada's longest interurban route. It proved a ground-breaking run that brought people from across North America to gawk, marvel at and, of course, ride the grandest public transit vehicles available.

Canada's longest interurban line opens

The inhospitable land between Vancouver and New Westminster – deep ravines and treacherous hollows, with grades of up to 11 per cent – made it perfect for a roller-coaster route, not a dead-straight interurban line. But hellish hills did not thwart the business minds behind this colossal venture. After several proposed routes, they agreed on one that would serve as a showcase for entry to New Westminster. It would travel from Columbia and 6th Street in that city through to Central Park (so named because Oppenheimer's wife came from New York City) in today's Burnaby and on to Vancouver's east-end area, Cedar Cottage (Commercial Drive, then Park Avenue) at 18th Avenue and into downtown Vancouver. The transit company would have to build costly trestles

STREETCAR RAILS TAKE SHAPE – In this view west on Powell Street from Main Street (then Westminster Avenue) in the early summer of 1889, Vancouver Street Railways Company's streetcar lines begin to take shape. The company confirmed its decision to use electric power rather than horses on August 9 that year, but Vancouver streetcars would not operate until June 1890.

PHOTO SOURCE: CVA: TRANS. P. 79 N. 45

– the longest was 86 feet (26 metres) high and 120 feet (36.5 metres) long – and carve a 100-foot-wide (30.5-metre) right-of-way out of swamp and heavy forest.

The company directors did not let the terrain scare them off, particularly if they thought it would ultimately bring them real estate profits. They convinced the route's surrounding landowners to donate as much of their holdings (eventually an average of under 7.5 per cent) as possible. The B.C. government also made a matching land grant of 10 per cent: 196 acres (79 hectares) that extended between the Earles Road and Park Avenue stations, north of the interurban route. Two of the company directors, Edmonds and Webster, had their own vested interests: each owned 1,000 to 2,000 acres (404.5 and 809 hectares) between Vancouver and New Westminster. [10]

The tram route followed Commercial Drive down Venables Street, Campbell Avenue and along the city's booming commercial district, Hastings Street west to Carrall. The Vancouver Electric Railway and Light Company agreed to build the portion of the line from Cedar Cottage to Carrall Street, which it could use for streetcar service. The interurban would run on the same line and have precedence in running rights.

After a trial run with champagne and dignitaries on September 29, the main portion of Canada's longest interurban line launched its inaugural run on October 1, 1891,

ROLLING BACK THE FOREST — In this westward view of Burnaby from Central Park at Kingsway - where SkyTrain flies overhead today - Westminster and Vancouver Tramway streetcar number 2 and one of the interurban cars pose momentarily during test running some days before the inauguration of service in October 1891. The streetcar, whose motorman grips the brake handle with authority, is still lettered "Westminster Street Railway" and sports a colour scheme reversed from the interurban's.

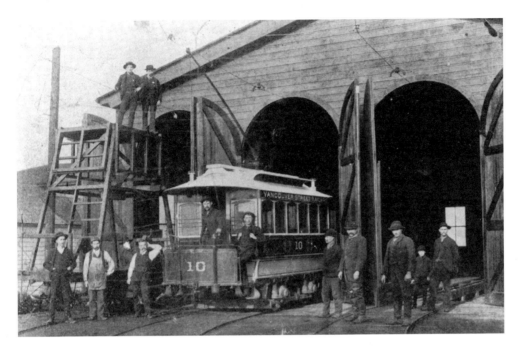

LAUNCH OF A NEW ERA — This photo was taken at Vancouver's first streetcar barn in 1890, almost two months before service began. Car 10, one of the first to operate in Vancouver, appeared revolutionary in its day, but decades later, the January 1920 edition of *The B.C. Electric Employees' Magazine* dismissed it as a "prehistoric car."

Standing atop the tower car are linemen Duncan Brown (left) and William Harkness. On the ground, from left, are line foreman James McPhee, an unidentified, newly hired carpenter, and chief clerk and timekeeper Teddy Parkinson. George Dickie, later to become B.C. Electric's master mechanic, sits on the front of the streetcar. The other men remain unidentified.

PHOTO SOURCE: BC HYDRO:
THE B.C. ELECTRIC EMPLOYEES' MAGAZINE,
JANUARY 1920, P. 5

from Vancouver to New Westminster (it was all but complete although it didn't actually reach Carrall Street until October 8). The interurban offered two round trips a day for 50 cents one way, 75 cents return. The 14.25-mile-long (22.9-kilometre) interurban run effectively doubled Canada's previous public transit track mileage.

Real estate advertisements quickly appeared in local papers, announcing the sale of acre blocks along the tram route. The ads made a point of mentioning that 17 trams – unbelievable! – would travel daily between New Westminster and Vancouver, perhaps a conflict of interest since real estate agents Rand Bros. placed the ads and C.D. Rand served as an officer of the Vancouver Electric Railway and Light Company.

The October 16 issue of the *News-Advertiser* reported on the fast acceptance of tram service in both Vancouver and New Westminster: "A special car arrived at the depot at 4:25 last evening with a party of vocalists from Vancouver to take part in the choral services at Holy Trinity Church. The regular through tram [interurban] cars are packed on every trip both ways to and from Vancouver."

The interurban proved to be a relaxing ride in grand style, unless certain motormen demonstrated bursts of speed between stations. At such times, "one could succumb to an interurban-type 'mal de mer' as the tram swayed violently from side to side as if threatening to jump off the tracks completely in protest at having to put on the effort of extra speed," writes historian Pixie McGeachie. [11]

GOLD DUST IN HIS EYES — Motorman Jack Hunter defined his pet hobby in the August 1921 issue of *The B.C. Electric Employees' Magazine* as "looking for a place where gold dust comes well over the ankles and nuggets are as big as apples." A part-time prospector, the transit employee came to Vancouver in 1876, later discovered a claim at the head of Knight Inlet, but lost it when he could not return to do the required assessment work. (Perhaps his long work days and transit schedule interfered.) The claim hit the market at $500,000 roughly 40 years later.

PHOTO SOURCE: BC HYDRO:
THE B.C. ELECTRIC EMPLOYEES' MAGAZINE,
AUGUST 1921, P. 5

The 50-minute tram service made only three stops between Vancouver and New Westminster. The first Vancouver stop was on Venables Street at Glen Drive. Known as Largen's Corner because of Largen's blacksmith shop, this stop had a switch or one-ended siding. The tram made its next stop at Central Park, which would soon have a substantial station. The new Central Park line revolutionized transportation in Burnaby, as it did elsewhere. Before that, the only public transit through this area was a horse-drawn stagecoach that provided a bumpy, uneven ride from New Westminster down Douglas Road to New Brighton Park (by today's Exhibition Park) in Vancouver.

The final stop was at the Westminster and Vancouver Tramway's power house, where a small company-built "village" housed employees. More than nine miles (14.5 kilometres) from Vancouver and almost 5 miles (8 kilometres) from New Westminster, this impressive red building had a four-stall barn for interurbans and streetcars, a boiler room, engine room, machine shop, store room and superintendent's office. Nearby, a large boarding house provided accommodations for about 30 engineers, train men, tram repairers and section men. The transit company provided several cottages beside it for married employees and their families.

Such infrastructure helped this interurban system gain a reputation as the best-equipped and "most perfect" one on the continent, hailed by experts from around the world. But in the summer of 1892, a smallpox epidemic hit Vancouver. The Westminster and Vancouver Tramways franchise forced the company to provide service, but there were few passengers. The company lost an enormous amount of badly needed revenue. By 1894, a global recession had hit, and investors panicked following the U.S. bank slump the previous year. After a glorious start, the Tramway company now looked like a poor investment; it had paid little of its capital and had no money to lay new track. Slow settlement along the route meant that hoped-for passenger numbers never materialized.

That year, two mishaps seemed to seal the fate of the fallen company. Car 15, en route from New Westminster to Vancouver, left the tracks just east of Cedar Cottage and rolled onto its side north of the line; there were no casualties. Then lightning struck the power house and damaged one of its dynamos. The transit company had no money for repairs – it had severely overspent in its high-flying launch of leading-edge technology. When it could not pay interest on company bonds, the Bank of B.C. refused to cover payments. After little more than three years, one of Vancouver's flagship transit boosters, the Westminster and Vancouver Tramway Company, went into receivership on August 10, 1894.

But the dream of bigger and better street railways did not die. A year later, Frank S. Barnard bought the company's assets for $280,000, acting for the Consolidated Railway and Light Company. Officials in both Vancouver and New Westminster

AN EARLY MEMENTO – Only five years after its incorporation, Vancouver in 1891 already had much to brag about, as depicted on this souvenir: a streetcar (upper far right) bisecting the city's busy Cordova Street, in this view west from Carrall Street; the wreck of the West Coast's most famous steamer, originally the Hudson's Bay Company's *Beaver*, against Stanley Park's Siwash Rock (upper right); and the renowned, much-photographed Hollow Tree in Stanley Park (lower left).

The souvenir provides two panoramic views of the city, the larger featuring a view of Granville Street north to the harbour. Vancouver at this time possessed a transcontinental railway terminal, a splendid streetcar system, and the promise of abundant natural resources.

PHOTO SOURCE: CVA: SC. P. 33 SGN. 121

HANGIN' ON THROUGH HISTORY – Passengers clamber onto the rear of one of Westminster and Vancouver Tramway's interurbans as it prepares to leave its Vancouver terminus on Hastings Street at Carrall. This photo was probably taken soon after interurban service started in October 1891. A one-way fare cost 50 cents; a return fare brought a welcome reduction to 75 cents. Even with this discount, these fares were extremely high for their time.

PHOTO SOURCE: CVA: SGN. 1085.2

LAUNCHING A LEGEND – Vancouver's first six streetcars – four of them shown here at the Barnard (later Union) Street car barn in 1891 – symbolized the ultimate in rapid growth and transit at the time. Valued at about $2,000 each, they were built by the prominent U.S. vehicle manufacturer, the John Stephenson Company. They received daily care and maintenance in this deluxe four-bay car barn. In this photo, car 10 still displays its factory-applied, obsolete lettering "Vancouver Street Railway," soon to be replaced by "Vancouver Electric Railway." This indicates the need to press the vehicle into service immediately to meet rapidly growing transit needs.

PHOTO SOURCE: CBMC: SC-90-1

thought that with this new burst of British capital, and the global economic recovery then underway, interurban service in the region could perhaps regain its old stature and flourish under stable leadership.

To boost patronage, Consolidated Railway offered perks to transit users. Settlers received reduced fares in 1895 while the company urged the provincial government to offer two additional benefits: more reasonable terms to those who bought government land, and the cancellation of stumpage fees for settlers who made cedar-shingle bolts as they cleared their land.[12]

A new twist came on November 22 that year. Another London-based company, The Railway Amalgamation Syndicate, bought out the Consolidated Railway and Light Company. This move spearheaded the hopes and vision of the Railway Amalgamation Syndicate's ambitious head, Robert Horne-Payne. This exceptional 24-year-old had managed to raise enough capital in England to make the purchase because he so thoroughly conveyed his enthusiasm for the street railway and interurban systems in both Vancouver and New Westminster.

However, after another accident, in which 55 people died on a streetcar when the Point Ellice bridge collapsed in Victoria, Consolidated Railway could attract no more investors; it went into receivership on October 13, 1896. But Horne-Payne did not give up his vision. After all, his company controlled the entire electrical utility systems of the Lower Mainland and Vancouver Island.

He sought financial backing from England and the following year created a new entity, B.C. Electric Railway Company Ltd. With head offices in London, England, B.C. Electric incorporated on April 3 and took over Consolidated Railway's whole system for $2.25 million on April 15, 1897. "Thus was accomplished the most rapid and effective consolidation of a single industry in the city's history," writes Vancouver historian Alan Morley.[13] Horne-Payne could not then have known that as chair of B.C. Electric, he would launch a transit empire that would shape the Vancouver region and the entire province for generations to come.

Once B.C. Electric took over the line, the company wanted to ensure high ridership. It introduced an advertising campaign, in conjunction with real estate companies, to entice new settlers to the area and encourage both domestic and industrial growth. It offered the added incentives of free transportation passes for a year, cheap land and industrial rates on freight and power. The scheme worked. The economy was improving, and settlement grew around the interurban line as houses, gardens and orchards started to appear between Vancouver and New Westminster.

By 1897, Vancouver was a modern city of almost 23,000 residents; New Westminster had roughly 6,500. The region was enjoying an economic recovery and British investors now looked favourably on electric interurban stocks. After the desperate recession years came a new period of solid development that continued until 1905. This lay the foundation for astounding future growth in the area's public transportation.

NUMBER-ONE MAN — The number on D. J. McLean's cap says it all: he was B.C. Electric's first motorman in seniority.

PHOTO SOURCE: BC HYDRO:
THE B.C. ELECTRIC EMPLOYEES' MAGAZINE,
AUGUST 1921, P. 2

It runs in the family

Generations of transit families began with the arrival of streetcars and trams to the Vancouver region. As in many other occupations, a son carried on the work of his father. (The involvement of daughters did not occur until many decades later.)

Pixie McGeachie writes of one early transit family, the Walmsleys.[14] Samuel Walmsley, who helped build Burnaby's Central Park interurban line, met Annie, his wife-to-be, at the interurban station in New Westminster in 1891. At age 23, Annie had just arrived in the area, and the two married within a short time. Unfortunately, Samuel died suddenly in 1895.

Annie later married William Farrand, who started with B.C. Electric as a dispatcher. He worked from a small building or "dispatch box" located at the interurban tracks between Wilson and Kathleen avenues. (With only one track in operation, and interurbans travelling in opposite directions, it was vital to keep records of their movements to prevent a collision. An important ritual emerged: the dispatcher and motorman exchanged a stick. When the motorman had the stick in his possession, he had the right-of-way. This simple, yet crucial, practice continued until another set of tracks was installed and precluded the need for this precaution.)

Meanwhile, Annie's son William Walmsley followed in the footsteps of his stepfather. Like William Farrand, he became a section foreman on the Burnaby Lake interurban line and served for more than 40 years.

The Competition: "The streets are blocked with wagons and cabs"

(complaint from Vancouver tourist, c. 1895)

For daily travel within Vancouver, early residents had limited choices beyond public transit. One's feet could provide free, dependable transportation, but the prospect of a long hike in mud and rain on rough, slippery boardwalks wasn't always appealing. Horse-drawn private carriages and taxis gave elite door-to-door service, but at a premium price. Bicycles, or "wheels," gave no cover from the elements and functioned as solo affairs; they wouldn't help a harried mother overloaded with packages and travelling with children, or a man with a heavy pile of luggage.

Alternatives for inter-city travel ranged from stagecoaches and trains to steamers. But a steamer could take all day, as did a wagon ride from Vancouver to Steveston at the turn of the century. Stagecoaches gave bumpy rides and could leave passengers with bruises, not to mention hours of delays if waylaid in mud.

Public transit gave people the option of travelling in a public conveyance at a relatively affordable rate. No other vehicles offered such accessible service within and beyond city limits.

Interurbans gave the impression of "unlimited power, speed and reliability," unlike the "snorting or hesitation" of still-to-come Ford automobiles, which sputtered and coughed like sick beasts of burden.[16] With seating for 64 passengers (in later cars), interurbans travelled at 50 miles per hour (80 kilometres per hour) and soon left any automobile driver eating dust. The public perceived them to be safe and fast; it would take at least a decade before private automobiles, and with them taxis, became competition for public transit. Eventually, however, the appearance of private jitneys severely curtailed streetcar ridership, resulting in drastic financial losses and union unrest.

Stagecoaches: mired in mud

Vancouver's oceanic mud in the early days could make stagecoach travel a nightmare of delays and inconvenience. On a downtown departure on a muddy day, for example, male passengers often had to get out and walk uphill on Granville Street to ease the load; otherwise, the stagecoach would sink into muck and be mired for hours.

In 1890, a daily trip from Vancouver to Steveston took two hours and cost 50 cents. The prejudices of the times meant that Chinese and First Nations people were relegated to the back seat.

Ships: Fraser River steamship service

Those who sought travel to nearby cities beyond Vancouver could choose between two steamship services. The C.P.R.'s *Beaver* left New Westminster for Chilliwack on Monday, Wednesday and Friday and returned the following days. The *Paystreak*, oper-

ANOTHER OPTION: STAGECOACH – Passengers complained of the bruising and discomfort of bumpy stagecoach rides, but people continued to use this mode of transport. In this 1900 photo, the planked streets of Steveston feature a vehicle of prime importance, the Steveston-Vancouver Royal Mail stage.

PHOTO SOURCE: CVA: TRANS. P. 72 N. 40

ated by the Royal City Navigation Company, left on Tuesday, Thursday and Saturday and returned the following days. New Westminster departures were at 8 a.m.; Chilliwack departures at 7 a.m.

The introduction of interurban service to Chilliwack eliminated the need for these two steamboats, which formerly made stops along the south and north sides of the Fraser River between New Westminster and Chilliwack. Soon interurbans were delivering mail, which previously came by steamship, to Chilliwack residents. The *Beaver* and *Paystreak* ceased operation on the run by 1913.

Trains: single fare a hefty dollar

The Canadian Pacific Railway operated a 25-mile (40-kilometre) run between Vancouver and New Westminster via Coquitlam. The twice-a-day trip, which cost a hefty dollar per single fare, ran every day except Sunday and took about an hour and a quarter. The train usually operated with three cars and sometimes as many as 300 passengers took the round trip in one day.

By contrast, an interurban train travelled directly between the two cities at a cost of only 50 cents and took almost an hour.

*July 2, 1907
Vancouver news-
paper ad promotes
a bicycle as
"rapid transit."*

Bicycles: same speed limit as a streetcar

Bicycles could get travellers to their destinations with no need for tracks, schedules or fares. Cyclists could venture into Stanley Park for a leisurely tour on the track at Brockton Point, a spot where no streetcar could enter. But with no protection from the elements, bicycles weren't always the best option in rainy Vancouver. They also required decent road conditions, which were limited in the city's early days. "Our side-walks were principally three planks wide," remembers city resident Ralph Shaw at age 95. "Each plank was about six by twelve inches. It was not conducive for bicycles."

The first bicycle in Vancouver reportedly arrived two years before the city's first streetcar. Bob Matheson, who ran a print shop on Hastings Street, imported the "bone-shaker" in 1888. Three or four years later, a group of residents formed the Vancouver Bicycle Club, which had 209 members by 1892; almost one-quarter were women.

Bicycles, like public transit, brought independence to women. A "wheel" allowed for quick getaways with no chaperone and proved a fashionable way to get about town. Former West End resident Kenneth Caple remembers: "One dear old lady who lived on Barclay Street could not ride, but wheeled her beautiful bicycle down to Robson Street for her shopping because it was smart and the basket on the handlebars was useful for parcels." [17]

Riding a bicycle safely in early Vancouver demanded steering clear of streetcars and their tracks. Jessie McQueen, a 39-year-old teacher in 1899, confided to her mother in a letter: "Have only been out twice on the wheel & am so canny & cautious, that

PEDAL POWER IN STANLEY PARK – Though many Vancouver residents and organizations lobbied over the years to extend streetcar service into Stanley Park, this fortunately never happened.

In this outstanding 1895 photo at Prospect Point, members of the Vancouver Bicycle Club pose at the height of the bicycle craze. During this period, women shocked the world by riding "wheels" while wearing divided skirts called bloomers.

NATIVE TRANSPORTATION – Coast Salish people had little need for streetcars. Here, they bring their canoes to the downtown foreshore of Burrard Inlet, near the foot of Richards Street, in 1890. Their traditional mode of travel contrasts with the industrial look of the newly arrived Canadian Pacific Railway in the background. The railway's depot stood a few hundred metres to the left, along the trestle.

PHOTO SOURCE: CVA: IN. P. 29 N. 10

it won't ever be my fault if there's an accident. Mrs. Macf. cautioned me yesterday to be careful of the [street]cars, but I'm that, all right – you can't get me any nearer to one than the other side of the street, when I'm on a wheel." [18]

Early regulations for Vancouver's bicycles, like streetcars, fell under municipal control. A July 1896 bylaw outlined that "no person shall ride or drive a bicycle at a pace not [sic] exceeding 8 miles per hour." [19] This matched the speed limit for a street-car on business streets at the time; the public vehicles could speed up to a startling 10-mile-per-hour (16-kilometre-per-hour) limit in residential areas.

A bicycle, like a public transit vehicle, proved a great equalizer in transportation, available to almost anyone regardless of income or status. This selling point appears in a July 2, 1907, bicycle advertisement in *The Daily Province*. Under the headline "Rapid Transit," the ad highlights the benefits of a bicycle "for all classes" and takes an indirect dig at streetcars: "You control your speed, your direction, your safety and have no annoying delays or stops."

Horse and carriage: only for the wealthy

Only the well-to-do in early Vancouver used a horse and carriage for regular travel. Businesses large and small, from corner grocers to Woodward's Department Store, made daily use of this transportation, providing deliveries and handy door-to-door service. The city's hotels used their own elegant buggies as private shuttles to pick up guests at the train station or escort them to an evening's entertainment. Tourists often rented horse-drawn cabs around Stanley Park. But horses proved a wild card for urban service; often skittish, they could bolt at sudden noises, and runaway carts were commonplace. Vehicles fell prey to mud, with wheels often stuck in deep ruts.

Not surprisingly, carriage owners complained about public transit; they charged that the streetcar rails posed a serious hazard to the safety of their horses and vehicles.

Fairview Line: "It was a positive disgrace"

> The Fairview line served an ungrateful stretch of dense bush whose raccoon and deer declined to give up private transportation.
>
> ***Eric Nicol**, Vancouver*

The opening of Vancouver's first streetcar line in Fairview on October 22, 1891, was less than auspicious. It reflected the ambition of the times: a big vision with disappointing results. Land speculators had used public transit as a key selling feature for this area south of downtown across to False Creek, named by a Canadian Pacific Railway surveyor. Realtors pushing for settlement touted the area as the up-and-coming Nob Hill community; their advertisements glorified the rugged region as "a gentle slope rising from the waters of English Bay." A more truthful version might have described steep slopes with a bleak but unparalleled view of False Creek's industrial heartland.

Fairview emerged as the first major residential subdivision developed by the C.P.R.; the company offered the Vancouver Electric Railway and Lighting Company 68 lots in exchange for streetcar service. Land values doubled and even tripled as lots went to auction, with an average selling price of about $380.[20] But when the humble, single-track transit line, all 2.75 miles (4.4 kilometres) of it, opened, more wildlife than humans occupied the surrounding region. Despite strong promotion for new residents, there were few homes for the Fairview streetcar line to serve. It kept running regardless; it crossed False Creek, climbed Centre Street (later renamed Granville) to Ninth Avenue (later Broadway), then headed east to Main Street, where it connected with the recently completed Mount Pleasant extension from Second Avenue. A transit employees' magazine recalled this early era: "Remember the dinky cars on Fairview, especially old 21 and 23 wobbling up and down and sideways all in a breath?"

The route featured one major annoyance: only single-truck (two-axle) cars could make the tight, sharp turns that angled through the railway trestle attached to the False

Creek Bridge. "Remember the old trestle bridge where the present Granville bridge now stands?" the same transit magazine recalled decades later. "This old structure had a kink in its middle and only single track dinky cars could get around it. That's why Fairview had only single track cars till the new bridge was completed in 1908 [1909 is correct completion date]."[21]

The less-than-resounding response to the line and surrounding development contrasted markedly with the far-reaching infrastructure required for the service. It demanded seven wooden bridges, some up to 150 feet (46 metres) long, to cross seven streams at a cost of $150,000.[22] As megaprojects go, this one cost five times its original estimate. The end result: the street railway company went bankrupt and could not even guarantee the original service requirements set out by the C.P.R. Transit service was suspended for almost a year in 1893–94, resuming in late April of the latter year. At the time, Fairview and neighbouring Mount Pleasant had only about 500 households, while many homes stood vacant in both areas.[23] These residents were outraged at cutbacks to their much-vaunted streetcar service.

FALSE CREEK SHUTTLE – Streetcars made the creation of Mount Pleasant possible, much of it visible in this southward view in 1893, which shows Main Street from the north shore of False Creek. Two landmarks on the brow of Mount Pleasant include the tower of the fire hall at Broadway and Quebec Street to the right, and recently completed Mount Pleasant School, whose castle tower stands directly above the front of the streetcar.

One of Vancouver's original streetcars makes its way across False Creek Bridge on its passage up steep Main Street to Broadway, two blocks beyond the top of the hill. The streetcar's trestle had been attached to the west side of the existing bridge for the launch of streetcar service on June 27, 1890.

Towards the end of the First World War, False Creek to the west of Main Street would be drained, creating space for the imposing terminal buildings and yards of the Canadian National and Great Northern railways.

1892

- A smallpox epidemic hits Vancouver. The transit system shuts down for almost two months due to lack of business.

- Vancouver's population hits 15,000.

- Vancouver's six-year boom ends and the Depression begins; the latter lasts for five long years. Mayor Cope announces that despite hard times, Vancouver has suffered few business failures compared to other cities.

- The deficits of Vancouver Electric Railway and Light Company run up to $1,300 a month; city council declines two separate offers to buy the company.

- Lightning strikes and destroys one of the dynamos in the Edmonds powerhouse, used by Westminster and Vancouver Tramway Company to power its streetcars and interurbans. Service is maintained but the company is left with no back-up power.

- Charles Woodward opens his first dry goods store at Main and Georgia on March 3.

The line's construction method, however, did make electric railway history. For the first time, fully charged electrical power was used to haul the trolley wire into place; previously, horses and tackle did the job.

The struggling suburb of Fairview finally hit its stride by 1907. Houses now filled the region, streets were vastly improved and Vancouver General Hospital had just opened nearby. Streetcars on Broadway between Granville and Main Street ran on newly laid double tracks, as did those on Granville from the False Creek Bridge to Broadway.

In mid-January that year, B.C. Electric scrapped its method of running streetcars in both directions from a Broadway-and-Main terminus and introduced a belt line where cars operated on a continuous route without switching ends. This gave more efficient, 20-minute regular service with four cars available every 10 minutes in rush hour on each of the inner and outer belts. Seven cars operated on each belt line with six-minute headway.[24]

Nonetheless, the Fairview line remained a challenge as residents complained vigorously about their service. One day after the new Granville Street Bridge opened in September 1909, Fairview dwellers lashed out at transit service, protesting that their promised new streetcars had instead been put on the Grandview run. "We were told we were going to have the best service in the city…[but] the service given today was the worst ever," complained a city alderman at a board of works meeting regarding the use of old, single-truck cars on the line. *The Province* reported: "It was a positive disgrace the way the Fairview cars crept along."[25]

The vagaries of this new line symbolized the contrasts of public transit in this early period; idealistic hopes and over-ambitious plans often outstripped the daily realities of the times. Some could argue that follow-through of transit plans meant promoting image over substance, yet without a grand scheme and the will to achieve it, public transportation could not lead Vancouver out of the backwoods and onto the world stage. Even then, the adage held true: If you build it, they will come. Maybe not immediately, but eventually.

Line construction feat a first for street railways

To a casual observer, it must have looked like mechanical madness. Take one of Vancouver's first streetcars, then couple it to a tower car and a flat car that carries a large spool of trolley wire. No horses required. Use the streetcar to push the other two cars along the track while a lineman feeds trolley wire over the tower car and attaches it to the fully charged guy wires overhead.

It sounds simple enough, but in its day, this procedure broke technological barriers, eliminating the need for previous horse-and-tackle methods. The visionary who came up with the idea was 34-year-old Angus MacDonald, the first lineman employed by the Vancouver Electric Railway & and Light Company. He successfully repeated his technique in 1893-94. He replaced the entire length of "kite-string" trolley wire on the New Westminster–Vancouver interurban line without schedule disruption. This feat undoubtedly involved some spritely dodging of oncoming interurbans, since the continuous wire lay loosely between the tracks on the ties directly in the path of regular trams.

Business Districts Rely on Transit: "We beg for an extension of the car line"

Unwittingly, in 1890, Vancouver was launching itself as a boom-or-bust metropolis. That year, 50 real estate agents and 42 grocers operated in the city. Three years earlier, only 16 real estate firms and 12 grocers existed.[26] The continuing growth of the street railway system echoed this trend; the steady appearance of more and more streetcars and ever more track meant the city was riding a wave of progress. Business leaders, transit executives and civic politicians forged full speed ahead – excitement and optimism overrode concern for costs.

Business operators in early Vancouver soon learned that increased profits relied on transit service. If a streetcar line did not pass a row of storefronts, that commercial block did not thrive. Streetcars and their links to the interurban line brought in droves

SOON AFTER START-UP – This electrical powerhouse, barn and two interurban cars, run by the Westminster and Vancouver Tramway Company, helped launch the longest interurban line in Canada in 1891. These Brill-built interurban cars were considered state of the art at the time.

The operation, photographed here soon after the start of service, stood in the wilderness more than nine miles (14.5 kilometres) from Vancouver, near today's Beresford Street between Mission and Griffiths avenues in Burnaby. The powerhouse also helped launch Burnaby; within its walls, the municipality – city today - of Burnaby was created at a meeting on October 8, 1892.

PHOTO SOURCE: CMBC: IC-10-14

1893

- The Hudson's Bay Company opens a new store at Georgia and Granville on October 6.
- Land held by Mr. Austin is assessed for tax purposes at $20 per acre; today, it's the Vancouver Golf Club on Austin Road.

of customers, and retail owners often wrote petitions requesting streetcar service to their area. Typical is one submitted in the late 1890s by property owners and residents in the city's Cedar Cottage area; they sought an extension from the Cedar Cottage interurban station down Commercial Street (later Drive) and east to Victoria Road (later Drive): "We beg to petition the B.C.E. Railway Co. for an extension of the car line. . . . Cedar Cottage is becoming a center of usefulness, already two Banks besides a large number of up to date stores." [27]

The city's first and most important business district was along Water and Cordova streets between Granville and Carrall streets, where Vancouver's streetcar service first began. Besides retail shops, most of the city's wholesale outlets were here, where there was easy access to the waterfront and railway. A less fashionable retail area grew along

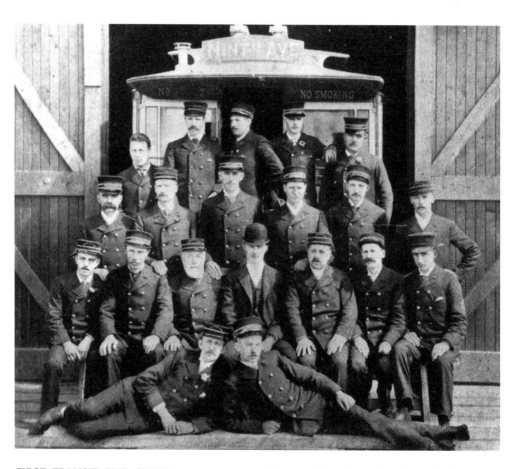

FIRST TRANSIT EMPLOYEES — Vancouver transit service in 1893 required only 20 motor-men and conductors. This photo, taken at the original car barn on Union Street, shows the full complement of on-board employees at the time (last names only available). From left, front: Durgan, Philips. First row: Cornwall, Marshall, Stevens, Hutchings (superintendent), James, Fowler, Rogers. Centre row: McQuaid, Fletcher, Baynes, McEwen, Collins, Wilcox. Back row: Davies, Jeffers, Paxman, Spriggs, Perry.

PHOTO SOURCE: BC HYDRO:
THE B.C. ELECTRIC EMPLOYEES' MAGAZINE,
SEPTEMBER 1923, P. 25

Westminster Avenue (Main Street), where Charles Woodward opened his dry goods store in 1892. Streetcar service had begun there two years earlier.

The third commercial area, still in its prime today, emerged to the west along the planked road known as Granville Street. Although in 1886 it was merely "a thoroughfare marked by wooden shacks, a few brick buildings and bordered by roughly cleared lots," [28] it would be developed with C.P.R. influence. The railway's luxurious Vancouver Hotel had opened in 1887 at Georgia and Granville, then on the outskirts of a growing city. Adjacent stood the opulent, 1,200-seat Vancouver Opera House, built by the C.P.R. and opened in February 1891. By 1895, multiple streetcars served this popular part of town as fashionable shoppers flocked to shops, theatres and other entertainment venues.

The C.P.R. eagerly sought to develop Granville Street (the company's senior officials,

1894

- Vancouver feels the impact of the Depression. The population drops, houses are boarded up and many residents return to the U.S. Many small merchants go bankrupt. In the words of historian Alan Morley: "For the first time, Vancouver saw misery on its doorstep and starvation in its streets."

- Writer/hobo Jack London receives free meals and handouts from Vancouver residents as he wanders across B.C.

- Discontinued streetcar service is reinstated on the Fairview and Powell Street lines.

- Hikers climb a North Vancouver mountain on October 12 and, after shooting a blue grouse there, name it Grouse Mountain.

- Massive flooding of the Fraser River hits New Westminster in late May 1894, resulting in a beef famine in Vancouver. Water rises up to the gas works on 12th Street. Vancouver–New Westminster tram has to change its timetable; it can't use its short route because the lower part of New Westminster is under water, reports the June 5, 1894 edition of *The Vancouver Daily World*.

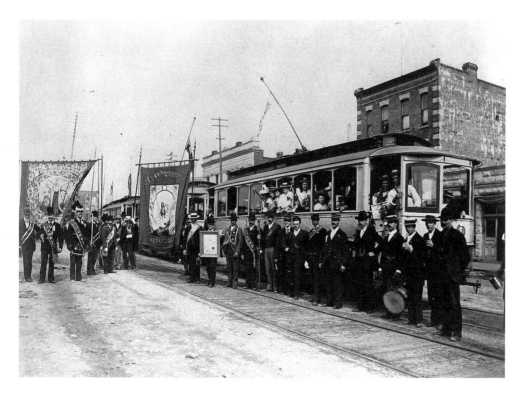

PARADE BOOSTERS – Even in Vancouver's early days, streetcars played a key role in the city's special events. Three interurbans, led by number 10, join a procession and street celebration on Hastings Street, c. 1892. This view looks west to Carrall Street, midway between Columbia and Carrall.

PHOTO SOURCE: HE COLLECTION

WORK CREW TAKES A BREAK – A substantial work crew poses with Westminster and Vancouver Tramway's only work car, number 4, at the company's car barn and steam plant in Burnaby in 1893.

Roderick Semple, the white-bearded man shown here, stood over six feet (two metres) tall and served as the company's first roadmaster. He also played Santa Claus for the children at Christmas, remembers his grand-nephew Fraser Wilson. Semple's wife, Minnie, ran the couple's 15-bedroom rooming house for employees or contractors who worked on the interurban line. Situated near the company power plant, the building also served as a public meeting place for several years since Burnaby had no other structure for this purpose. [29]

PHOTO SOURCE: CVA: TRANS. P. 117 N. 73

Donald A. Smith and Sir William Van Horne, owned two of the city's largest privately held properties, both on Granville north of downtown). The railway company was instrumental in situating the Bank of Montreal's main office on Granville.

Another Canadian institution, the Hudson's Bay Company, had opened a Granville Street branch in 1889. Four years later, the company consolidated its two stores and opened a full department store across from the Vancouver Hotel.

As the city's power centre shifted, the transit system scrambled to serve these influential businesses. Track expansion and the later introduction of more and larger streetcars provided a symbiotic link to the region's ever-increasing commercial presence. The rise of Granville Street as Vancouver's new downtown core paralleled the growth of the city's public transit system.

But by the mid-1890s, the powerful entrepreneurs at the street railway company allowed their enthusiasm for development to overshadow their financial resources and the grim reality of the city's recession. The company had problems raising funds after its Fairview expansion flopped and expenses far outstripped profits. It depended on support from its power base in England, but depressed bond markets there left overseas investors wary of any iffy projects in this headstrong colonial town. After such a glorious beginning, it looked as if the upstart city and its prestigious street railways had gone too far, too fast.

Labour Scene: "40 cents for a day's work"

EARLY MOTORMAN — H. W. Vanderwalker, or "Van," started as a motorman in 1898, then worked as a ticket clerk and later a cashier at B.C. Electric's Prior Street ticket office.

PHOTO SOURCE: BC HYDRO:
THE B.C. ELECTRIC EMPLOYEES' MAGAZINE,
AUGUST 1921, P. 25

The No. 20 line . . . was the first streetcar route into the developing industrial and working-class districts of the city's East End. . . . The streetcars swayed past the hotels and row cabins of retired campworkers and rumbled by the locales of now nearly forgotten labour struggles. They pitched and yawed around corners, braked down hills and rattled past most of the docks and mills and industries of the Vancouver waterfront.

Rolf Knight, *Along the No. 20 Line*

Motormen and conductors got an extra treat when their streetcars reached Denman Street in 1895: neighbourhood women served them tea and cake. Back then, Denman lay on the city outskirts, a bleak frontier amid tangled bush. At the time, only 12 streetcars operated on six miles (10 kilometres) of track in all of Vancouver.

In this early era, transit employees endured working conditions as challenging as the uneven tracks they rode. Conductors and motormen worked $10\frac{1}{2}$ to 11 hours every day in streetcars with few comforts; a motorman had to contend with extreme weather, from rainstorms to snow, while riding in a car's open vestibule.

TRANSIT OLD-TIMER — Even at 83, his age when pictured here, John Perry worked for B.C. Electric as the company mail messenger. He started as conductor in 1891 at age 53, and lived for the next 30 years at 391 Hamilton Street. Perry arrived in Vancouver with his wife via South Dakota and Ontario, after sailing from his native Scotland in 1866.

PHOTO SOURCE: BC HYDRO:
THE B.C. ELECTRIC EMPLOYEES' MAGAZINE,
FEBRUARY 1921, P. 30.

IMPORTANT SALE.

ELECTRIC TRAMWAY.

NOTICE is hereby given in pursuance of a certain indenture, dated 25th October, 1892, made between the Westminster and Vancouver Tramway Company and the Montreal Safe Deposit Company, as trustees, that tenders will be received by the undersigned, at his office, in the City of New Westminster, British Columbia, up to noon of

SATURDAY, the 24th DAY of NOVEMBER, 1894.

For the purchase of the said Tramway and all the property of the said Tramway Company comprised in the said indenture.

The Westminster and Vancouver Tramway Company's lines of tramway extend throughout the City of New Westminster, in the Province of British Columbia, and between that City and the City of Vancouver.

Conditions of sale, and full particulars as to property, may be obtained at the office of the Montreal Safe Deposit Company, or from Messrs Corbould & McColl, Solicitors, New Westminster, B. C.

GORDON E. CORBOULD.
Solicitor for the Montreal Safe Deposit Company

New Westminster, 10th August, 1894.   1798-92

Transit Employee Job Duties

Motorman: No cruise control

- operates the streetcar
- punches the time clock at each terminus
- hands in the running card (as per time clock) at the end of each shift
- bleeds condensation out of air tank, when necessary
- obeys conductor's bell signals
- sets the front destination signs and route number sign

Since the motorman was ultimately responsible for the streetcar's operation, his duties surpassed those of the conductor. Their respective jobs required teamwork: the motorman did not rank ahead of the conductor.

Conductor: Feather duster and broom required

- takes fares
- sells tickets and passes
- closes and opens the door or doors
- signals the motorman by pulling the bell: one pull for "stop"; two pulls for "go"; four pulls for "back up"
- takes and gives transfers, which have a one-hour limit with no stopover
- punches transfers to indicate the terminus the car has left and at what time
- calls out street names
- calls out "Move to the front of the car" when necessary
- does the track switching
- is responsible for setting the curtain
- sets the rear destination signs and route number sign

A handbook called *Rules for Conductors and Motormen*, published around 1900, outlines the multi-tasking required by conductors:

> The conductor must report for duty in full uniform at least ten minutes before the time for starting, having a sufficient supply of tickets, transfers and change, his box slip, punch and accident blankets, and, when running an open car, his whistle; and also inspect his car to see that everything is clean and in proper shape, that proper signs are on his car, and that his feather duster and broom are there.[32]

Inspector: Vehicles must run on time

- ensures that vehicles run on time
- reroutes, terminates or reschedules streetcars if emergencies arise
- deals with streetcar failure by phoning the "bullpen," whence a call would be made to the car barn to activate a new crew and attendant car

Inspectors (later called supervisors) were stationed at four locations: Main and Hastings streets, Robson and Granville streets, Broadway and Granville streets, and Broadway and Kingsway.

In the words of a transit newsletter: "A motor-man driving in the rainy season would probably have his top coat wet for five or six weeks, there being no opportunity to dry it."[30]

Conductor John Perry started with transit in 1891, earning 17 cents an hour. He got 18 cents for the next two years and reached the maximum of 20 cents an hour by the end of his third year. Four years later, wages ranged from 20 to 30 cents an hour, and it took 10 years to achieve maximum pay, conductor John McDonald remembered in 1925. In 1895, employees received a Christmas bonus of $60; the annual bonus amount depended on the company's success that year. That year, it was possible to buy a building lot on Broadway for $400.

1895

[I]nside of an hour every real-estate man in the place would know him and his business in Vancouver and probably whether he had any family or a hereditary disease [once any man stepped off the train].

A British visitor, 1895, from Doug Sladen's
On the Cars and Off

- Transit construction crews lay a double-tracked streetcar line on the two blocks of Hastings Street between Carrall and Cambie, Vancouver's thriving hub.

- The first mailboxes are installed on Vancouver streets.

FIVE YEARS' RUNNING – Transit employees and passengers pose with a streetcar on Main Street near Pender in this delightful 1895 view, five years after service began. Thankfully for the riders and motorman, the sun is shining; the vehicle's open-air style offers little protection from the elements.

PHOTO SOURCE: BC HYDRO: A0010

McDonald recalled that in those days, it took patience to serve as a spare or "extra," hoping for a chance to work on board a streetcar or tram. Sometimes it meant waiting for several days with no work or pay. He said: "Often for days the extras would only get a two-hours' special on Robson or Davie, earning forty cents for a day's work, with an occasional last shift, although many a day was a blank from six a.m. to six p.m."[31]

Women on Transit: They provoked "a dickens of a row"

Vancouver transit officials got an earful from women regarding one of the city's early street-cars. Female passengers in 1895 refused to sit on the seats of car 25, which ran on Denman Street, because they could not extricate themselves under layers of skirts and petticoats. City archivist Major Matthews wrote of the car: "It had lengthwise seats, but so hollowed that women, when once seated, could not rise again. The idea was to stop people sticking their feet out. There was a dickens of a row; women would not use the seats."[33]

Unfortunately, the women's views left little impact. They lacked the money, political will or population base to implement a change, so Vancouver's street railway system kept operating car 25. The discomfort of a handful of "lady riders" hardly seemed a priority considering the demands of the city's rapid expansion.

Early transit documents do acknowledge the unique demands posed by a female passenger; her skirt, for instance, could drag her to death if it caught on a streetcar when she disembarked. The circa-1900 handbook *Rules for Conductors and Motormen* gave the following instructions to conductors: "When a lady leaves the car, he will see that her dress is entirely clear before giving the signal to start."[34]

HATS TO THE SIDE – The late Sid Gregory, a retired transit employee in his nineties, remembered the early days when women had to tip their wide hats sideways to board the streetcar. (Gregory joined B.C Electric on May 1, 1894, and was the first to sign the charter of local 134 of the Amalgamated Association of Street Railway Employees of America, more commonly known as the Street Railwaymen's Union or S.R.U.)

PHOTO CREDIT: HEATHER CONN (FROM HE COLLECTION)

A RIDE ON THE SIDE – Streetcar 25 poses grandly on Denman Street with most of its windows wide open in this 1895 photo. Its two long seats on each side of the car allowed for ample standing room, but made it difficult for seated passengers to rise, particularly, as in this case, without stanchions.

PHOTO SOURCE: CVA: M-3-18.2 TRANS. P. 118 N. 74

The Stanley Park Line: "A brewery at each end"

Thousands of turn-of-the-century visitors and residents used streetcars to reach Vancouver's largest natural leisure site: 960-acre (388-hectare) Stanley Park. However, the single-track car line to the park was no deluxe trip. One pioneer remembers the bumpy route "with its little single truck cars, on whose platform no Scotchman wearing a hard hat would ever ride."[35] Nevertheless, it sure beat the only other means of park access for those without a bicycle or carriage: long walks on slippery boardwalks through mud and rain.

Streetcar rides to the park, which began in 1895, soon became a popular transportation option. In fact, only four years after transit started in the city, some residents already requested an extension of streetcar service down Robson Street to the park. They wrote in an 1894 petition to Consolidated Railway Company, B.C. Electric's predecessor: "[We] residents here would find it [service to the park] very convenient, and it would also enable the residents in the middle and East Wards to enjoy the Park and English Bay, which at present, through the distance, they are debarred from doing."[36]

PASSAGE TO THE PARK – Car 21, at Stanley Park in 1900, draws citizens for a return journey from their day's recreation. By this time, Stanley Park has already achieved international recognition and many tourists flock to have their picture taken inside the park's famous Hollow Tree.

How pleasant it must have been to take a streetcar ride to glorious Stanley Park, then uncluttered with automobiles and coin-operated parking machines.

PHOTO SOURCE: CVA: ST. PK. P. 39.2

A shrewd property developer, William S. Johnson, who owned about 100 lots near Stanley Park, moved to cash in on the demand for streetcar service to the park. He asked the Consolidated Railway Company in 1895 if it would give away free transit passes for two years to those who bought his first 20 lots. He proposed the following money-back guarantee as an added incentive: "Should these lots sell freely we are prepared to pay you $25 for each ticket so issued."[37] It is not known whether the transit company took him up on his offer.

Consolidated Railway itself lobbied to get streetcar service into Stanley Park, but the city turned down this request in 1896. That same year, the company used a tunes-and-transit strategy to woo patrons to the park; it hired the 15-piece Vancouver City Band to play Sunday concerts in the park for eight dollars per performance.

Streetcar service to Stanley Park continued to expand and by 1897, Pender Street was extended to Stanley Park; locals quickly called this 1.23-mile (two-kilometre) line "the Stanley Park line." It ran west from Granville Street on Pender into Georgia and then down Chilco Street, where it connected with the existing Robson line.

The streetcar line on Powell Street, which ran to Stanley Park in 1895, once bore the distinction of having a brewery at each end; one stood on the edge of today's Lost Lagoon, then a marsh. A streetcar conductor reminisced about the brewery proprietor in 1925: "Mr. Millar . . . often invited the car crew to tread his sawdust floor and sample his foaming jug free."[38]

Meanwhile, Vancouver residents continued to demand streetcar service within Stanley Park. Citizens in 1903 put pressure on city council to extend the streetcar line from the park entrance at Georgia and Chilco streets to Brockton Point; this would cover about three-quarters of a mile (1.2 kilometres) and require a new 800-foot (244-metre) bridge. B.C. Electric had already made a rough survey for such a route, but general manager Johannes Buntzen vigorously opposed the idea and permanently squelched any such plans in late October that year.

Tours to Stanley Park from the downtown waterfront (today's Gastown) began in 1903. The city's first sightseeing streetcar, operating in 1903 and 1904, provided this novelty service for 25 cents.

1896

[T]he streets of bituminous rock pavement and the macadamized roads of Vancouver are excellent, the permanent sewerage system is an admirable one, and the tram car facilities, brightly lighted thoroughfares, first-rate drinking water, and brushed-up appearance of things in general contribute vastly towards the comfort of residents and visitors alike.

The Province, **August 29, 1896**

- Advertising appears on streetcars for the first time.
- The street railway company builds bathing sheds and a small pavilion at English Bay to promote streetcar travel.
- The post office pays $150 to allow postal workers to ride on streetcars "at all hours of the day when in uniform."
- Motorman George Martin starts with Consolidated Railway; he later recalls a popular saying at the time: "In 1910, Vancouver will have 100,000 men."
- Population estimates for that year are Vancouver 22,800; New Westminster 6,550; Victoria 19,300; and all of B.C. 146,000.
- Vancouver council sets 25 as the maximum number of cows per owner within city limits on October 26.
- Burnaby hires its first police officer on November 7 at a rate of two dollars a day.

Safety Issues: Teamsters should "take great care not to leave horses standing on the street"

Whether dodging livestock on tracks or avoiding a bolting horse and carriage, Vancouver's first transit passengers often took safety into their own hands – literally. Since all the early streetcars had only hand brakes, it proved routine to ride with the motorman and sometimes help him brake the car. Nevertheless, derailments occurred more frequently than the public probably suspected.

In later years, to minimize such mishaps in North Vancouver, B.C. Electric installed a safety switch, reinforced with sand, between 2nd and 3rd streets. This provided some measure of protection for downhill vehicles that faced the steep, hair-

CITY'S FIRST CONDUCTOR — J.J. Jeffers, who received a designation of No. 2 employee on his cap, remained Vancouver's first and longest-employed conductor. He retired from transit service in 1921.

PHOTO SOURCE: BC HYDRO
THE B.C. ELECTRIC EMPLOYEES' MAGAZINE,
AUGUST 1920, P. 28

raising grades of Lonsdale Avenue. Otherwise, all that transit employees and passengers could provide were their own prayers.

In Vancouver, a skittish horse-and-buggy team could prove hazardous to streetcars. A warning appeared in the *Vancouver Daily News-Advertiser* on June 28, 1890: "Teamsters and all people having horses should, now that the street cars have commenced running, take great care not to leave horses standing on the street without being securely tied. With a little care many accidents will be prevented." The Saturday edition of the same paper reported triumphantly after the first day of transit service: "No accident occurred, not even a runaway, the horses surprising people by the way they took to them [streetcars]." [39] Contrast this with later years, when a motorman's accident report in 1898 outlined how a bull knocked a streetcar off its tracks and then casually sauntered away. [40]

Cows, horses, dogs and other roaming creatures proved a recurring menace for transit vehicles, especially on the interurban lines. As early as September 1898, a woman sued B.C. Electric for $5,000 in damages for a broken arm after the streetcar she was riding derailed from hitting a cow at night. [41] An animal's death resulting from collision with an interurban usually provoked outrage from its owner. Even as late as 1910, one man sought claims of $225 per animal after a B.C. Electric freight car killed his three prized heifers. [42] By late October that year, the company's legal department responded with a notice

AN EARLY INTERURBAN – This circa-1895 view shows a Westminster and Vancouver Tramway interurban car loading passengers on Hastings Street, just east of Carrall Street. This spot was the car's Vancouver terminus. The offloading activity around the car, prior to its departure, reflects the significance of this interurban line, the only civilized transport between two of B.C.'s most important cities.

PHOTO SOURCE: BHS

MAY DAY PARADE – A streetcar and two interurbans accompany a parade on Columbia Street in New Westminster on May Day in 1896. This location, at the 6th Street intersection, marked the terminus of the New Westminster-to-Vancouver interurban operation. The two interurban cars are still in the yellow paint job of the Westminster and Vancouver Tramway, while the streetcar has already been repainted in successor company paint. The streetcar, also at its ter-minus, operated up Columbia, past Queen's Park, to its upper terminus at 6th Street and 6th Avenue.

Notice the double-ended siding just before the intersection. The four-storey structure is the Douglas & Elliott Building. The sign for the Consolidated Railway Company, the operator of streetcars in New Westminster, Vancouver, and Victoria, is visible in the alcove behind the telephone pole at the far right.

PHOTO SOURCE: CMBC: SS-90-8

posted along its tracks with the warning "Keep Your Cattle Off the Track." It notified livestock owners that they were liable to a 20-dollar fine per offence if they "willfully" left a gate open or took down a fence, resulting in their animals roaming on B.C. Electric property. [43] (The company had built fences and cattle guards along the Central Park line, as far east as Jubilee station, by 1903.)

Meanwhile, Vancouverites repeatedly requested B.C. Electric to install new fend-ers ("cow-catchers") on streetcars for public security. Newspaper articles condemned delays in the installation of these safety features and city council resolved to bring this to the company's attention in November 1897. Since the start of transit service in

JUST ANOTHER DAY IN THE OFFICE? — Two prominent men in B.C. history appear here in 1896 in an informal pose. Such depictions are rare for this period; VIPs were usually only photographed at special events in dressy attire, or at least in an official capacity. The setting is 163 Cordova Street, just after the amalgamation of the Consolidated Railway & Light Company.

From left, are C. Rummel, who later took charge of the company's light and power department in New Westminster, and Frank S. Barnard, who became B.C.'s lieutenant-governor in 1914 and was knighted in 1918. Barnard, the street railway's general manager at the time of this photo, became B.C. Electric managing director

in the province when the company formed in 1897; he resigned a year later, but remained a member of the company's directorate until he died in 1936. To Barnard's right are office worker Jack Priestman, and Johannes Buntzen, who was appointed B.C. Electric's general manager in 1897. A year later, he became the company's managing director for B.C. and remained until 1905, when he left for London as chairman of the board. He died in 1922. At the extreme right is a Mr. Wilcock, accountant, who left the company soon after this photo was taken.

PHOTO SOURCE: BC HYDRO: *THE B.C. ELECTRIC EMPLOYEES' MAGAZINE,* JUNE 1923, P. 9

Vancouver, passengers never hesitated to voice their gripes and to remind B. C. Electric that they were part of the system too; strongly worded petitions and highly charged letters clearly revealed that transit users held a distinct sense of ownership of the system and wanted input on its use, even for relatively minor issues.

Transit users, however, had little control over safety and discomfort issues. For instance, city residents complained before 1898 that some streetcar track and roadbeds were in such bad shape that they had to move residences to avoid vibrations caused by the public vehicles.

Some of the city's poorly maintained bridges, roadbeds and track prompted concerns from B.C. Electric for the safety of its passengers. The company's general manager, Johannes Buntzen, lamented to his London boss, in September 1898 correspondence, that the company had stopped using Granville Bridge because "the whole of the bridge, swing and all, has practically been condemned."[44]

Understandably, this loss of service riled residents in Fairview, who were now stranded; they had to walk across the bridge every time they needed to access the lone streetcar to Robson and Granville or connect with the Fairview line. In the face of this ever-growing public discontent, Buntzen complained to his superiors: "[T]he few people living there have given the Company more trouble than the rest of the citizens put together."[45]

Freight: "Settlers' effects carried free when accompanied by someone"

> BC [Electric] inherited a thriving freight business from the Tramway Company [in 1897], which had run into trouble not because of lack of business, but only by its lack of rolling stock.
>
> **BC Hydro Power Pioneers,** *Gaslights to Gigawatts*

I n its early days, public transit soon discovered a cash cow for its interurban line: freight service. The influx of settlers between Vancouver and New Westminster, and their resulting need to transport goods, belongings and produce to their new homes, proved highly profitable for B.C. Electric.

IN THE GOOD OL' SUMMERTIME – A throng of male passengers, almost all wearing a stylish hat and suit, fill a streetcar on Granville Street at Dunsmuir in the summer of 1896. Superinten-dent Tom Barnet stands at the front of the car, which is under the direction of motorman W. R. Jamieson and conductor William Eaton.

PHOTO SOURCE: CVA: TRANS. P. 7 #2 N. 10

1897

While the citizens of cities elsewhere vented their spleen against czars and petty potentates, the people of Vancouver cursed an oligarchy whose palace was a carbarn, whose temple was an aromatic silo of gas produced from coal, and whose benevolence was limited to providing, on foggy nights, the red light on the rear of the streetcar that served as bellwether for a flock of private vehicles feeling their way home.

Eric Nicol, *Vancouver*

- Vancouver adds a new 1.23-mile (2-kilometre) streetcar line, which soon becomes known as "the Stanley Park line."

- Klondike gold fever hits Vancouver; city council agrees on November 15 to spend $2,000 to advertise the city as an outfitting point for the gold fields.

- The "movies" come to Vancouver on August 2 with an Ethiopticon Kinetoscope moving picture exhibition at Market Hall, along with Edison's "wonder speaking phonograph."

- Pauline Johnson reads her poetry on October 21 at Homer St. Methodist Church.

- Almost 2,000 Japanese fishermen, a third of the total fishing population, operate on the lower Fraser River.

The popularity of freight service, and its resulting high demand, had resulted in complaints about the mishandling of packages by a B.C. Electric predecessor, Westminster and Vancouver Tramway. Correspondence in July 1897 indicates that the company's Hastings Street office was "very often left without anyone in charge; parcels may thus be brought in when nobody is at the Office and taken away again, or left in some place where they may be not noticed." [46]

Even with such haphazard service, settlers continued to use freight delivery and pickup on a daily basis. They soon learned they could use the tram line to transport their eggs, chickens and market crops for sale in the cities, which boosted existing freight business and was guaranteed to make the New Westminster – Vancouver run a money-maker.

In response to the rising demand, B.C. Electric quickly posted its rates and regulations. A "Notice to Settlers Along the Tramway Line" appeared on September 1, 1897, signed by general manager Johannes Buntzen. It read:

On, and after, 1st September, 1897, Settlers' effects and supplies, not exceeding Fifty pounds for each person, will be carried free, as baggage, when accompanied by, and in charge of, someone. Any excess baggage beyond fifty pounds will be charged for at the rate of 10 cents per 100 lbs, or fraction thereof.

Settlers' effects and supplies shipped as freight, and not accompanied by anyone in charge, will be carried at the rate of 10 cents per 100 lbs, or fraction thereof, at Owner's risk, and the Company will not be responsible for any goods left at any Way Station.

As of this notice date, it cost $2.50 per ton of merchandise carried between Vancouver and New Westminster. For 1,000 to 2,000 pounds (454 to 907 kilograms) of goods, the price was 12.5 cents per 100-pound (45.5-kilogram) load, or fraction thereof; any load between 1 to 21 pounds (.45 to 9.5 kilograms) cost 20 cents, to a maximum of 1,000 pounds. Each can of dairy cream received a 30-cent charge, with empties returned free between Vancouver and New Westminster. [47]

Businesses and farmers also cashed in on this new transportation trend, which avoided the time-consuming use of skiffs and flat-bottomed scows, or the need to connect with a stagecoach. For instance, freight trains hauled cord wood and shingle bolts

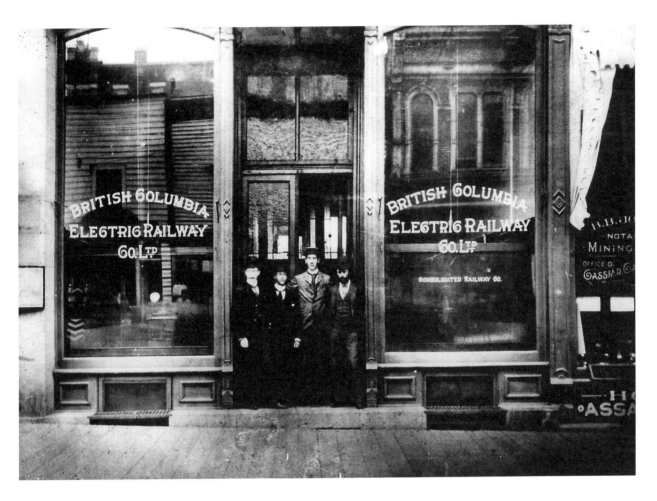

NEW BUSINESS BEGINS – Soon after the incorporation/creation of the B.C. Electric Railway on April 3, 1897, the company opened this Vancouver office at 163 West Cordova Street. (B.C. Electric operated all streetcars and interurban service in the Lower Mainland and on Vancouver Island.)

This photo was taken in 1897, likely not long after the office opened. The name of Consolidated Railway Company, which previously ran these systems, still appears on the right window.

PHOTO SOURCE: CMBC: SS-90-13

to Vancouver from Burnaby and South Vancouver, and brought in bricks from New Westminster. Cliff's Can Factory in Burnaby became a major freight customer. Several sand and gravel pits along the interurban line also generated lots of business. Most farm goods and dairy products from the Steveston region went to market in New Westminster via the interurban line.

NOTES

1 *The B.C. Electric Employees' Magazine*, April 1922, p. 8.

2 Ewert, *The Story of the B.C. Electric Railway Company*, p.14.

3 *The Buzzer*, Aug. 9, 1935, p. 1.

4 *The Province*, March 29, 1957, p. 4.

5 Kloppenborg, ed., *Vancouver's First Century: A City Album, 1860 – 1985*, p. 38.

6 Ewert, *B.C. Electric Railway Company*, 1986, p. 25.

7 Morley, *Vancouver – From Milltown to Metropolis,* p. 110.

8 Nicol, *Vancouver*, p. 105.

9 Mount Pleasant binder, p. 55, Vancouver Public Library, Special Collections.

10 Ewert, *B.C. Electric Railway Company*, p. 19.

11 McGeachie, *Bygones of Burnaby: An Anecdotal History*, p. 21.

12 Roy, "The British Columbia Electric Railway Company, 1897–1928: A British Company in British Columbia," p. 38.

13 Morley, *Vancouver,* p. 117.

14 McGeachie, *Bygones of Burnaby*, p. 28–29.

15 *The B.C. Electric Employees' Magazine*, August 1921, p. 2.

16 Sladen, *On the Cars and Off*, p. 384.

17 *Vancouver Historical Society newsletter*, April 1977, p. 7.

18 July 2, 1899 letter from Jessie McQueen to her mother, from Jean Barman, Professor of Educational Studies, University of B.C.; original in BC Archives.

19 Taylor, *The Automobile Saga of British Columbia, 1864–1914*, p. 23.

20 Roy, *Vancouver*, p. 30.

21 *The B.C. Electric Employees' Magazine*, July 1932, p. 17.

22 Ewert, *Story of the B.C. Electric Railway*, p. 22.

23 Roy, *Vancouver*, p. 30.

24 Ewert, *Story of the B.C. Electric Railway*, p. 74.

25 *The Province*, Sept. 8, 1909, p. 10.

26 Roy, *Vancouver*, p. 19.

27 B.C. Electric Railway, Petitions, Box 158-8, University of B.C., Special Collections.

28 *The Daily Province*, Sept 18, 1912, p. 15.

29 McGeachie, *Bygones of Burnaby*, p. 22.

30 *The B.C. Electric Employees' Magazine*, May 1919, p. 15.

31 *The B.C. Electric Employees' Magazine*, Dec. 1925, p. 10.

32 BC Hydro Power Pioneers, *Gaslights to Gigawatts*, p. 26.

33 Major Matthews collection, City of Vancouver Archives, Book 178, p. 118.

34 BC Hydro Power Pioneers, *Gaslights to Gigawatts*, p. 26.

35 Nicol, *Vancouver*, p. 85.

36 April 20, 1894 petition, B.C. Electric Railway, Petitions, Box 158-9, University of B.C., Special Collections.

37 Taylor, *The Automobile Saga of British Columbia*, p. 40.

38 *The B.C. Electric Employees' Magazine*, December 1925, p. 10.

39 BC Hydro Power Pioneers, *Gaslights to Gigawatts*, p. 26.

40 Correspondence from Johannes Buntzen to F. Hope in London on Sept. 10, 1898, B.C. Electric Railway records, Accidents file 146-4, Box 146, University of B.C., Special Collections.

41   Sept. 6, 1910 correspondence, B.C. Electric Railway records, Box 2, University of B.C., Special Collections.

42   Correspondence, BCER, Oct. 26, 1910.

43   Roy, "Electric Railway," p. 59.

44   Correspondence from Buntzen to Hope, Sept. 7, 1898.

45   Correspondence from Buntzen to Hope, 1898, p. 267.

46   July 13, 1897 letter from Buntzen to H. Hemlow, B.C. Electric Railway, Letter Books, General, 1897, p. 179.

47   B.C. Electric Railway, Letter Books, General, 1897, p. 81–83.

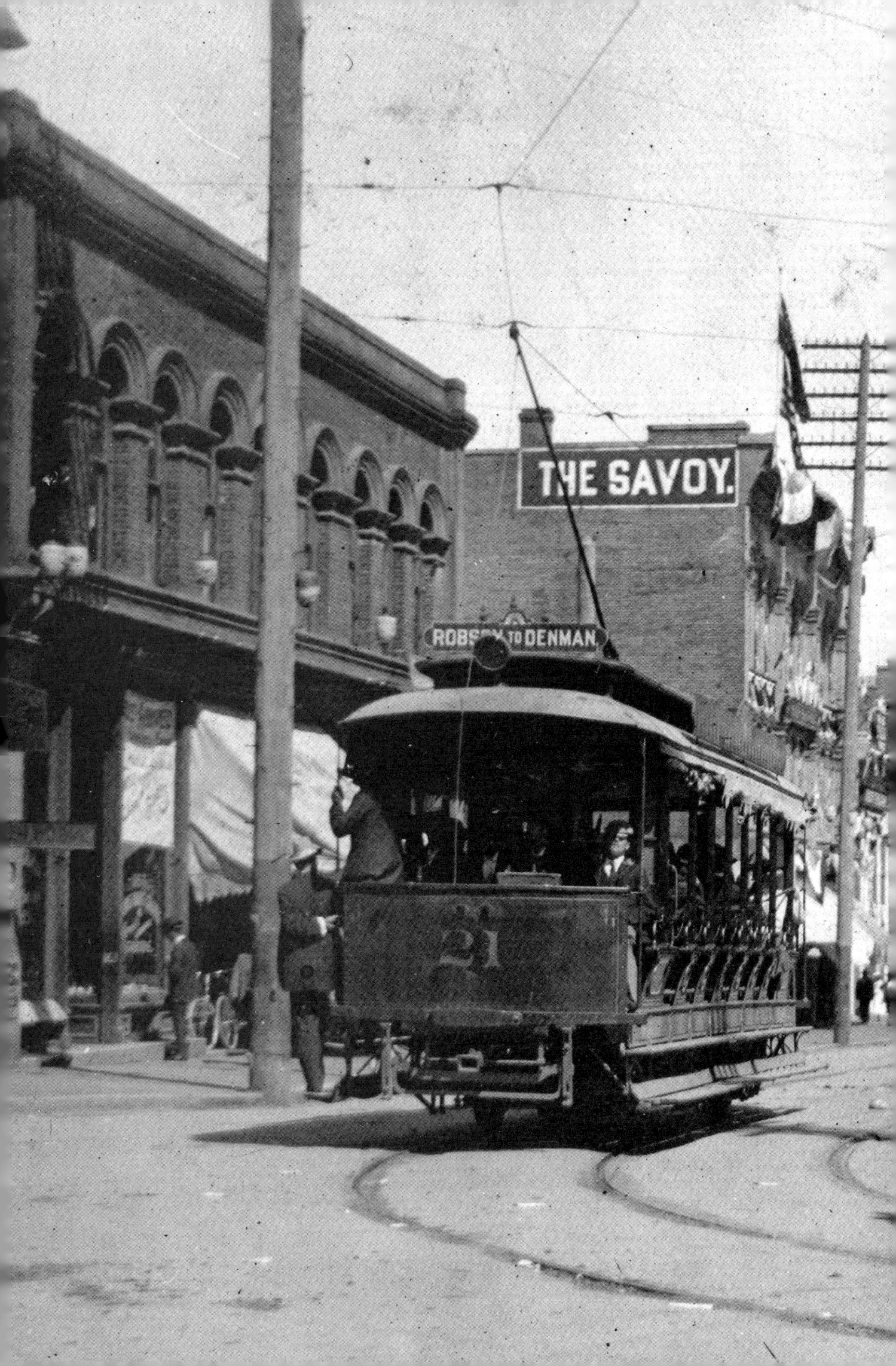
THE SAVOY.
TO DENMAN
21

CHAPTER TWO

Growth to Greatness
1898 – 1903

TURN-OF-THE-CENTURY TWOSOME — This superb study, c. 1900, reveals two typical early streetcars: open car 27, built in 1896, and conventional closed car 24, built in 1890. Both single-truck (two-axle) cars would be obsolete within five years, when B.C. Electric began building larger, double-trucked streetcars in its New Westminster shops; such was the city's fast pace of progress. Car 24 was sent to North Vancouver in 1906, along with three other Vancouver streetcars, to begin B.C. Electric's operation there.

In this photograph, the streetcar crews wear sporty summer-issue caps. Car 27 displays a bulkhead painted a distinctive gold.

From Woebegone to Award-Winner in Five Short Years

The franchises of the company were in chaotic condition, the steam generating plants inadequate and unreliable, rolling stock mostly obsolete, tracks and roadbed in bad shape, and terminals and repair shops utterly insufficient for their purposes, [in] whole producing a set of conditions under which the average man would have broken down.

The first decade of B.C. Electric's life,
Gaslights to Gigawatts

"Vancouver has benefited immensely . . . amply proved by the increased receipts of our Company"

Most glorious ventures that achieve success have stared in the face of potential doom at some point. By 1898, B.C. Electric was no different – it had inherited a mess. Although the street railway system in the Vancouver region had proven itself by then, it was still on shaky ground. Bankruptcies and corporate changes had not spawned overwhelming trust in the future of street railways in this port city. As a new company, B.C. Electric had to show both investors and the public that streetcars and interurbans had a solid future in the area.

Among company officials, a positive vision prevailed between 1898 and 1903. The London-based company took on its challenge with enthusiasm and was prepared to take some risks. It laid much more streetcar track in Vancouver, struck deals with realtors and land-seeking settlers, gave out free passes to politicians and civic VIPs and laid the groundwork for the momentous decade of transit glory to follow.

In 1898, company officials had to contend with high expectations from all corners. This was, after all, the era of the Klondike gold rush, when brash dreams filled the hearts of many. Members of the first local transit union, formed during this period,

1898

[A] mining madness seized Vancouver . . . In 1898, every hotel and lodging-house was crowded to capacity; tents were pitched in every water-front lot . . . and stranger sights than ever before were to be seen on the skid road . . . contracts were let for new mansions in the West End and for new business blocks in the heart of the city, and newspapers increased their circulation beyond belief . . . Vancouver had started its climb back to prosperity.

Alan Morley, *Vancouver*

- Gold fever flourishes in Vancouver as the Klondike gold rush continues.
- By 1895, Vancouver has 17,862 residents; by 1900, 24,750.
- The entire downtown section of New Westminster burns in a great fire on September 10 and 11, leaving hundreds homeless.
- B.C. Electric introduces coloured lights to Vancouver's streetcars on June 8 for better identification: Pender Street cars use a green light, Fairview white, and "main line" cars, red. Soon afterwards, the company scraps this confusing system.
- *The Province* newspaper office installs Vancouver's first long-distance telephone line on March 28, two days after publishing its first daily edition (it started as a weekly in Victoria in 1896).
- Vancouver's first pay phones are installed at English Bay on August 6; a local call costs five cents, the same as street-car fare.
- Canada's first motion picture theatre opens on Cordova Street.

negotiated a raise for street railway workers. Expectations had risen significantly. It was no longer enough just to provide transportation; after eight years, everyone from passengers and patrons to employees wanted more service and better value for their dollar.

B.C. Electric was determined to deliver. As more and more people continued to pour into Vancouver, and real estate fervour grew, company officials realized that more track was needed to service expanded neighbourhoods and business areas. The work of laying more track grew from a flourish to an orchestrated frenzy within two years.

Around 1898, B.C. Electric received the title to 68 lots that the C.P.R. had promised to its predecessor, the Vancouver Electric Railway & Light Company. This real estate deal came with a price; in exchange, B.C. Electric agreed to run a 20-minute service between Fairview and the downtown area. This goodwill gesture appeased disgruntled Fairview residents who had previously felt abandoned when their line was temporarily discontinued.

The Klondike gold rush gave Vancouver's transit system a welcome flush of revenue. City council had agreed in November 1897 to spend $2,000 to advertise the advantages of Vancouver as an outfitting point for the gold fields; it circulated 50,000 pamphlets to promote the city for this purpose.[1] A year later, Johannes Buntzen, B.C. Electric's general manager, wrote to his London superior: "Vancouver has certainly benefited immensely by the advertising done, as I think is amply proved by the increased receipts of our Company."[2]

After the gold rush, B.C. Electric continued an advertising campaign aimed at cashing in on Vancouver's growing reputation as an enticing place to visit and settle. The company advertised the area and offered free transportation to new settlers around 1900. These special inducements came in cooperation with real estate agents, who subdivided land into one- and two-acre (.4- and .8-hectare) parcels. At the same time, B.C. Electric created streetcar service via Davie Street to English Bay, which helped popularize the scenic spot as a destination point for swimming and picnics.

The success of B.C. Electric hinged on increased ridership and good relations with civic politicians and the community at large; Vancouver city council decided where street railways could be built and regulated factors such as vehicle speed and maximum fares. To further their cause, B.C. Electric liberally gave out free annual passes to most city officials, including mayors and aldermen, all members of civic police forces, some members of the B.C. Provincial Police and top officials of the fire departments. In 1900, B.C. Electric executive F. S. Barnard insisted that all members of the B.C. legislature receive free passes. The post office, meanwhile, paid $150 a year so uniformed postal workers could ride the cars "at all hours of the day."[3]

BLACKSMITH'S HELPER – W. Kerfoot joined Vancouver's street railway company on November 5, 1898. He worked as blacksmith's helper at the Kitsilano street-car shops and remained there until his retirement on May 31, 1932.

PHOTO CREDIT: HEATHER CONN (FROM HE COLLECTION)

CABOOSE AT YOUR SERVICE – The cataclysmic fire of September 10 and 11, 1898, destroyed New Westminster's entire business district and a large section of the residential area. B.C. Electric set up its one caboose, still lettered for Westminster and Vancouver Tramway, at the corner of Tenth Street and Columbia as a temporary depot.

PHOTO SOURCE: CVA: TRANS. N. 88.2

1899

- B.C. Electric begins a program to close in the vestibules of its open streetcars, a long-overdue plan that takes nine months to carry out.

- The six-block, double-tracked streetcar line on Denman Street, reaching English Bay at Davie Street from Robson, is completed.

- Vancouver passenger receipts for the year ending March 31 are up $22,378.16 from the previous year.[9]

- W.H. Armstrong introduces Vancouver to its first horseless carriage, a steam-driven automobile.

OH, TO BE ON BROADWAY – By the time conductor John Perry's photo was published in a 1919 transit employee magazine, he was 81 and had worked for 30 years in Vancouver's transportation business. (Perry is second from left.)

This 1899 photo, taken at Broadway and Main, shows a Mount Pleasant streetcar and Perry's uniformed co-workers, from left: motorman H.W. Vanderwalker, who later became cashier at the Prior Street car barn; Perry, later a messenger; conductor Shand; and motorman Tibbs.

Vanderwalker started as a motorman in 1898, became ticket clerk in 1907, then worked as cashier at the Prior Street ticket office three years later. The employee magazine reported: "He is always addressed familiarly as 'Van' by all who know him and can be seen any day still going strong behind the wire cage of the ticket office."

PHOTO SOURCE: BC HYDRO:
THE B.C. ELECTRIC EMPLOYEES' MAGAZINE,
MAY 1919, P. 15

To meet growing demand, B.C Electric feverishly expanded its streetcar tracks across Vancouver in 1900. It rushed through an improvement of the Powell Street line, double-tracked and extended the Main Street line, and completed three other track work projects.

By 1897, the company was operating 13 double-ended streetcars across the city. It would enhance its interurban service with the opening of a new depot in New Westminster on March 26, 1900. The one-storey brick building, located on the south side of Columbia between 8th and Begbie streets, featured offices, a waiting room and a covered bay with two tracks for the interurbans and streetcars. It looked as if public transit was here to stay. (Service survived, despite a devastating, city-wide fire in New Westminster in 1898.)

Around this time, B.C. Electric began to use names, rather than numbers, to identify the interurban coaches. Former Westminster and Vancouver Tramway's number 17 became "Burnaby" and number 13, "Richmond." The New Westminster–based vehicles, which arrived in 1899, were given names: "Vancouver" and "Westminster."

Of wages and work: a union local forms

B.C. Electric needed more than a folksy image to satisfy its hard-working employees. Transit staff in New Westminster, spurred by a desire for increased wages, decided to unionize in 1900. On January 19, they formed local 134 of the Amalgamated Association of Street Railway Employees of America. (Known informally as the Street Railways Union, the union had been founded on September 15, 1892.) The 37 members of local 134 soon negotiated a new contract with B.C. Electric and won a two-cent-an-hour wage increase, raising the rate to 22 cents an hour. At the time, motormen and conductors worked a 10¼ hour day, seven days a week, at 20 cents an hour. No one received the unthinkable luxury of paid vacation.[4] (Sid Gregory, the union's

A STREETCAR COMPETITOR? – This basic buggy, driven by gasoline-powered steam, was Vancouver's first automobile in 1899. Bought from Stanley Bros. of Newton, Massachusetts, it was known as the Stanley Steamer and cost $1,000, with delivery. W.C. Ditmars, an accountant for Vancouver Engineering Works, purchased the revolutionary vehicle in February that year for his partner W. H. Armstrong of Armstrong & Morrison, a construction/contracting firm.

Here, driver George Taylor, accompanied by his wife, holds the curved tiller that steered the car; they are at 816 Burrard Street. The new vehicle posed little threat to streetcars and interurbans at the time; it had a two-cylinder engine, wire wheels with pneumatic tires, and a pedal-operated bell. The engine and boiler sat under the seat with a water tank in the rear. Armstrong used the buggy for about two years, then sold it to W.G. Tanner of Victoria, B.C. Automobiles did not gain popular use in Vancouver until about 1913.

PHOTO SOURCE: CVA: TRANS. P. 28 N. 21

FOREMOST FOREMAN – Thomas F. Tokely started as foreman of the car barns in New Westminster in September 1899. He retired in 1932.

Hand-painted, gold-leaf logo: B.C. Electric gains a name brand

One man's creative flair and patient work added distinctive style to B.C. Electric's image in the early days. (Today, we'd call it corporate branding.) Eli Egriphan Nimrod Sampson Joseph Jeffrey Maneer handpainted, in gold leaf, the numbers and lettering on all Vancouver's streetcars and interurbans from 1899 to 1926. He also designed the scripted company logo that B.C. Electric used for 35 years. [10]

Like many transit employees, the work ran in the family. Maneer passed on his sign-writing skills to relative Fraser Wilson (Maneer was second cousin to Wilson's father), who, in turn, designed the masthead for *The Buzzer*. (This free news brochure, published by B.C. Electric, first appeared as an on-board giveaway in June 1916.) [11] Wilson's father, and his grand-uncle Roderick Semple, also worked in local transit.

Maneer's lengthy mouthful of a name spawned endless ribbing. As a boy, young Wilson and his friends liked to pester Maneer by chanting his full name again and again.

first financial secretary, was the first to sign the local's original charter. He had started on May 1, 1894, with the Westminster and Vancouver Tramway Company, sweeping out streetcars and the car barns for a dollar a day. He worked his way up as conductor, motorman, timekeeper and ticket agent and by 1911, was appointed general agent of the freight and passenger department in New Westminster. He retired in 1946 as a general agent of the New Westminster transportation division.)

By 1901, B.C. Electric claimed that it had the best-paid employees of any company in Canada. Four hundred regular staff worked for the company in Vancouver, New Westminster and Victoria, and they could now even take Sundays off. This was a luxury that had not existed the previous year.

Consolidation brings greater security

B.C. Electric built only one new streetcar line in Vancouver in 1901: a single track on Main Street south from Ninth Avenue (later Broadway) to 16th Avenue; 16th Avenue formed Vancouver's boundary with the municipality of South Vancouver. But haphazard additions of streetcar lines, regardless of their rapid appearance, did not ensure a stable future for the transit company. Since the lease for each streetcar line expired at a different time, the fate of transit service relied too heavily on the whims of city council. B.C. Electric needed a more secure, guaranteed street railway presence.

The company convinced Vancouver city council in 1901 to consolidate all its street railway franchises, which created a more attractive climate for investment capital. The agreement, dated October 14, made the company's Vancouver operations subject to purchase on February 11, 1919, and every five years thereafter. In return for the new arrangement, B.C. Electric agreed to pay a higher percentage of its earnings to the city, extend existing streetcar lines on Main Street and on

Powell, and obey city rules regarding maximum fare, minimum service and speed limit (8 to 10 miles/13 to 16 kilometres per hour). [5]

Around 1903, a truly informal announcement marked a new interurban stop in east Vancouver. A man painted the word "Grant" in black letters on a board and nailed it on a stump by what is now Grant Street; back then, Park Avenue (later Commercial Drive) was just thick wilderness. This meant that passengers inbound from New Westminster had gained an additional stop within Vancouver. Along this route, some stops were just patches cut out of forest with no platform.

B.C.-built cars a first

Amid such humble improvements, the biggest news, by far, in 1903 was the construction of two elegant, state-of-the-art interurban cars, built in B.C. Electric's own car shops by the best local craftsmen in only two months. The company had opened a remarkable car-manufacturing plant in New Westminster in February that year. For the first time, the pioneering company could build its own cars, rather than rely on U.S. and eastern Canadian manufacturers. This was a gutsy move that gave the transit

EARLY TRANSIT STAFF — Vancouver's motormen and conductors pose at Barnard (later Union) Street with several of the city's first streetcars in 1899. Seated in front with dog: Frank Foster. Front row, from left: J. Frizzell, Anderson, Grant, G. Lenfesty, McCann, Snider, C.E. Bennett, A. Keith, W. Braim, E. Manning. Second row, from left: J. Howes, G. Cameron, T. Routley, McNab, G. Martin, Tibbs, J. Barton, Abe Ross, R. Brunt, J. Perry, C. Tanner. Back row, from left: J. Paxman, H.W. Vanderwalker, J. Marshall, H. Gibbs, McLennan, R. Brerdon [listed elsewhere as Brereton], Ross, A. (Paddy) Davis, J. Jeffers, J. Clode, G. Sherman, J. Gardiner. Mechanic on car: Louis Peterson. Missing: D. McLean.

PHOTO CREDIT: BC HYDRO:
THE B.C. ELECTRIC EMPLOYEES' MAGAZINE,
JUNE 1922, P. 17

WHEN CORDOVA HELD TOP SPOT – Two-year-old streetcar 21 has just wheeled onto Cordova Street, eastbound from Cambie Street, in July 1899. At the time, Cordova was Vancouver's busiest, most highly developed shopping street. Carrall Street in the distance marks the eastern end of this thriving district.

PHOTO SOURCE: CVA: STR. P. 209 N. 127

A WILD-WEST WAGON – In this splendid rare photo, these hatted men pose with a B.C. Electric tower, or line, car in 1899. The company's first electric-powered line car, numbered L.1, would appear in 1900, rendering horse-drawn work vehicles such as this one obsolete. Notice the gears, immediately under the roll of trolley wire, used to raise the platform to the height of the trolley lines.

PHOTO SOURCE: BC HYDRO: A0400

company autonomy and efficiency – which would prove invaluable in the heady decade to come.

"Delta" (later 1203) and "Surrey" (later 1204) were widely admired by the media and public alike. Until then, no one had ever used B.C.'s Douglas fir and cedar for vehicle finishing. The two trams, styled after full-size railroad coaches, were like no others on the continent. B.C. Electric entered them in New Westminster's annual exhibition, where they garnered the highest manufacturers' award. *The British Columbian* did not hold back its praise:

1900

- Vancouver has 24,700 residents, Burnaby about 400.
- Thirteen double-ended streetcars operate daily regular service on the Vancouver lines.
- The first regular ferry service begins May 12 between North Vancouver and the Vancouver waterfront on the south side of Burrard Inlet.

> *In the handsome passenger cars, the frame is built of Douglas fir, cedar and maple – all native woods except the maple. The use of British Columbia woods for car finishing was never tried before, and the expedient was considered risky by experts. But after making some experiments, Superintendent Driscoll felt quite safe in proceeding, which he did with most satisfactory results, and in "Delta" and "Surrey" it is generally admitted that the company has two of the handsomest and best equipped electric cars in America.*

It was further reported, with a twinge of patronizing eastern bias, that at this show, the cars "attracted a great deal of attention, and were somewhat of a surprise to Eastern people, who could hardly believe anything so handsome could be produced from so-called soft woods."[6]

The British Columbian gave B.C. Electric ample credit for the weighty contribution that its car shops and top-quality employees had made:

> *A large and constantly increasing staff of skilled mechanics is employed at the carshops, to whom the highest current wages are paid. The establishment of this institution has added a couple of score of families to New Westminster's population, and from present indications it will mean much more in the near future.*[7]

Indeed, the street railway company had created an enviable reputation and position to define the future of transit in the region. Bolstered by its classy trams and two locally built locomotives, it could move both people and freight on a grand scale. Passenger business on the interurban line was growing phenomenally and B.C. Electric built its first line dedicated solely to freight in 1903. That marked the first year in which the company publicized the freight hauled during the year: 6,158 tons.[8]

In five short years, B.C. Electric had shifted from a financial risk on precarious footing to a visionary operation with increased revenues and world recognition. The fledgling corporation had transformed from ugly duckling to graceful swan. Success had finally arrived for the transit system. Vancouver's greatest years of glory awaited. . . .

Salmon for dinner? Oh, the shame!

What happened if you smuggled a salmon onto a turn-of-the-century streetcar in Vancouver and your secret leaked out? Public humiliation.

Today's diners consider a salmon meal a special treat, but in the summer of 1900, local residents deemed it a lowly choice for guests. Back then, salmon were so plentiful that they were free or cost a mere nickel. For most households, such a deal was still too good to pass up. Decades later, one Vancouver man recalled the unpleasant aftermath of his wife's request to bring home a salmon for dinner.

He boarded a streetcar with his "secret" hidden in newspaper, hoping no one would notice his fishy cargo. But events did not turn out as planned. The passenger explained his embarrassing predicament:

> It [the salmon] was under my arm, and in the crush to board the conveyance, my arm was squeezed and the slippery salmon squirted out of the paper, tail first ... We had been caught in the act, we were guilty of the indignity of carrying home so worthless a trifle as a salmon, and what was worse, there could be no doubt, it was our intention to eat it when we got it there. Awful!" [12]

THE GOOD OLD DAYS? — Conductor 36, name unknown, was reportedly debonair and "the pride and joy of all lady passengers." But Vancouver's early transit years left him with memories of crude conditions, not fun times. He joined B.C. Electric in 1900 and gave an interviewer this disgruntled account two decades later in the August 1921 edition of the employee newsletter:

> I often hear the remark, "the good old days." If scrambling along the side of a car when old numbers six and ten were up-to-date [cars], blowing a whistle to stop and start the car, no closed vestibules, sitting on the bench as an extra from 6 o'clock in the morning until 5 at night for five consecutive days without getting a run and without remuneration, for there was no minimum guarantee – if such days were good, compared with the present, I miss my count.

PHOTO SOURCE: BC HYDRO
THE B.C. ELECTRIC EMPLOYEES' MAGAZINE,
AUGUST 1921, P. 23

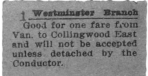

Dupont Street: "Gambling goes on promiscuously all over Vancouver"

W ith brothels, gambling dens and saloons only steps away from downtown streetcar service, Vancouver's early public transit undoubtedly provided access to numerous diversions. However, many who ventured such anonymous rides would likely hail from the city's more comfortable homes in the West End

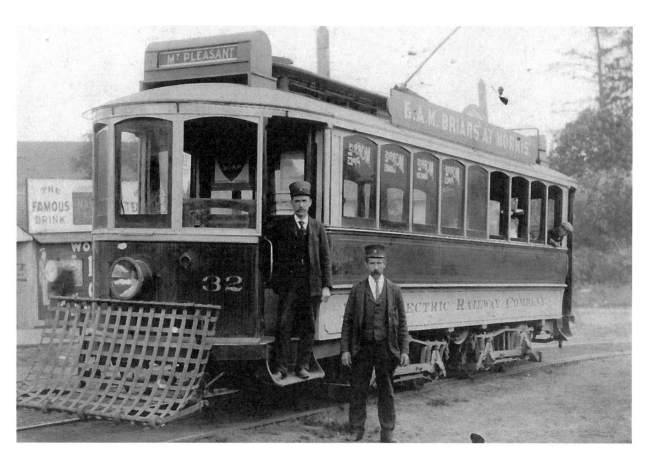

A TRAM TRANSFORMED – Streetcar 32, shown here at the turn of the century, began its life as an interurban coach for Westminster and Vancouver Tramway. B.C. Electric refurbished and rebuilt five of these vehicles in 1900 and placed them into streetcar service. This view shows former W. & V. T. number 12 soon after its renewal.

B.C. Electric shipped this streetcar across Burrard Inlet in 1910 to operate on North Vancouver's new Lynn Valley line. Scrapped four years later, car 32 was one of the first double-trucked (four-axle) cars to be withdrawn from service.

PHOTO SOURCE: VPL: SC-00-3

STREETCAR SIMPLICITY – Car 26, built in 1899, proceeds along Granville in this northeast view from Robson Street, photographed in the early 1900s. St. Andrew's Presbyterian Church, at the corner of Georgia and Richards streets, appears in the distance to the right.

PHOTO SOURCE: CMBC: SS-90-6

ON-THE-GO PROMOTION – The Morris brand of pipe tobacco receives top billing on this 1900 streetcar. Motorman W. M. Braim and conductor Dick Brereton pose with their vehicle at Broadway and Main (then 9th and Westminster avenues). This view, with few passengers, offers an excellent photographic study of one of the finest streetcars of its day.

PHOTO SOURCE: BC HYDRO: A0009

or elsewhere; the mostly transient males who frequented cheap downtown hotels could easily walk to their debauchery.

At the turn of the century, the city's seedy waterfront teemed with single men, mostly sailors, mill hands and seasonal labourers, who earned good wages in construction or logging. By 1886, 46 saloons and hotels operated in the city's waterfront area alone.[15] A city resident complained in a letter to the editor of *The Province* four years later: "Everyone knows that gambling goes on promiscuously all over Vancouver, in clubs, in hotels, in saloons, in rooms connected with saloons and in private houses. Not a night passes, that it is not indulged in."[16]

Before 1897, public transportation's head office on Barnard (Union) Street stood within easy reach of temptation. Despite strict rules regarding no gambling or drinking on the job, transit employees could pursue such pleasures in their off-hours. Like any other residents, they had an entertaining, and often conflicting, variety of diversions to choose from. Mount Pleasant pioneer Reuben Hamilton recalls the early 1900s:

> *What did we do with ourselves on a Saturday night in Vancouver? . . . [W]hiskey was 10 cents a glass and a good schooner of beer [went] for a nickel . . . we could roll the dice for the Toms and Jerrys, and play Chuck-Luck, Fan-Tan, and lottery on old Dupont Street in Chinatown. On the street corners the I.W.W. [Industrial Workers of the World] would be singing "Solidarity Forever"; a religious group singing "There is Honey in the Rock for you my brother" and music from the Salvation band [playing] "We will understand each better when the mists have rolled away."*[17]

A streetcar offered the perfect inexpensive way to travel to a colourful corner of Vancouver. For those who sought discreet encounters at midday or midnight, public transit also provided a less visible form of transportation than a waiting carriage.

Opium salons and other "dens of vice" flourished in Shanghai Alley, where Carrall Street extended into False Creek and "a long string of red lights told all too plainly the nature of the resorts."[18] (Opium was legally manufactured and peddled on Dupont Street until local sale of the drug became illegal in 1908.) The quest for sex focused on Dupont Street, the original name for Pender Street between Main and Cambie. By August 1906, 153 prostitutes and 41 brothels thrived on this street, with one favourite "luxury house" address known as "The White House."[19]

DOUBLE DUTY FOR THE KIDS — Motorman Alex Innes proved better than a babysitter on his streetcar and interurban runs. "His reputation is so good, the women folk on the Sapperton-Edmonds line . . . put their children on his car, knowing they will be looked after," reported the February 1925 issue of *The B.C. Electric Employees' Magazine.*

Alex started with B.C. Electric as a stoker at the Burnaby powerhouse steam plant, then transferred to the position of motorman in 1900. He maintained an unblemished record in his 25 years of transit service.

PHOTO SOURCE: BC HYDRO:
THE B.C. ELECTRIC EMPLOYEES' MAGAZINE,
FEBRUARY 1925, P. 25

1901

- B.C. Electric employees form their first local of the International Brotherhood of Electrical Workers, which organizes men who work on the overhead wires and electrical rail lines.

- One new streetcar line is built: a single track on Main Street south from Broadway to Sixteenth Avenue, Vancouver's boundary with the municipality of South Vancouver.

- The Duke and Duchess of Cornwall and York, later King George V and Queen Mary, arrive in Vancouver on September 30.

BRIGGS GOT THE BUMPS — Joe Briggs started with B.C. Electric as motorman no. 33 in 1901, "receiving instruction . . . in the art of coaxing one of fifteen cars . . . over the bumps and mud holes around town." [13] After 10 years, he became inspector and then depot master at Mount Pleasant streetcar barn.

At the company's Prior Street car barn, car repairer Joe Berry began work that same year. Retired car repairer Ted Gardner remembered working with Berry in later years; Berry remained with B.C. Electric until after the Second World War.

PHOTO SOURCE: BC HYDRO:
THE B.C. ELECTRIC EMPLOYEES' MAGAZINE,
MAY 1921, P. 14

Dupont Street grew so popular that city traffic patterns changed. In the first few years after Vancouver incorporated, carriages bound for New Westminster had headed east on Cordova or Hastings, then south on Westminster Avenue (later Main Street). After Dupont Street grew in notoriety, more and more carriages began to take a short cut through this steamy street, transforming it into a major thoroughfare. It enjoyed no direct transit service, however; the closest the streetcar got was to Hastings Street, only a block away.

Meanwhile, some Burnaby citizens deemed certain passengers, whether of public interurbans or private vehicles, "the undesirable class of females." *The Columbian* reported on March 16, 1900: "It seems that, on Saturdays and Sundays especially, women of the demi-monde class are in the habit of visiting . . . road-houses, on the New Westminster-Vancouver road, and the language of some of them is, to say the least, an abominable outrage on the law abiding-respectable community of Burnaby." (This likely referred to Douglas Road, now known as Canada Way.)

Almost three weeks later, the same paper reported that Burnaby Council had appointed a constable with "special instructions to keep a keen look-out for any misconduct on the part of either drivers or occupants of oft times furiously driven rigs, which especially on Sundays, carry flauntingly along the inter-urban highroad females of certain and doubtful class, who . . . have carried Sabbath desecration in the suburbs to a most annoying extreme." [20]

Judging morality was not the mandate of Vancouver's early public transit operations. B.C. Electric and its predecessors opened their doors to all manner of passengers, as long as they did not prove unruly or dangerous. From the heart of the city to the suburbs, public vehicles carried saints and sinners alike, as long as they all paid the proper fare.

BROTHELS AND BOOZE – Part of Vancouver's red-light district, with an opium "factory" on the left, appears in this circa-1906 photo, which looks westward along Pender Street from Columbia Street. (Photos of this part of early Vancouver are rare.) This section of Pender, some seven blocks east of glamorous Granville Street and one block from a streetcar line, was known as Dupont Street at the time. The carriage trade shown here is likely of a different sort than what frequented Granville Street.

PHOTO SOURCE: CVA 677-530

The Interurban: "I presumed it would always be with us"

> Kids walked everywhere, except the more adventuresome who would steal a ride on the interurban. The system was: climbing up the back steps on the devil strip side, hanging on for dear life and hoping the tram would stop at the rider's station.
>
> **The Discovery Project for South East Vancouver,**
> ***Collected Memories***

The old interurban trams, more than any other early vehicle, seem to hold a special place in the hearts of many Vancouverites. Old-timers speak lovingly of the camaraderie on board, when friendly conductors took shopping orders from housewives in the morning and delivered the goods in the afternoon to a waiting family member at a tram stop.

A MADE-IN-B.C. DISTINCTION – "Delta" and "Surrey" were the first of their kind to be built in B.C. In this photograph, taken on September 28, 1903, builders pose with "Surrey" on 12th Street at B.C. Electric's recently opened shops, where the car was built. ("Delta" was completed one week earlier.) Highly skilled tradesmen built both cars in only two months. This car began operating immediately on the Central Park line between Vancouver and New Westminster. It featured etched-glass upper windows and decorative paint work, with a large cow-catcher at each end.

PHOTO SOURCE: CMBC: IC-10-2

Many recall the childhood delight they experienced when riding the trams, sometimes sneaking free trips. Others describe with admiration the fine details and workmanship of these well-crafted vehicles. Transit enthusiasts rave about the trams' reliability and their forging of transportation routes for decades to follow.

Whether for historical value or just plain nostalgia, many rue the day that these trams stopped running in the Lower Mainland. But they are not gone forever. Today, restored trams 1207 and 1231 operate on a short False Creek route while efforts are underway to revive other interurbans that once gave daily service in this region.

1902

- No streetcars operate for six weeks due to winter snow.

- The first passenger train arrives in Steveston on July 1, operated by the C.P.R., primarily to serve the canneries. Three years later, B.C. Electric leases the line and converts it from steam to electricity.

- The Edison Electric Theatre, believed to be the first permanent cinema in Canada, opens in Vancouver.

DRIVE-THROUGH DECOR – In this westward view from Cambie Street, a streetcar has just passed through the Japanese arch on Hastings Street, one of many erected across the city to celebrate the visit of the Duke and Duchess of Cornwall and York in October 1901. (Vancouver boasted a population of 27,010 at the time.)

There was great excitement over the arrival of the royal couple, who would remain in B.C. from September 30 to October 3. In Victoria, the Parliament Buildings were outlined for the first time with long strings of lights.

PHOTO SOURCE: CVA: SGN 881

In a look at the past, one Vancouver pioneer provides her memories of the tram:

The platforms were heavy, weather-beaten planks. The little station shelters were painted "railroad red." Inside, a single wooden bench. On the side of each building, a white board with black lettering gave the name of the station – Cedar Cottage, Lakeview, Collingwood West and East, Park Avenue, Central Park. . . . The interurban was part of our lives in a more relaxed age.

Slowly, it emerged from the depths of its dim, cavernous terminal at the corner of Hastings and Carrall; packed with commuters of all kinds. Shoppers, many from Woodwards food floor, boarded with large boxes of groceries. Then, through the coach's swinging doors, to the smoking section, there men sat with newspapers and pipes. Along Hastings, it would take its place among the streetcars, trundling up Commercial to Cedar Cottage.

After this, it came into its own territory. The interurban became "king of the road" and had a free line all to itself. Generally, two coaches would be linked together, swaying up the track. We waited at the Central Park Station. The conductor would be standing on the steps, ready to jump down and help us board. Once we were seated, he came to collect fares. We paid according to a zone system.

Our conductor was a splendid figure in his navy serge uniform. It was like an elegant three-piece suit, with metal buttons; and always, the watch and chain of the railroad man. Of course, his cap was trimmed with gold braid.

The tram announced its arrival at each station by blowing a whistle. Often, we ran the last yards to Central Park platform, as that sound warned us – our transport had left Park Avenue and was rushing our way.

When I was a kid, I presumed the interurban would always be with us – scooting by on a track above our heads at Collingwood West, or down below the high embankments, where we played at Collingwood East.

We marveled at this wonder of transport as it flashed past. Our interurban was always on time. Our aged and very young were helped on board by caring and friendly railroad employees.

Rattlers and boneshakers gone

Cheerful conductors, clanging bells and teetering old streetcars full of chatty standees: Vancouver's two-person streetcars inspired nostalgia from a local newspaper columnist in the late 1970s. He reminisced with an air of wistfulness and appreciation:

Gone...are the two-man street cars, affectionately known as "rattlers" or "boneshakers." There was ample room on the boarding platform for passengers to stand watching the conductor opening and closing the doors manually, punching individual transfers, selling strips of tickets, and making change up to two dollars for cash patrons, although he'd do his best to handle a five-spot without grumbling. And the cars stopped at every corner. The skipstop plan was not in vogue.

The remarkable thing was that these ever-busy conductors were happy at their jobs, and chatted cheerfully with standees, even if one inadvertently stepped on the clanging backing-up bell. All the while he had to keep a wary eye out for disembarking passengers so he could pull the stop cord in time. All had to leave by the rear as motormen were ensconced in their own curtained-off precincts. [21]

WHEN MEN WERE MEN – This circa-1902 view shows a crew laying tracks for one of the city's longest streetcar lines at the time, which extended along Powell Street. Twenty-five years later, one transit employee reminisced in the January 1927 issue of the company newsletter that this photograph depicted a period "when men were men and Vancouver was small."

PHOTO SOURCE: BC HYDRO: *THE B.C. ELECTRIC EMPLOYEES' MAGAZINE,* JANUARY 1927, P. 4

A MADE-IN-B.C. TRIUMPH – This cutting-edge car-manufacturing plant in New Westminster stood west of 12th Street at today's Stewardson Way. After it was destroyed by fire in August 1904, an even larger shop was built. Almost 200 streetcars and interurban coaches were built there, the last in 1914.

The "Richmond" interurban car shown here became car 1205 and remained in service until December 1953. Car 71, shown next to a single-truck streetcar, was only the third double-trucked car ever built in the shop, and it operated until 1952.

PHOTO SOURCE: CMBC: IC-10-7

TRAM FRONTRUNNERS – B.C. Electric had already built four interurban cars by 1904 and two of these appear here, approaching their Vancouver depot at Carrall Street. In this 1903 view, the vehicles are coming west on Hastings Street, about to cross Columbia Street.

By this time, Vancouver has started to look like a big city, with enormous growth waiting in the future.

PHOTO SOURCE: GEORGE E. TIMMS PHOTO, VPL 5250

1903

- B.C. Electric's hydro plant on Indian Arm delivers the first hydroelectric power to Vancouver on December 17.

- B.C. Electric delivers its first company-built streetcars, 50 and 52, on August 2, under the guidance of master builder Thomas Driscoll.

- B.C. Electric announces on August 8 that "main line" streetcars will soon exclusively use Hastings Street, rather than the original route along Powell, Carrall, Cordova, Cambie and Hastings. Cordova Street merchants complain that this will result in a loss of business and a drop in property values.

- B.C. Electric focuses its whole year's track-building program on the intersection of Main and Hastings. This creates the company's only "grand union" set-up, which means that a streetcar can make both left and right turns or go straight through – a rare achievement on any system at that time.

- A steel cable suspension bridge, the first commercial tourist attraction in North Vancouver, is being built over the Capilano Canyon.

- The Carnegie Library opens at Hastings and Main on October 1.

- The Royal Vancouver Yacht Club forms.

- Woodward's Department Store opens on November 4, 1903 at Hastings and Abbott streets.

Today, I stand at Joyce [SkyTrain] station, on a platform resembling something made with a meccano set. But, far up the line, I hear a clickety-clack, and the old interurban whistles for my station![22]

Another area resident, former Port Moody publisher Tom Browne, shared his own nostalgia about the interurban and the striking role it once played in daily life:

Vancouver never again will have rapid transit the equal of those trams that ran single, double and triple-headed . . . They sped on, night and day, front-end flags stiffened out against the breeze, their whistling for stations carrying hauntingly for miles.

On frosty nights, the overhead wires spat sparks as the trolley rolled along them, a sight of surpassing brilliance which kids of the day must well remember . . .

Passengers boarded without paying fares. They were collected en route. It was a sight to see the conductor, in gold-braided cap, moving up the car, legs braced against the sway from the roadbed, making change from the pocket of his blue serge suit.

GRANVILLE STREET IN ITS GLORY — Substantial stone buildings, street lighting, paving and a host of electric wires attest to the new status of Granville Street, which has already outstripped Cordova Street by the time of this 1903 photo. In this view south from Hastings Street, a streetcar dominates; a horse cart and a few bicycles hardly add up to serious competition.

PHOTO SOURCE: CVA: STR. P. 335 N. 296

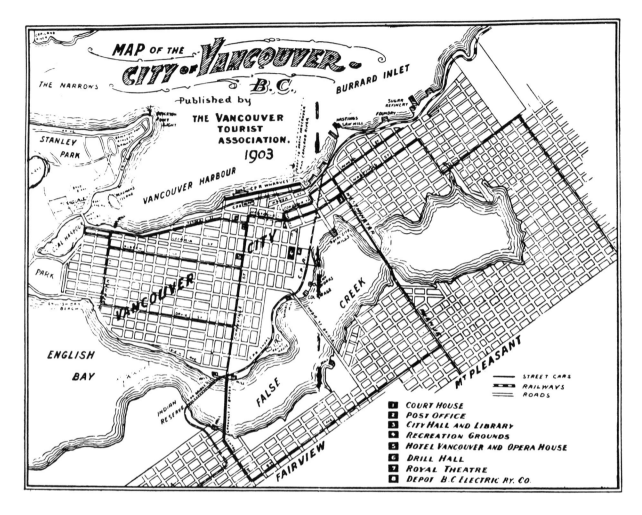

A MAP TO THE WORLD – Vancouver's street railway lines, and the city's most important sites, services and industries, adorn this 1903 map, published by the Vancouver Tourist Association as a way to promote the city.

The fares he collected, with a cheery greeting for those he knew, were rung up on a dial, which he altered manually. The dial tabulated the trip's takings, differentiating between cash and settlers' tickets. These were 10 to a book and cost 70 cents, with transfer privileges coming and going on city car lines. This seven cent fare was good to Marpole. [23]

NOTES

1   City Council minutes, Nov. 15, 1897, Street Railway Company, City of Vancouver Archives.

2   Aug. 20, 1898 correspondence from Buntzen to Hope, 1898.

3   Taylor, *The Automobile Saga of British Columbia,* p. 40.

4   Ewert, *The Story of the B.C. Electric Railway Company*, p. 41.

5   Ewert, *B.C. Electric*, p. 44.

6   Ewert, *B.C. Electric*, p. 49.

7   Ewert, *B.C. Electric*, p. 49.

8   Ewert, *B.C. Electric*, p. 49.

9   Ewert, *B.C. Electric*, p. 38.

10 McGeachie, *Bygones of Burnaby*, p. 24.

11 Ewert, *B.C. Electric*, p. 130.

12 *Collected Memories – A Guide to the Community Markers of South East Vancouver,* p. 234.

13 *The B.C. Electric Employees' Magazine*, May 1921, p. 14.

14 May 28, 1897 letter from Buntzen to R. Lewis, Electric Railway Letter Books, General, University of B.C., Special Collections.

15 Keller, *On the Shady Side – Vancouver 1886–1914*, p. 6.

16 *The Vancouver Daily Province*, Jan. 30, 1900, p. 10.

17 Mount Pleasant binder, 1957, Vancouver Public Library, Special Collections.

18 Kloppenborg, ed., *Vancouver – A City Album*, 1988, p. 38.

19 Keller, *On the Shady Side*, p. 70.

20 McGeachie, *Bygones of Burnaby*, p. 27.

21 Browne, *The Vancouver Sun*, April 8, 1978, p. 6.

22 *Collected Memories*, p. 124.

23 Browne, *The Sun*, April 8, 1978, p. 6.

CHAPTER THREE

Glory!
1904 – 1912

WESTERN CANADA'S LARGEST STREETCAR BARN – This February 1904 photo shows the newly completed Prior Street car barn, at the time the largest one west of Toronto. Located at Main (formerly Westminster Avenue) and Prior streets, it is pictured here in a northwestward view. It was 264 feet (80 metres) long on Main Street and 120 feet (37 metres) wide. The largest one-storey structure in Vancouver, it had nine parallel tracks with a 45-car capacity, an electric hoisting apparatus, four full-length repair pits and two skylights 18 feet (5.5 metres) long.

Here, 38 uniformed streetcar employees pose by the macadam road, plank sidewalk and crossings. Car 25, third from left, displays an exterior ad for Sweet Caporal Cigarettes. The Mount Pleasant car (extreme right) bears a cotton banner that reads "Band Concert, Stanley Park, Sunday afternoon, three o'clock." (The awning at the building's right rear belongs to the shop of George Aldrid, where transit staff bought tobacco, fruit, etc.)

PHOTO SOURCE: CVA: BU P. 212

Vancouver: "Supreme and Peerless City of Canada"

Transportation speaks probably more pronounced than anything else of the commercialism of any centre and surely we are peculiarly blessed in this respect. The old hackneyed saying that "all roads lead to Rome" could be aptly applied, at the present time, to our city.

Vancouver mayor James Findlay,
Saturday Sunset, **October 19, 1912**

Public transit "like something of a miracle"

These eight years had an enormous influence on the city of Vancouver. Remarkable buildings, constructed with detailed splendour and style, created an enviable downtown core. Magazine headlines of 1909 tell the story: "Many Great Buildings Being Constructed"; "Population of Vancouver Doubled in Five Years"; and "Vancouver – A City of Unlimited Possibilities."[1] Fuelled by the credo "Do it now and make it look great," a flurry of expansion permeated every facet of city life from the laying of streetcar tracks to clearing land to the start-up of businesses and the speculative sale of prime properties.

At the same time, an exploding network of new transit lines laid the foundation for Vancouver's present-day public transportation service. Between 1905 and 1913, the length of single track laid by B.C. Electric increased seven-fold: from 52 to 358 miles (85 to 580 kilometres).[2] Public vehicles, built locally with local timber for the first time, served the flood of newcomers who brought goods and skills and families to the young city. Streetcars and interurbans were the primary, and often only, way to get

LOYAL EMPLOYMENT — Many Vancouver transit employees stayed with the company for decades. A significant number of the motormen and conductors in this 1908 photo still worked with B.C. Electric 15 years later. From left, front row: F. Embleton; Billy Wilson; Jim Robertson; R. Rigby; W. Reach; Stan Moore; J. Thomas. Second row: Joe Graham; Turner; J. Reid; Joe Briggs; A. A. Walker; J. Mowat. Third row: unknown; Rowlands; Bacon; Lester; Chapman; Archer. Top row: B. Leveson and R. Campbell.

PHOTO SOURCE: BC HYDRO:
THE B.C. ELECTRIC EMPLOYEES' MAGAZINE,
MARCH 1923, P. 17

to work, attend cultural and sporting events, go on a family or recreational outing or run errands.

Public transit was both a necessity and a factor in urban growth. For those in outlying areas, it was essential, accessible and affordable, and it provided a mobility to all levels of society that was unavailable until this time. Transit vehicles were the miracle machines of this pivotal era. They ran on the magic of electric power. They brought comfort and convenience to hard-working citizens, and their craftsmanship added a dash of luxury to everyday lives.

Labour: "The street railway was a great provider of jobs"

A steady paycheque with benefits and perks seemed little short of miraculous at a time when most people depended on transient, seasonal labour to survive. Early street railway workers in the Vancouver region enjoyed the luxury of stable employment while most men worked long hours and hard days at construction, mining, logging or fishing.

As one fringe benefit, B.C. Electric employees paid a flat rate of 50 cents a month for their electricity, with no meters. As a result, many left their lights on day and night,

1904

- Vancouver public transit operates 36 single-truck, double-ended streetcars (12 convertible and 24 closed); two line cars (L1 and L2); two snowplows; two dump cars; and one flat car.

- Streetcars operate for the first time on electricity generated by water power from Lake Buntzen, starting June 4.

- B.C. Electric opens its Main Street substation to power streetcars. Frequent electricity shutdowns and outages leave Fairview line cars inactive, waiting for "juice."

- Frank and Fred Begg start the first car dealership in Vancouver. Industrialist John Hendry buys the first gasoline-powered car.

SOON TO BE OBSOLETE – Two Davie (English Bay) streetcars are about to pass in this glorious 1904 view of a bustling Hastings Street, looking east from Richards Street. The approaching car (right) is one of the few remaining open cars.

These single-truck (four-wheel) streetcars would soon be replaced with double- trucked, or eight-wheeled, cars, the city's first large street-cars, which began arriving the following year. The demands of Vancouver's booming population were about to exceed the carrying capacity of the city's early streetcars.

With these demands came high expectations from passengers, as revealed in a petition to B.C. Electric, sent four months after the Kitsilano streetcar line began service on July 4, 1905: "We, the undersigned patrons of the Kitsilano Street Cars beg to call your attention to the discomfort of the open ended cars running on the line. We think that it would add greatly to the comfort of both passengers and employees if doors instead of iron gates were placed on these cars similar to the doors on the main line cars." [3]

PHOTO SOURCE: VPL 5211

which drew criticism from the public. As another bonus, motormen and conductors received dashing caps and uniforms with brass buttons that many kept even after they left the company.

With ever-expanding demands for more transit service, employment at B.C. Electric jumped from 425 in 1905 to more than 1,000 in 1911. As one modern observer writes: "The street railway was a great provider of jobs. . . . To thousands of British Columbians it was [a] matter of pride that they had the best urban transportation system west of Toronto run by a well-established, well-financed, well-respected private company."[4]

Still, the transit jobs that served the public were no picnic. Motormen and conductors had steady jobs, but their pay was low, less than that of many tradespeople. By 1911, street railway employees brought home less average annual earnings than carpenters, bricklayers and even trainmen. "I started at 22 cents an hour, 10 hours a day, 365 days a year," said George Thompson, who began work for B.C. Electric in 1912.

Motormen and conductors could earn extra money by delivering merchants' goods to housewives along their routes. "Dixie Ross, the big grocer, would come out with a

A look back at brake shoes and bumpers

Every job has its shop talk and unique quirks that evoke a shared bond among workers. One transit employee reminisced about this aspect of his street railway past in the July 1932 issue of *The B.C. Electric Employees' Magazine*:

"Remember the old tin signs—red for Robson, yellow for Davie, white for Fairview, and so on—fastened onto the front and rear ends of the cars just where the new advertising cards are now [in 1932]?

"Remember the way those brake shoes used to climb the wheels, chatter, and stop the car with an awful jolt in spite of the most careful handling?

"Remember the signal lights on single track operated by a rope that hung from the guy wire? On windy days it was often some job to grab that rope!

"Remember the P.M. rush hour and the loads on the rear bumpers and the roof? Things were prosperous then and even those passengers didn't grumble at the accommodation—or lack of it. But that was probably because they were hard to get at with the farebox."

20 YEARS OF SAFE SERVICE – Like any transportation outfit, B.C. Electric had its share of both speed demons and safety-conscious staff. Motorman Aleck Matheson typified the latter. He started with the company in 1904 and maintained an accident-free record, or "clean sheet," for the next 20 years while driving streetcars in the city and for the Lulu Island branch.

Matheson attributed his success to good luck, but a company newsletter gave credit to his "99 per cent carefulness." Simply put, he never took chances.

PHOTO SOURCE: BC HYDRO:
THE B.C. ELECTRIC EMPLOYEES' MAGAZINE,
JULY 1924, P. 27

IN FOR THE LONG HAUL – This 1908 photo captures a number of B.C. Electric's long-time streetcar motormen and conductors. They're posing at Vancouver's Prior Street car barn, at the northwest corner of Main and Prior streets.

The seniority numbers on the employees' caps reveal their longevity of service; number 140 is the highest number, but lowest status. It means that 139 people have worked longer than this man.

PHOTO SOURCE: CVA: TRANS. P. 115 N. 70

KITS BEACH IN WINTER – The first large streetcar built by B.C. Electric, in 1905, eight-wheeled car 72 waits at lonely Kitsilano Beach before making its way back to its eastern termi-

nus at the corner of Frances Street and Victoria Drive. Harris is today's Georgia Street.

PHOTO SOURCE: HE COLLECTION

IN THE HEART OF NEW WEST – Streetcars serve New Westminster's main thoroughfare, Columbia Street, in this 1904 view east from 8th Street. The Windsor Hotel (right) marks the corner of Columbia and Begbie streets, while the track at right curves into B.C. Electric's interurban depot, built in 1900. This facility was replaced in 1911 by a two-storey depot, which stood slightly west at the corner of 8th and Columbia.

New Westminster's streetcar lines all arrived at, and operated on, the length of commercial Columbia Street.

PHOTO SOURCE: GEORGE E. TIMMS PHOTO, VPL 6748

A 1905 Steveston interurban line ticket

Frankenstein worked in the field

For a year, this monster-to-be laid track for B.C. Electric, spending 10-hour days digging ditches, shovelling coal, clearing land or working with surveying parties. He earned $2.50 an hour. When he came to Canada from Britain to seek his fortune before the First World War, the name on his passport said William Henry Pratt. However, millions of moviegoers later came to know him by his stage name: Boris Karloff.

Pratt really wanted to be an actor. He wound up with on-stage work in Nelson, B.C., where he was by no means star material. He admitted: "I mumbled, bumbled, missed cues, rammed into furniture, and sent the director's blood temperature soaring. When the curtain went up, I was getting $30 a week. When it descended, I was down to $15."[8] Nevertheless, he followed his passion and, under his new stage name, went on to portray a frightening Frankenstein in countless Hollywood movies.

load of provisions and ask us if we could drop it off at such-and-such a corner," remembers one former B.C. Electric employee. "We got 15 cents and some housewife got her groceries faster. We did the same with meat and liquor."[5]

Non-Caucasian workers had no such access to extra payment or to the jobs themselves. Asians earned half to a third of what Caucasian labourers did, and most employers upheld strict rules against hiring Asians; legislation and public sentiment supported this stance. For instance, all Vancouver city contracts contained a clause forbidding contractors to use Chinese labour.[6]

Despite these hiring prohibitions, Caucasian workers resented competition from Asians and race riots kept the groups divided. Canadian Pacific Railway president William Van Horne saw Asians as a valuable source of labour and criticized any laws that restricted their employment, but he stood in the minority. Local library and archival sources provide little indication that Asian labourers assisted in track-laying, construction or any other aspect of street railway work.

British Columbia had established itself as a province with growing unionism by 1903. A strike in February that year by the United Brotherhood of Railway Employees resulted in the province's first sympathy strike, which, in turn, prompted the formation

KEEPING CURRENT – Newly laid streetcar tracks dominate the intersection of Main and Hastings streets in this 1904 view. This routine work of track renewal formed part of a huge push for new transit infrastructure, including construction of the Prior Street car barns and the need to rework curves to accommodate new double-trucked streetcars. Ongoing track work was essential to maintain daily regular service.

Visible in this view to the southwest is the towered Carnegie Library, which still remains today. Vancouver's former city hall, to the left, is long gone.

PHOTO SOURCE: CMBC: SS-00-3

Passenger puts literary inspiration on the line

Sometimes, an appreciative passenger just wants to write a poem — not always the stuff of literary legend, but a simple tribute to a trusty vehicle that provided reliable service, safety and a modicum of comfort. Following is the contribution of Mrs. L. L. Vance, who paid homage to car 89 almost five decades after it first started service in Vancouver in 1905. Her "Queen of the Fleet" was a large, double-trucked streetcar built in New Westminster.

Ode to Car 89

When gas lights glowed upon
A new gadget called a fone,
In Merrie England, Ireland and Wales,
Victoria graced the throne.
And out in Vancouver, folks were adaze
By a wondrous new car line,
And Queen of the Fleet, so young and gay,
Was car Number 89.

That she was a belle in her youth
'Tis true, nobody will deny;
She frolicked up and down the streets,
So pleasing to the eye.
And Grandmother rode her to church one day,
When she was just a bride,
McDonald, McTavish, McLeod and McQuirk,
Rode her just for the ride.

The years have passed and my Grandmama
Rests peacefully in her grave,
But the 89 goes on and on,
With a heart that's weak, but brave.
Arthritis is in her wheels and she long
Ago earned her rest;
She creaks and groans as she trudges on,
Trying to do her best.

So retire her now, while she still can go
With a shred of dignity;
Don't be unkind, or curt, or harsh,
Have a bit of a ceremony.
Admit she's been loyal, staunch and true,
Admit that she's been fine;
Then hope and pray that you can run
As long as did car 89. [9]

of the Employers' Association, with corporate members such as B.C. Electric Railway. The Employers' Association vowed to support strikebreakers, lobby governments to oppose union demands, and take legal action against labour leaders and those who threatened business property. By the following year, the association had 103 members. [7]

By 1911, more than 6,000 labourers in the Vancouver region went on strike in six different work stoppages. A general strike occurred in sympathy with the building trades, but B.C. Electric employees did not join the job action. By that time, the Employers' Association claimed to have 90 per cent of Vancouver's businesses as members.

The following year marked the peak of the city's early union movement, even though only 15 per cent of Vancouver's work force was unionized. The unions excluded all Asians, most seasonal migrants and women, and many unskilled labourers.

During the frenzied pace of progress between 1904 and 1912, B.C. Electric's unionized workers provided a steadfast force of guaranteed labour. Transit employees did not emerge as radical members of the union movement, but provided the backbone for an amazing growth industry. With their crisp uniforms and a strong public presence, the motormen and conductors put the spit and polish, so to speak, on Vancouver's glory years. Their colleagues in the car barns and in the field ensured that vehicles arrived on schedule and stayed in good repair. Theirs was an admirable team effort.

TRANSIT PREDOMINATES – There are no automobiles, few people and several horse-and-buggies visible in this circa-1904 view of Granville Street, looking south from Hastings Street. (The Georgia Street crossing appears in the distance.) This was a time of relative simplicity, before the larger streetcars that appeared in 1905 and 1906.

PHOTO SOURCE: CMBC: IC-10-7

Transit as a White Man's World: "No Oriental labour employed"

Chinese labourers

Although no Chinese labourers helped to clear land and lay tracks for the interurban lines, they were hired, through the Chinese woodcutter Lee Deen, to supply the power house with fuel. Many had previously served on crews to build the B.C. portion of Canada's national railway and had earned a reputation as solid, hard workers. Yet they had endured cruel taunts and meagre pay for their railway work, well below that of

SERVICE TO DOWNTOWN – Fairview (F) streetcar heads west from Hamilton Street in a view that reveals the vibrancy of Hastings Street in 1905. Power poles, wires and an assortment of solid brick buildings show the city's development. A few horse-drawn vehicles are still operating but streetcars are well used by this time.

PHOTO SOURCE: CVA: STR P. 308 N. 259

their white co-workers. (In the region's early decades, laws denied Chinese manual labourers full employment and allowed them to work solely as contractors; their only other job options were primarily houseboy, laundry man or restaurant help. Vancouver's Chinese population was almost totally male; immigration laws regarding Chinese women were not in place until after the First World War.)

Condescending attitudes towards Asians were commonplace during this period. In one account, a white woman's attempt at a humourous exchange with a Chinese labourer, employed by Lee Deen, backfired. On rainy days, Chinese workers were invited to have their lunch on the verandah of the Griffiths Avenue home of Minnie and Roderick Semple, the interurban line's first roadmaster. Minnie's sister Catherine McRae apparently remarked to an approaching young Chinese man, "Heap lainy day to-day, eh, John?" It turned out that he was a Victoria College student working to earn his tuition who later became a barrister. "Grandma was always polite to racial minorities after that," admitted McRae's grandson Fraser Wilson. [10]

Daily newspapers regularly featured editorials and advertisements full of anti-Asian vitriol. For instance, on October 1, 1891, the same day that the interurban made its inaugural run between Vancouver and New Westminster, a *Daily World* advertisement warned readers against eating "coolie sugar." It stated that such "foreign sugars" contain "great numbers of disgusting insects, which produce a disgusting disease. . . . Use therefore, only Home Refined Sugars, they are absolutely Unadulterated, Pure and Cheap."

Meanwhile, only Caucasian men worked as transit conductors, motormen and maintenance crew. However, one young Asian passenger received special treatment from transit employees in 1892. Before Burnaby opened its first school, Lee Deen's son had to travel to New Westminster to attend school. The tramway company arranged for a pass for the youngster. During school days, the conductor of the interurban passing the steam plant at the appropriate time was directed to stop, walk down to Deen's house, take charge of the boy, and put him on the interurban. Upon reaching New Westminster, the interurban was to stop in front of the school, the conductor was to take the boy by the hand and pass him over to the teacher at school. The process was reversed in the afternoon. (This occurred during a period when people at a Burnaby council meeting had proposed that Chinese residents be excluded from schools, stating that the Chinese government should pay for its citizens' education.)

After an altercation occurred between an Asian man and a Scandinavian on the Sapperton streetcar line in the early 1900s, B.C. Electric's general manager Johannes Buntzen wrote to company official F. R. Glover, stating that any person who paid a fare to ride on a company vehicle was entitled to the courtesy of staff and to an "unmolested" ride; the passenger's racial origin should have no bearing on the quality of service they receive.

In another incident around 1903, a Chinese cook, who worked on a large estate in Burnaby near today's Patterson and Marine Drive, took the first interurban from Vancouver to Patterson station, then walked down the hill to the estate. One morning, an angry man came up behind the cook and cut off his queue (pigtail). D.C. McGregor, the estate owner, wrote a strongly worded letter to Buntzen, complaining of this outrage. Buntzen responded that B.C. Electric employees were to ensure the safety of all passengers and that the offending individual was facing prosecution.

1905

[B.C. Electric general manager] Mr. Buntzen used to come on the car, cheerfully show his pass and pass the time of day with the conductors," reminisced conductor John McDonald about transit service in 1905. "I have heard it said that he would jump off the car at a curve and shake hands with the greaser [track oiler] and ask about his welfare."

The B.C. Electric Employees' Magazine,
December 1925

- Regular interurban service begins July 4 on the Vancouver-Marpole-Steveston interurban line from the north False Creek foot of Granville Street, with hourly service from 7 a.m. to 10 p.m. The interurbans or "electric rolling palaces" have standing-room-only crowds; return fare from Vancouver to Eburne (Marpole) is 40 cents and a return fare to Steveston 85 cents (30 and 75 cents, respectively, on Sundays and holidays).

- Twenty-six streetcars, a new series of large, double-trucked vehicles, provide regular service on the Vancouver system.

- R. H. (Rochfort Henry) Sperling becomes general manager of B.C. Electric, effective July 1.

- The city hosts its first automobile club race around Stanley Park on Labour Day. Eleven cars begin, only five finish; the latter are all Oldsmobiles.

NO FINER PASSENGER VEHICLE – "Richmond," magnificently painted in jade green and gold, is pictured in the summer of 1905. The car was constructed in B.C. Electric's own shops in New Westminster, expressly for the company's new Vancouver-Marpole-Steveston interurban line. As business expanded, B.C. Electric rebuilt this car, and its 16 named sisters, to allow their coupling together. The growth spurt of 1912 prompted a vehicle refurbishment, which resulted in the "name" interurbans being numbered 1200 to 1216. This car became 1205 and served the Lower Mainland every day for another 42 years.

PHOTO SOURCE: CVA: OUT P. 685 N. 292

However, these attitudes did not extend to the transit company's hiring policies. Like most employers of the day, B.C. Electric maintained a policy of no non-white labour in its power-generation end of business. Under a heading "No Orientals Employed," *The Daily Province* states on April 29, 1905:

> *One important fact . . . in connection with all the work which has been carried out in this province for the British Columbia Electric Railway Company, is that there has been no oriental labor employed. Nothing but skilled white labor has been engaged both on this tunnel and in the preparatory work at the camps. Not even a Chinese cook has ever worked a day in either of the camps. This was one of the provisions of the contract, and is in line with the general policy inaugurated by Managing Director Buntzen.*

Laws, popular sentiment and the media of that period supported such attitudes. During this time, white labourers protested – and in the early 1900s rioted – if they felt their jobs were threatened by Asian contractors.

Japanese labourers

Although photos of this period show Japanese men felling trees and working alongside Caucasians in outdoor manual work, it is unlikely they provided contract labour for the city's first transit companies. Like the Chinese, they were legally prevented from formal employment. (Legislation had denied Japanese the vote in Canada in 1886.)

Japanese immigrants, mostly single men in their twenties, first appeared in Vancouver in the early 1890s and many worked in sawmills. By the early 1900s, some served as labour contractors. These entrepreneurs hired out their own countrymen, yet no reports confirm any Japanese contracts with B.C. Electric. The unskilled Japanese Canadians usually ended up with "the least desirable and most perilous" jobs.[11] The Japanese also worked for a lower wage than even the Chinese: roughly $1.00 a day compared to $1.50 to $2.00 a day.[12] (In 1911, a white streetcar conductor or motorman earned $3.50 for a 10¼-hour day, while a white carpenter earned $5.00.)

The involvement of Japanese workers in white society was deeply curtailed following anti-Asian race riots in Vancouver in 1907. By this time, 4,000 Asians, both Chinese and Japanese, lived in the city and many were the victims of harassment and discrimination. Efforts were made to end, or limit, further Asian immigration. By this time, B.C. Electric still maintained its official policy of not hiring Asians.

DENIED EMPLOYMENT – Asian labourers, other than Chinese woodcutters and fuel suppliers, were denied street railway jobs in Vancouver's early years. In later years, Japanese or Chinese helped to clear land in non-transit-related work, earning less than their white counterparts. Here, Japanese loggers remove a stump around 1910; such photos are rare.

PHOTO SOURCE: JAPANESE CANADIAN NATIONAL MUSEUM
94/85.017A-B, A-B: P8

STANDING TALL — A work crew takes a break near today's West Boulevard and 57th Avenue in the spring of 1905, while preparing a C.P.R. line for electrification. Built by the railway in 1902, this line ran from Vancouver to Steveston. B.C. Electric leased and electrified it three years later for interurban use. This interurban service between Vancouver and Marpole would continue to 1952.

Asian passengers on transit

The railways of the day restricted seating of Asians to certain cars – they could not mingle with the white passengers.[13] At the time, some movie theatres ushered non-white patrons to the least desirable seats. At other establishments, "No Orientals" signs appeared in the window. A 12-year-old Japanese girl, accompanied by white friends, was refused admittance to a swimming pool. Japanese couples were turned away from a high school alumni dance. (Even in the 1920s, a United Church minister refused to shake the hand of a Japanese Boy Scout.)[14] At the time of Vancouver's race riots, "contact with the white community was nonexistent except for a fragile tie with the Christian church," reports author Roy Ito in *Stories of My People*.

Amid such discrimination, it is not difficult to surmise that public transit vehicles upheld an atmosphere of segregation. "You knew your place," says Vancouverite Jim Wong-Chu, who has thoroughly researched the city's historical treatment of Chinese residents.

Even as late as 1952, a patronizing tone regarding Chinese passengers appears in a transit employee newsletter:

> *When it comes to riding transit vehicles, the Chinese don't take a back seat to anybody. And by that we don't mean they refuse to sit in the rear of the bus, but that they are good passengers. . . .With this our operator takes a large breath and continues in a more serious vein.* [15]

Still, Asians did use transit in Vancouver's early days. Chinese farm help and Japanese cannery workers were reported to use the interurbans. Former *Vancouver Sun* columnist Tom Browne remembered the farm workers as tram passengers:

> *Chinese truck farm workers – very fine people – would eat sweet pine nuts, spitting the reddish hulls onto the floor. They would sit back contentedly, chat among themselves in sing-song voices, smiling, and drawing at cigarettes rolled by hand with brown straw-paper covering. They fashioned the smokes like funnels, so there would be little, if any, tobacco wasted when they were burned to the butt.* [16]

Entertainment: "The elite used the trams extensively"

Vancouver's well-heeled set lived a life of elegance and high style during the city's glory years. They flocked to gala openings, garden parties, ballroom dances and the city's best restaurants. Vancouver historian Alan Morley writes in *Vancouver – From Milltown to Metropolis*: "Businessmen, once content with the cherry-colored walls and stuffed pheasants of the Leyland Hotel dining room, now lunched at their clubs, or amid the somber magnificence of Allen's Restaurant or the Strand Hotel; the latter had a cuisine and a wine cellar of truly Parisian standards, even importing French artichokes from California. Service in the cafes and restaurants was impeccable." Society women, meanwhile, hosted teas and luncheons or outdoor concerts in flowing gowns and flowered hats, squeezing as many private club functions as possible into days of scheduled leisure.

REAL ESTATE BUST — He went from rags to riches to rags . . . well, almost. Transit service provided stable, bankable income for conductor Ben Young, who started on B.C. Electric streetcars in 1905. He left the company five years later with enough money to make "quite a clean-up" in the real estate frenzy of the day, according to the October 1921 issue of *The B.C. Electric Employees' Magazine*. However, he lost most of his fortune to a "Lord Somebody" who disappeared off to England supposedly to sell timber rights. Ben returned to work at transit in 1917.

PHOTO SOURCE: BC HYDRO:
THE B.C. ELECTRIC EMPLOYEES' MAGAZINE,
OCTOBER 1921, P. 29

Public transit vehicles played a part in the social life of everyone – trend-setters to tramps. Residents in Steveston and other outlying areas took interurbans to see popular attractions at Vancouver's theatres on weekends. Vancouverites rode the trams on occasions such as New Year's Eve performances at Steveston's Opera House.

The interurbans themselves reflected the style-conscious sensibilities of the Edwardian era. Each vehicle offered etched-glass windows, decorative luggage racks, a private smoking compartment, brass fixtures and comfortable seats – the epitome of travel in style. "The elite in fashionable Kerrisdale used the trams extensively," one old-timer remembered in the 1970s. "Seats swung both ways and coteries of them would sit facing each other to chat affably as the tram rolled toward the depot, located first on the old Granville Bridge from a ramp off Third Avenue, later on Davie near Richards." [17]

Vancouver's streetcars provided more utilitarian transportation that brought thousands of people to the entertainment centre in the city's downtown core. On Granville Street and blocks nearby, residents and visitors could enjoy the latest opera, vaudeville, concerts, live theatre and silent movies. In 1904, Charlie Chaplin and Houdini starred at the newly opened Orpheum. The venue, which headlined Will Rogers in 1908, was part of an active vaudeville circuit and rivalled the Pantages Theatre in Los Angeles. For most audience members, these popular events were only accessible by streetcar – they would have missed such attractions otherwise.

"I can remember riding in the old streetcars with open grills at the back," recalled Abbotsford resident C. Chalowski. "We went to the Beacon Theatre where Fields is now on Hastings Street, and watched silent movies and stage acts (heard my first talking movie there also) . . . and attended operas at Gore and Hastings. The Rex Theatre where the Army and Navy is now cost us a whole 10 cents. . . . At the Broadway Theatre we got candies free." [18]

Vancouverites who sought a cheaper night on the town could still hop a streetcar for a Saturday night flick or a few beers away from the downtown hub. One old-timer remembers:

In 1914 you could buy two ice cream cones for a nickel at the ice cream parlour. . . . The butcher was named Barber and the barber was named Butcher. . . . At the old Dreamland Theatre you could watch the Perils of Pauline for 10 cents or sit in Marin's theatre . . . and listen to the Player Piano accompanying the silent movies. Can you visualize Fraser Street as a plank road and tobogganing all the way down to Marine? [19]

1906

- B.C. Electric hires its first female employee, Ethel G. Golightly, as a ticket and transfer counting clerk at $40 a month.

- Streetcar service begins to the Grandview area, running from Hastings and Main to First Avenue and Commercial Drive.

- Electricity becomes commonly available to North Vancouver on August 15 after fir poles are erected to support power cables across the Second Narrows.

A RARE SET-UP – One of B.C. Electric's splendid new double-trucked streetcars, heading north on Main Street, approaches Carnegie Library at the corner of Main and Hastings in 1906. The city hall stands just to the left.

This intersection, the only B.C. Electric junction of its kind, offered something rare on any streetcar system of that day: a "grand union" set-up. It allowed streetcars to make left or right turns or cross straight through. The company created the junction to better serve Hastings Street, which was growing commercially, and to move some of its streetcars off lagging Cordova Street.

PHOTO SOURCE: VPL 3426

OPULENT OPERA HOUSE – This deluxe opera house rivalled any in the world when it opened in 1891. (The building's grand opening occurred only a half-year after the launch of the city's streetcar service.) Owned and operated by the Canadian Pacific Railway, it remained Vancouver's only theatre until 1898, and inspired a tradition of staged artistic entertainment in the city. Stripped of most of its finery, it would last into the 1970s as International Cinema.

Passengers depended on public transit to get them home safely after an evening's entertainment; when streetcar service did not meet their standards, they voiced their views in clear terms.

In January 1905, 140 East End residents signed a petition requesting that B.C. Electric add an extra Powell Street car after the final performances at the Vancouver Opera House. Otherwise, they faced "a long walk from Westminster Avenue [Main Street] East, through the rain" in the dark.[20] General Manager Johannes Buntzen responded by letter that he would try to arrange for such a late-night car and would notify transit-users through a newspaper ad where the vehicle's layover spot would be. However, he admitted difficulties in timing the vehicle's arrival since "it is impossible to ascertain from the Opera House staff when any particular performance will be over." He added: "[We] have considerable trouble at times in endeavouring to accommodate the theatre goers without blocking up the line for the regular traffic."[21] Then as now, transit executives had to use their best juggling skills to keep vehicles on their regular schedule while addressing the needs of special-interest groups in search of a good time.

North Vancouver: "Whisked along the street at a good brisk speed"

When the first streetcar in North Vancouver made its trial run on August 29, 1906, a B.C. Electric superintendent appeared at the municipal hall and invited councillors for a trip. "[I]t did not take long to finish up the business of the meeting, adjourn, grab a hat, climb aboard the waiting car and be whisked along the street at a good brisk speed. To say that the ride was enjoyed by all is putting it mildly." [22]

The Daily Province trumpeted the event on its front page, noting that any bystanders who could not squeeze onto the packed car had to watch enviously as the "swiftly-moving car and its enthusiastic and joyous load" passed them by.

CRUISING IN A CONVERTIBLE — Motorman Fred Hoover and conductor Dan McDiarmid pose with open-air "convertible" car 31 at English Bay in 1905. Transportation photos of this period rarely record the presence of women; yet here, female passengers look on from this Ottawa-built vehicle.

PHOTO SOURCE: BC HYDRO:
THE B.C. ELECTRIC EMPLOYEES' MAGAZINE,
NOVEMBER 1919, FRONT PAGE

Open-sided streetcar 25, a castoff from Vancouver's system, officially launched service in North Vancouver on Labour Day, September 3. Throughout the day, 2,047 passengers piled on to ride the roughly 1.33-mile (2.1-kilometre) track from the foot of Lonsdale Avenue to 21st Street. At the time, North Vancouver had 1,000 residents and 250 houses; lots on Lonsdale were selling for $100 a foot.

Several derailments and a small crash, which prompted employees to hide the damage with a Union Jack and continue service, did not deter the enthusiasm of passengers and staff on opening day. *The Daily Province* reported: "At the close of operations, sighs of satisfaction were given, and everyone present joined in singing 'The End of a Perfect Day.'"[23]

From the outset, streetcar service on Lonsdale proved a remarkable feat in both engineering and operation. The road had steep grades of almost 10 per cent in places, more suitable for a cable car than a streetcar. The line required 800 fir poles to support the trolley wire and "some of the largest of British Columbia's forest giants" (215 feet/65.5 metres high) to support six power cables that carried electrical current from Lake Buntzen to Vancouver across the Second Narrows channel to North Vancouver.

Four days after service began, North Vancouver's newspaper, *The Express*, published the first streetcar schedule. At the time, six tickets cost 25 cents. Within weeks, the number of trips per day jumped from 36 to 50, except for Sunday, when two streetcars provided 20-minute service.

Over the years, service expanded to three distinct lines: Capilano, Lonsdale and Grand Boulevard (later Lynn Valley). The Capilano extension opened on May 1, 1911, the same day that 20-minute ferry service began from the foot of Lonsdale.

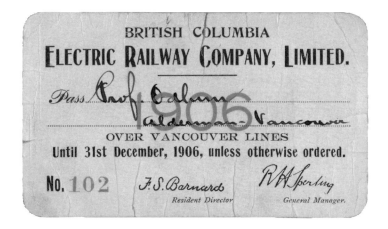

NORTH SHORE SERVICE – Streetcar 25 (left), open on only one side, was the first official streetcar to operate in North Vancouver. Shown here on 1st Street at Lonsdale Avenue in 1906, the car would soon be destroyed in an accident.

Number 14 (right), the first streetcar to run in Vancouver 16 years previously, would give North Vancouver six more years of service. North Vancouver's city hall dominates the scene.

PHOTO SOURCE: CMBC: SCR-05-P

Two weeks later, the first two of North Vancouver's 13 new double-trucked streetcars began arriving, complete with cherrywood interiors and rattan seats.

Despite occasional accidents, the streetcars continued to grow in popularity. Full-capacity service could not handle the flood of passengers on holiday weekends. Transit in North Vancouver had a huge impact on the leisure patterns of Vancouver's residents. City-dwellers could ride north-shore streetcars to reach the Capilano suspension bridge, hike up Grouse Mountain, or explore Lynn Canyon and its suspension bridge. In simple terms: "The streetcars had made the best of nature available on a platter." [24]

ANOTHER TRAVEL OPTION – A mere handful of cars, like this Oldsmobile photographed at Ladner's Landing in 1906, operated in Vancouver during this period. Streetcars and interurbans remained the primary, and often only, choice of transportation for most people. At the steering wheel of this four-cylinder model S is Dr. A. R. Baker, owner of Vancouver Automobile Company. Beside him, with goggles, is William M. Stark. Behind Dr. Baker is Robert Kelly, of the wholesale grocers Kelly, Douglas and Company. In the centre rear is B. W. Greer, former C.P.R. general freight agent. C. B. "Charlie" Worsnop sits at the right rear.

PHOTO SOURCE: CVA: TRANS. P. 55 N. 89

All-Weather Service: "Waiting for connections in wet and cold weather is a great waste of our time"

Like today's mail carriers, early Vancouver's transit employees aimed to provide service in all manner of weather. Exposed to the elements in open-air vehicles, they made their way through mud, rain, fog and snow. Frequent thick fogs, bolstered by the smoke of home sawdust burners and coal-burning fires, kept many onboard streetcar staff operating in near-zero visibility. Heavy snowfall could sideline streetcars and interurbans for days, stranding thousands of passengers who were left to trudge through high snowbanks on foot.

After a snowstorm hit Vancouver in early January 1901, streetcars managed to resume service quickly. *The Province* reported on January 2 that year: "Seldom has

Vancouver been visited by such a snow storm as that which commenced on Monday evening, and continued throughout the night . . . In the city proper it lay a foot thick . . . . The streets were almost deserted of vehicular traffic . . . . Street cars were not to be seen . . . . No passenger cars were run throughout the day, but towards evening a few [street]cars got out, and crawled over the down town lines . . . . The street railway people worked all night." Six days later, after about 30 inches (76 cm) of snow had fallen, *The Province* called this "one of the most prolonged storms ever known in the history of Vancouver."[25] The following year, heavy snowfall kept Vancouver streetcars from operating for six weeks.

Little mention is made of major storms until the next decade, when four interurban cars were left snowbound on the Central Park line on January 11, 1911. Two years later, when January brought continued snowfall, Vancouver's transit system received a new snowplow to add to its existing three.

Winters also brought flooding, which created havoc on streetcar tracks. One old-timer remembers flood conditions on the wooden bridge that crossed False Creek at Main Street (then Westminster Avenue):

THE FOG ROLLS IN – Mist obscures the grand C.P.R. station at the north foot of Granville Street in this 1906 view, taken from just north of Dunsmuir Street. One of B.C. Electric's new double-trucked streetcars, built in New Westminster, has just stopped at Pender Street.

PHOTO SOURCE: CVA 677-529

A RIDE THROUGH RICHMOND – One of B.C. Electric's 17 named interurban cars heads for Steveston through the farmland of Lulu Island in 1907. The car threads between two power poles, braced to prevent them from skewing in the soft, fertile soil of the Fraser River delta. B.C. Electric started this interurban service in 1905, opening Richmond to settlement and allowing the canneries in Steveston to flourish. Freight service, as on all the company's interurban lines, was an immediate feature of this line's operation.

PHOTO SOURCE: VPL 2146

During the high tides of winter the tracks would be constantly flooded, and . . . to make electrical contact between trolley wire and rails through salt water is impossible. Accordingly, the streetcars used to come zooming down Mount Pleasant hill with all stops out, and just before the flooded section was reached, the conductor, hanging out over the track, would haul down the trolley and the car would slush madly through two feet of water on its own momentum. One day, a car stalled right in the middle, and then Vancouver had a horse car, for a team was needed to pull it out. [26]

Cold weather made life miserable for early streetcar conductors, who rode in an open vestibule. One former passenger, Abbotsford resident C. Chalowski, commented: "I can remember riding in the old streetcars with open grills at the back, and in the winter the fog rolled in. The conductor sat on a stool with his overcoat, scarf and gloves on!" [27]

Transit employees weren't the only ones who suffered in bad weather. A harshly worded petition, signed with hundreds of names, to the head of B.C. Electric in the mid-1890s complained: "[C]hanging cars and waiting for connections in wet and cold weather is a great waste of our time and not conducive to the good of our health." [28] By 1910, the people who lived and owned businesses on Fraser Street south of 25th Avenue were demanding that streetcars should run directly from Vancouver to Ferris Road (today's 49th Avenue) so passengers could avoid transferring at 25th Avenue. It is not recorded whether their request was granted.

STILL A GO IN SNOW – In a view south from Pender, a line of streetcars inches along downtown Granville Street in 1908. These dependable vehicles maintained a schedule in most kinds of weather; automobiles, bicycles and wagons are noticeably absent.

Notice the advertisement for ice skating at Trout Lake; passengers could access this activity via Grandview streetcars or the interurban line to New Westminster through Cedar Cottage.

PHOTO SOURCE: GEORGE E. TIMMS PHOTO, VPL 7136

NO AUTOMOBILES IN SIGHT – A streetcar has the road to itself in this view of snowy Edmonds in a later period, 1913. (Few photos exist of Vancouver's early streetcars in snow.) It's heading towards the streetcar line to the right along 12th Street to downtown New West-minster. The photographer is standing on the platform of Edmonds station. The long-razed Edmonds block reflects the developing neighbourhoods of eastern Burnaby.

PHOTO SOURCE: BHS 230-8

1907

A city of vast commerce, a city of myriad beautiful homes – prosperity and happiness blended – will sum up the supreme, and now visible, possibility of Vancouver, the peerless city of Canada.

B.C. Saturday Sunset, December 14, 1907

- Only 175 automobiles are registered in all of British Columbia.

- The Asiatic Exclusion League leads a mob of 15,000 through Chinatown and Japantown, resulting in beatings, damaged homes and stores.

- B.C. Electric receives a petition from 24 Cedar Cottage residents to change the name on the interurban station at Cedar Cottage to "Sowania." R. H. Sperling, the company's general manager, responds that "it would require an almost unanimous petition . . . to induce us to make a change of name."[29]

ALWAYS A PHOTO OPPORTUNITY – Officials perform a symbolic sod-turning ceremony on August 26, 1907, to mark the start of construction of the interurban line between New Westminster and Chilliwack. They're standing in today's Surrey at the southeast corner of Old Yale Road and the track; this became the location of the interurban's South Westminster station.

R.H. Sperling, B.C. Electric general manager, is at the far left; W.H. Keary, New Westminster's mayor at far right; F. R. Glover, Sperling's assistant, second from left; D.J. McQuarrie, B.C. Electric's New Westminster superintendent, is second from right.

PHOTO SOURCE: CMBC: IS-00-1

WEST END WAYS – A streetcar, built locally by B.C. Electric, crosses Nicola Street and heads eastward on Davie through the elegant West End in 1907. Davie Street is double-tracked here, prepared for heavy transit use. The West End was well supplied with streetcar service on Davie, Denman and Robson streets, with English Bay close at hand. This exclusive neighbourhood, laid out between downtown and Stanley Park, was Vancouver's most prestigious residential area.

PHOTO SOURCE: CVA: STR P. 87 N. 407

1908

- Forty-eight streetcars provide regular service on eight lines in Vancouver.

- Vancouver has 228 miles (367 kilometres) of city streets; 12 miles (19.3 kilometres) are paved with wood blocks and 104 miles (167 kilometres) are macadamized. There are 58 miles (93 kilometres) of cement sidewalks, according to Eric Nicol's *Vancouver*.

- Newly opened nine-storey department store David Spencer, at Richards and Hastings, competes with Woodward's, just three blocks east. A Spencer's advertisement in January 16 newspapers announces that a special interurban car from New Westminster will bring shoppers to its "white-wear" sale.

- Canada's first gas station opens on Smithe Street at Cambie on January 1, 1908.

- The first tourist bus service begins in Stanley Park.

OFF TO MARKET – Car 75, built by B.C. Electric in its New Westminster shops in 1905, drops off passengers at Vancouver's original market circa 1908. This building could well have remained a heritage structure, but its odd location, north of 1st Avenue on the west side of Main Street's S-curve, doomed it to a short life.

PHOTO SOURCE: GEORGE E. TIMMS PHOTO, VPL 4990

Freight: "Transit customers served from the cradle to the grave"

[By 1908] The interurban to New Westminster was the lifeline for groceries bought by Vancouver housewives at the Valley market center [sic]. Running through forest punctuated by clearings of settlers, around the stations, and past the odd poultry farm, the trip cost ten cents and took three-quarters of an hour. The tramline to Chilliwack brought in produce and took out picnickers, with a daily "Milk Special," while the Cemetery line had its terminus at the Mountain View Cemetery — the B.C.E.R. [B.C. Electric Railway] served its customers from the cradle to the grave.

Eric Nicol, *Vancouver*

Names like "Flying Dutchman," "Strawberry Special" and "Sockeye Limited" evoke an exciting time in the region's transportation history, when Lower Mainland communities were linked for the first time. They were the dedicated freight cars of the interurban lines, carrying fish, produce, milk, mail and settlers' worldly goods to and from Vancouver. The daily service opened new markets for canneries and for farmers and growers who previously relied on wagons or barges to reach city buyers. Today, Vancouverites still enjoy produce from many market farms that were established at this time.

Completed in 1910, the 64-mile (102.7-kilometre) New Westminster–to–Chilliwack portion of B.C. Electric's interurban line brought rail freight and passenger service to the Fraser Valley for the first time. (The Chilliwack train was known as "Creeping Lina.") The service drastically curtailed steamboat business on the Fraser River and opened inland areas to settlement; one result was the city of Langley. B.C. Electric's new right-of-way also allowed the company to bring electricity to communities in the valley.

B.C. Electric's freight business grew hand in hand with the rapid increase in population and commercial development. Between 1911 and 1912, the company's freight totals more than tripled, from about 78,000 to 256,000 tons.

AN EIGHT-SIDED WORKHORSE – Locomotive 900, built in B.C. Electric's New Westminster shop in 1907 and shown here in 1910, featured a unique, octagonal cab. The locomotive would soon be downgraded to switching work after the arrival of new, large steel locomotives from England and from Baldwin Locomotive Works in the eastern U.S.

PHOTO SOURCE: BC HYDRO: A0927

BEFORE FREIGHT WAS BIG – This double-ended freight car, photographed in 1905, operated between Vancouver and New Westminster on the Central Park interurban line, which was built in 1891. Built in 1903 by B.C. Electric and initially numbered 7, the car was later renumbered into the express car series as 1801. In 1911, renumbered 507, it inaugurated daily freight service, two trips each way, on the Burnaby Lake interurban line.

PHOTO CREDIT: CMBC: IF-40-3

Strawberry fields forever

B.C. Electric launched its "Strawberry Special" freight trains in 1903 with new and larger cars to handle this specialized fruit crop. Burnaby, well known for its strawberries, was a major producer and its loads hurtled along the interurban's Central Park line. (The Burnaby Lake line did not open until June 12, 1911.) Locals dubbed one of these strawberry-laden freight cars "the Flying Dutchman" because its side curtains often came undone and flapped dramatically in the wind.

Sockeye run on the rails

Take a Steveston car and ride with it until it has carried you to the cannery village by the Fraser. Your ride will take you from nearly all that is familiar, and in the end you will find yourself where the speech of five tongues meets you with a pleasant shock.

Duncan and Susan Stacey,
Salmonopolis – The Steveston Story

The "Sockeye Limited" service, sometimes referred to as the "Sockeye Special," began with an hourly run between Vancouver and Steveston, when B.C. Electric leased the C.P.R.'s tracks in 1905. (The C.P.R. had offered twice-daily service between 1902 and 1905.) The interurban cars operated from False Creek to the Steveston canneries via Eburne (it became Marpole in June 1916). On the return trip, the line ran alongside Railway Avenue, on the west side, to Granville Avenue, east along Granville to Garden City, and north across a trestle over the north arm of the Fraser River into Vancouver. That year, B.C. Electric electrified the line for their interurbans, at the same time bringing electric light to Steveston.

One unidentified source, whose views reflect the overt racism of the times, remembers the line just before B.C. Electric took it over:

It ran through a slit in the forest after it passed about 16th Avenue, and emerged again at Eburne. There were no houses that I can recall between those two points, but, after a while, a store started at the corner of what is now Boulevard and 41st Avenue. The train carried those who had formerly travelled from the canneries by stage, and included many Chinamen and Indians; all went in the day coach together with whites, and sometimes it was not as pleasant as it might have been; also many Japanese. [30]

Besides its utility, the Sockeye Limited was an exciting ride, as recounted by humourist and historian Eric Nicol in *Vancouver*:

Probably the fastest and most exhilarating interurban ride was the "Sockeye Special" to Steveston, the flats of Lulu Island permitting quick acceleration with few curves. In its heyday the interurban was a cathartic experience; the cars, which often ran two in tandem, had cane seats so slippery that a sharp curve slid a small boy's buttocks sideways in sweet surrender to centrifugal force. The windows – barred to discourage defenestration on one side and decapitation on the other – were surmounted by panels of stained glass, a basilican touch only slightly profaned by ads for Heinz Apple Butter and Fit Rite Clothes, and entirely redundant to the youngster aware that he was careening at speeds beyond the power of mortals. The drivers of the interurbans were a breed apart, and knew it. To a man, they were filled with a kind of divine rage at the restraints of track and stops. Halted by the despicable requirement of picking up a passenger, both train and driver throbbed in a paroxysm of frustration, and the boarding party not uncommonly stumbled in its haste to scale the high steps before the brakes yielded to the massive surge to go sixty. [31]

A FREIGHT HUB – Express freight interurban car 1802, its back to Moncton Street, appears ready to leave Steveston for its run to downtown Vancouver in this 1910 photo.

B.C. Electric's substantial Steveston depot and attached freight building had been built by the C.P.R. when it opened this railway line in 1902. B.C. Electric leased and electrified the line in 1905. First-rate interurban passenger service would operate for another 48 years beyond the time of this photo.

PHOTO SOURCE: RA: 1986 49

AN ABUNDANCE OF ACTIVITY – This September 15, 1908 view of Granville Street, looking north from Dunsmuir Street, reveals a city on the move. A Davie streetcar advertises roller skating as it makes its way to its Denman and Davie streets terminus at English Bay. To the right is the Bank of Montreal.

Lulu Island farmers were eager to use the interurban and received special rates from B.C. Electric. For more than a half-century, until 1958, trains ran on a half-hour basis. Eventually, the Lulu Island section had 19 interurban stations: Tucks, Bridgeport, Sexsmith, Cambie, Alexandra, Lansdowne, Ferndale, Garden City, Brighouse, Lulu, Riverside, McCallan Road, Blundell, Francis, Woodwards, Cottages, Branscombe, Steveston Wye and Steveston.

Milk and mail on the move

B.C. Electric was operating a special milk and vegetable train by the spring of 1911; it carried 5,200 gallons (23,640 litres) of milk to Vancouver every day and returned the empty cans to the Fraser Valley at night. (Milk freight was measured in pounds and each milk can weighed 100 pounds [45 kilograms]; a cream can weighed 20 pounds [9 kilograms].) "For those who lived in Burnaby near the Central Park line, the noise of the 'milk train' whizzing by was a familiar sound several times a day," remembers historian Pixie McGeachie in *Bygones of Burnaby*.

After the introduction of the interurban line, two Chilliwack creameries turned from making butter and cheese to the more lucrative business of selling milk and cream to residents of New Westminster and Vancouver. Before the interurban, Chilliwack had exported no fresh milk; after the interurban, Chilliwack imported the butter it needed.

B.C. Electric had already started a milk train service earlier, and launched the shipment of small freight, between New Westminster and points on the way to Cloverdale and Jardine, just east of Milner, on July 1, 1910.

Harriet Woodward, who ran Burnaby Lake's post office for 45 years, walked to Edmonds and Kingway every day to pick up incoming mail and give outgoing mail directly to the interurban conductor. This took considerable effort since childhood polio had left her dependent on leg braces and canes to walk. However, before the tram came through, Woodward had to hitch her horse Pansy to a cart and "carried and fetched the mail in every kind of weather." [32]

Express packages and letters travelled in the front car of an interurban multiple-car train. This baggage-express car carried settlers' belongings or parcels. Anyone who bought goods in Vancouver and did not wish to carry them home could take them to the downtown tram office. For a small fee, the freight tram, which travelled at night, would leave the parcel in the designated station. The next morning, the owners of the packages could pick them up at their convenience.

This delivery system proved so successful that some interurban stations lacked enough space to handle the freight. Users of Edmonds station in Burnaby sent a petition to B.C. Electric in April 1910 requesting a new station; the result was a large, dedicated freight building.

Although freight sometimes remained for days in the station, few items were ever stolen, according to B.C. Electric employee Hugh Stewart. But merchants, residents

People You Should Know

lives have been so full and varied tha storage of detail has long since become an unbearable burden. At the time Ted was a private and the battalion photographer, Churchill, was a lieutenant and a war correspondent. The unit was in action in Mahmund, in the heart of the frontier hills. Somehow the Churchill sector was cut off by the marauding natives and it looked pretty much like somebody else was going to have to make the "We shall fight on the beaches" speech years later.

But the remaining "Buffs," Ted included, thought different. They waged a "blood-and-guts" struggle out there that is still echoing through

SERVED WITH CHURCHILL – E.S. "Ted" O'Donovan, who started as an interurban motorman in 1908, previously fought in India with the same British battalion as Winston Churchill. He served as a private in the frontier hills of Mahmund in 1895; Churchill, then a lieu-tenant and war correspondent, acted as the battalion's photographer. O'Donovan emigrated to Canada and joined B.C. Electric as a motorman, where he remained until his retirement in 1939.

PHOTO CREDIT: HEATHER CONN (FROM HE COLLECTION)

and other freight shippers/receivers who used the Jubilee station in Burnaby had less faith in the system. In 1911, they petitioned B.C. Electric for "a suitable warehouse for the reception and discharge of freight, one which may be placed under lock and key and so situated that a [horse] team can be loaded direct from same....[T]he present shed is too exposed to the elements and freight left in same over night is absolutely at the mercy of any marauders who may pass by."[33]

Real Estate: "A business street cannot exist without a carline"

The **B. C. Electric Railway** have **NOW LET THE CONTRACT** for the **EXTENSION** of the **CAR-LINE** on **WESTMINSTER AVENUE** from the **BODWELL ROAD** to the **FERRIS ROAD** through the **"GOLD LOTS"** and the **CONTRACTORS** start work within **2 WEEKS.**

Do you **REALIZE** that when this **CAR SERVICE** is completed that the prices of these lots **MUST JUMP?**

Your time to buy is **NOW** before the price is **ADVANCED.**

$100 cash and balance in **3** years secures you a lot; easier terms if you want to build.

Maps and prices on application.

Office On the Ground:
Tel. 5089   Open Evenings   **EDWARD GOLD**   Office : 441 Seymour St.
Tel. 1923

A September 1, 1909 real estate ad warns Vancouver readers that lot prices "must jump" when streetcar service is completed.

Whereas the Canadian Pacific Railway more or less established the City of Vancouver, and influenced the direction of its downtown and inner-suburban development, the BC Electric Railway Co. "laid out" the rest of the city. Its electric tram lines through the suburbs and its Lulu Island and Fraser Valley interurbans had the Midas touch for many real estate promoters, and determined the location of nearly all the main streets outside Vancouver downtown.

Michael Kluckner, *Vancouver: The Way it Was*

A spectacular real estate boom swept Vancouver from 1907 to 1912. Anyone with a little extra cash wanted to buy into the craze. A 1930s transit employees' magazine wrote in its look back to 1907: "Remember the one topic of conversation, on the cars and off – real estate? Not a man on the job who wasn't a real estate owner – he had paid something on a lot somewhere."[34] Speculation fever allowed dozens of realtors to put up their shingles and prey on unsuspecting immigrants and newcomers, claiming that stump-filled swamps were prime residential property.

One buyer, Albert Foote, bought land unseen and recalled years later what he and his wife saw when they visited their lot just off Earles Road in 1909: "After working my tortuous way through the jungle of uprooted stumps to the rear of the lot I discovered the horrifying fact that the back end of the property was submerged in a sluggish swamp, under about two feet of water."[35] At least he didn't have to walk to his property; he could reach it by the New Westminster tram – the only vehicle access at the time.

BOUNDARY RD AND PARK AVE STATION

UNPARALLELED SERVICE – An interurban car approaches Park Avenue station in 1908. This view looks south on Boundary Road to Kingsway; Burnaby is to the left.

This area was already well settled, thanks to the interurban, which took passengers the six miles (10 kilometres) to Vancouver in under half an hour, or an equal distance to downtown New Westminster in even less time. (The latter route was faster because it did not have the same amount of running time on Vancouver's busy urban streets.) With the recent double-tracking of the Central Park line for heavy use, the overhead street crossings, such as the one shown here, had been upgraded from wood to concrete.

PHOTO SOURCE: CVA: STR P. 356 N. 316

Transit access was a key element in selling property during Vancouver's glory years. Land prices were tied to proximity to a streetcar or interurban line. One 1909 ad for lots in Burnaby's Central Park region touted properties with access by "eight-cent Carfare" with "transfers to all parts of the city."[36] Another included an artist's idyllic rendition of Eburne (Marpole) townsite and noted that this residential/commercial area "was in the midst of a settled community and NOT in the backwoods." It pointed out the area's attractive transit features: "The junction of the THREE Electric Railways is south of the general store at the foot of Fourth St. while there are stations at [the] foot of Granville Street on Townsend Road – TRAVELING ACCOMMODATION galore."[37]

Thanks to public transportation, early Vancouverites could live away from their place of employment. This opportunity allowed many new communities to be established within and around the city. Tradespeople, shopkeepers, dock workers and other working-class residents settled the east-end community of Grandview.

Similarly, the availability of streetcar service to Hastings Townsite in 1909 launched a steady influx of working-class men and women into this area; two years later, with 2,300 residents, it amalgamated with Vancouver. Meanwhile, new streetcar lines in South Vancouver enabled employees of downtown and False Creek's mills and businesses to make South Vancouver their home.

Public transit even altered the long-established demographics in the West End. Once streetcar service began to serve this exclusive stronghold of imposing mansions,

THE BOOM IS ON – Eastbound streetcar 151 takes on riders at Hastings and Main around 1909. Hastings Street east of Main is just coming into its own as a commercial thoroughfare. Population growth was so great at this time that B.C. Electric's car-building shops in New Westminster could not keep up with the demand for vehicles. Consequently, this streetcar was built by John Stephenson Company in the eastern U.S.

the area soon provided affordable accommodation for the working class. "The coming of the Denman, Davie and Robson street car lines connected the West End to the downtown area and ended the era of the well-to-do who had built fine houses for themselves here," says a Vancouver Historical Society newsletter. "As the clerks and workers needed by Vancouver's growing commercialism came to the West End, small apartment houses rose to accommodate them."[38] At the same time, the C.P.R. had decided to open up an elite subdivision, Shaughnessy Heights.

If a transit line did not yet exist in a particular area, real estate ads urged potential owners to buy immediately since land values would jump dramatically once a transit line came into place. One 1909 *Daily Province* advertisement appeared two weeks before contractors even began to build a streetcar extension on Westminster Avenue (Main Street). It queried: "Do you REALIZE that when this CAR SERVICE is completed that the prices of these lots MUST JUMP?"[39]

In the same promotional vein, a real estate ad for Victoria Road Heights in South Vancouver told potential buyers: "The electric car line now building on Victoria Road is projected past the property, and the cars will soon be running almost to these lots, affording speedy and cheap transit to the city." It added as a prompt: "Purchasers buying now are sure to reap a good profit on an early rise in values."[40]

The growth of street railways did indeed drive up real estate values, sometimes quadrupling the price of a property overnight. Between 1909 and 1911, "assessments increased twenty-fold and on the streets where the rails would be laid, the price of lots rose from $200-$500 to $500-$2,000."[41] Commercial properties jumped even higher. In 1905, a city block near Stanley Park sold for $1,500; five years later, a small section of it went for $125,000. In 1887, before transit arrived in Vancouver, the site of the Dominion Trust building sold for $750; by 1911, it had hit $100,000.[42]

Not just realtors, but Vancouver business operators fully recognized that streetcar access was vital to their success in attracting customers. The Hastings Street East

Property Owners Association, for instance, vowed that it would not build business premises until "a good car service" was in operation. The group wrote to B.C. Electric in 1907 to request an extension of the streetcar line along Hastings Street East. Their letter states: "In a City growing as rapidly as Vancouver, a business street cannot exist without a carline … [W]ith an efficient car service it will only be a matter of a few years for this street to become a fine thoroughfare adorned on either side with stately buildings."[43]

Property owners in suburbs such as South Vancouver, who saw public transportation as vital to their survival and growth as a municipality, wrote a criticism-filled petition to get their point across:

No similarly situated suburb of the size of Vancouver on the North American continent is placed at such a disadvantage through lack of transportation facilities as

DOWNTOWN AT YOUR SERVICE – Five streetcars, on double track, serve the needs of Vancouver's growing population in this southward view of Granville Street, taken in 1908. That year, the city had 228 miles (367 kilometres) of city streets, none more impressive than the section between Georgia Street, at the top of this view, and Cordova Street, at the bottom. The photo is taken from high in the Canadian Pacific Railway's terminal building.

PHOTO SOURCE: CVA: BU P. 16.1

1909

Vancouver was burnt to a cinder 23 years ago, and now she numbers 100,000 [sic] people. Who can fail to wonder? . . . Vancouver is now being propelled forward by forces which are unabating, and are continually augmenting.

Vancouver Mayor Douglas,
***B.C. Saturday Sunset*, September 25, 1909**

- Vancouver's first pay-as-you-enter streetcars enter service on August 29.
- Vancouver officially renames Ninth Avenue as Broadway, a name that is already in common usage.
- B.C. Electric's interurban service is extended from Eburne (Marpole) to New Westminster and regular service begins on November 15.
- Vancouver's population is 85,387.
- Vancouver's first skyscraper, the Dominion Bank Building at Hastings and Cambie, is completed; it is locally known as the tallest building in the British Empire. Its architect trips on the stairs and falls to his death down the building's central core.

Instant job offer

One lucky immigrant found a Point Grey transit-related job in 1910 with no effort at all. That year, B.C. Electric sought recruits to clear land to build the company's Point Grey power substation. A company employee stopped Harold McColm, newly arrived from London, England, on the street and asked him if he wanted a job. He replied, "yes" and immediately received an axe, saw, level and canvas bag, and started cutting down trees to make a clearing. He stayed with the company for the next four years and after serving in the First World War, returned to B.C. Electric to work as a conductor.

A September 14, 1910 real estate ad promotes the land's proximity to transit lines.

South Vancouver . . . [T]he settlement of this beautiful locality is retarded and those already settled there are inconvenienced and discouraged by such lack . . . [T]he great influk of population to our city . . . are compelled to pay exorbitant [sic] rents because of the inaccessibility to these suburbs on account of such lack of transportation facilities . . . The present [interurban] connection via Lulu Island branch with Vancouver is altogether too circuitous, too tedious, too lengthy, and therefore too costly.[44]

By 1905, South Vancouver had its first streetcar line, the cemetery line, which ran from 16th and Main, south to 33rd Avenue, and then east to Fraser. New streetcar lines sprouted across Vancouver's uninhabited areas from October to December of 1909, designed to attract more settlement. Real estate ads extolled the terminus of a transit line as a reason for buying property nearby. One such *Daily Province* ad, which appeared on September 4, 1909 under the no-nonsense bold heading "Money in Tramline Terminals," declared the benefits of buying a lot at the streetcar terminus at Westminster Avenue (Main Street) and Ferris Road (49th Avenue East), and Seacome Road (Prince Edward Street): "The investor who places his money in such terminals is bound to make money and lots bought in our property . . . offer an investment absolutely without parallel . . . Right here will be the greatest move."

An August 20, 1910 realty ad in *The Daily Province* under the headline BURNABY NEW TRAMLINE stated bluntly: "The new tramline through Burnaby which passes between Burnaby Lake and Deer Lake is being rushed to completion and cars will be running very soon, when acreage will double in price."

By 1911, South Vancouver had 16,126 residents, making it the third largest "city" in B.C. Its population continued to grow as 200 families

LITTLE SIBERIA – This rare view, circa 1908, depicts the southern edge and industrial heart of what New Westminster residents called "Little Siberia": the area along 6th Street north from 11th Avenue in eastern Burnaby. George Leaf's store is on the left, with Cliff's Can Factory, a major stop for New Westminster streetcars, on the right. A streetcar approaches in the distance, while hexagonal-shaped locomotive 503 waits on the can factory's spur. The streetcar has come from Edmonds and Kingsway, where it connected with the Vancouver-New Westminster interurban line, and is destined for Columbia Street in downtown New Westminster.

PHOTO SOURCE: BVM: BV 995.10.1

THE HEART OF DOWNTOWN – Five streetcars and a horse-drawn wagon provide transportation at the key intersection of downtown Vancouver in 1908: Granville (southwards) and Hastings streets. The streetcar to the left is a four-wheeled remnant of earlier, less-demanding transit times. In the distance, a streetcar swings westward onto Pender Street for the trip to Stanley Park. Solidly constructed buildings and well-dressed citizens typify Vancouver at this time, far removed from its early boom-town years.

PHOTO SOURCE: PHILIP T. TIMMS COLLECTION, VPL 5236

a month moved in. Real estate developers lobbied for new public works and services in this fledgling region. Realtors sought property buyers, while transit officials sought paying passengers. The two groups soon learned that they could combine their respective interests for mutual benefit and hopefully, profit. In fact, ratepayers gave B.C. Electric a very generous 41-year franchise and tax concessions in return for an agreement to lay more street railway lines.

The area around Deer Lake in Burnaby was supposed to be a posh residential district served by the Burnaby Lake interurban line. Examples of fine houses built in this period are the Burnaby Art Gallery and Hart House Restaurant. (When he built his house, Hart was a prosperous New Westminster real estate dealer; he lost his fortune when the boom collapsed around 1912.)

Vancouver's early real estate boom levelled off just after 1911.

Point Grey: Transit plans prove too grandiose for this former "wasteland"

A realtor's rose-coloured glasses can transform any stretch of swamp or lonely land into an Eden of untapped potential. The start of Point Grey was no exception. The area was deemed "an impenetrable waste" in 1895, but after its incorporation on January 1, 1908, it shifted from a "wasteland logged-over and be-stumped" to an upscale, exclusively residential region within four years. [45]

The C.P.R. was eager to develop its landholdings in this region, which now encompassed more than half the area previously part of South Vancouver. This development opened a new area for the city's rich and powerful, Shaughnessy Heights, which featured especially large lots and, ultimately, opulent homes. A *Province* ad on September 26, 1912 commented about a similarly prosperous area in this new municipality: "Who would not return each morning to the routine of city business refreshed and rejuvenated by the healthful life on Point Grey's heights 'where sunshine and fresh air meet'?"

Transit service was an integral part of planning for this "mecca of the elite." [46]

A 1908 engineering report made an extravagant proposal for two continuous circular streetcar routes, a western and eastern belt, with two additional streetcar connectors to serve the area. At the time, these links would have served more trees than passengers, since there were few residences in the suggested locations. The western belt would operate from 16th and Alma to 4th Avenue, along Chancellor and Marine Drive (then South Boulevard), and back. The eastern belt would run from 16th Avenue at Johnson Road (later Blenheim) down Marine Drive to Eburne (Marpole), up Hudson to 49th Avenue, and up Laurel to 16th.

For the western belt, the report recommended single-truck Brill streetcars, which could each seat 32 people and make the belt trip in 30 minutes, including stops. It con-

MAKING WAY TO POINT GREY – The construction of a new streetcar line on Dunbar Street south to 41st Avenue is well underway in this 1913 photo, four years after the first line went into Point Grey. The line shown here would open up a prime residential area in Point Grey for immediate development. Locomotive 952, built by B.C. Electric in New Westminster in 1911, pulls a company dump car; a construction crew works hard alongside.

PHOTO SOURCE: BC HYDRO: A0939

cluded: "Two cars operating in opposite directions providing a half hour service should be sufficient for a time." Double-trucked Brill cars were proposed for the eastern belt; these could carry 48 passengers and make the 11-mile (18-kilometre) round trip in 45 minutes, including stops.[47]

As if caught up in the area's expected burst into grandeur, this transit vision ensured that a streetcar line would never lie more than three-quarters of a mile (1.2 kilometres) from anywhere in Point Grey, with or without residents. However, this ambitious dream did not go ahead, undoubtedly due to expense and slower-than-expected settlement.

Instead, B.C. Electric opened a new double-tracked streetcar line on Fourth Avenue between Granville and Alma in October 1909, originating the two-mile (3.2-kilometre) service at Granville and Smithe. It took almost another year before Point Grey ratepayers passed bylaws, submitted by their council, for a streetcar-line franchise, roads, parks, a sewage system and water connections in July 1910.

Track was installed almost to the university endowment lands in 1910 and service opened on this new line on February 25, 1911. (This line, along with the one on Granville, would cease operations the following year due to a franchise disagreement between B.C. Electric and the municipality of Point Grey. The line reopened in September the same year after the dispute was settled.)

Point Grey also gained some new transit extensions. The Shaughnessy Heights line extended on Granville Street from 16th Avenue (the boundary between Vancouver and Point Grey) to 25th in October 1911. The following September, the Oak Street line was extended from 16th (the boundary) to 25th. Just over two months later, the Sasamat line was extended along 4th Avenue, west to Drummond Drive.

Nearby streetcar lines helped to entice settlers to Point Grey. Even for more monied residents, choosing property in Point Grey meant considering commuting distance to and from the downtown core. Realty ads in *The Province* always highlighted easy access to transit service, as in the following on September 26, 1912: "Streets are perfectly made, water, light, telephone, street car service – all at your door." A 33-foot lot in a "superb situation," selling for $850 in 1912, stood a "block from Oak Street carline," read a *Province* ad on September 13, 1912. The next day, *The Province* ran another advertisement, which promoted "lots on open roads/cleared and graded" for $800; the ad's headline "POINT GREY/ CAR LINES" was its biggest feature. Then, as now, subtlety did not rate high in promotional copy.

Observation Car: "Party on wheels" gives sightseeing a twist

An open-air observation car debuted in Vancouver in 1909, delivering sightseeing with a twist every summer from May 24 to Labour Day. It was a party on wheels: two arches of lights twinkled in the dusk over tiered seats; two whistle toots provided greetings at every block. The tour came with corny jokes, dog tricks, vaudeville acts and the option of a souvenir photo. Conductor/raconteur Teddy Lyons guided tourists and locals on a two-hour showcase of neighbourhood talent, regaling them with an ever-changing repertoire of one-liners. "I used to admire Teddy Lyons with his megaphone," remembers Ralph Shaw at age 95, then a Mount Pleasant resident. "I saw him passing by frequently. [He was] very popular. Fascinating."

Passengers on car 124 watched amateur performers, from jugglers to magicians, present their acts at pre-arranged spots along the route. Not all entertainers had talent; some over-eager mothers pushed their tots into the limelight. One of these happy kids remembers years later: "We didn't even have to do anything – just stand and look cute and they'd throw us pennies and sticks of Wrigley's. It was really exciting."[48]

A TOURIST TOUR DE FORCE – Observation car 124, poised on Robson Street facing Granville Street, prepares for a two-hour sightseeing extravaganza c. 1913. The popular trips made stops throughout Vancouver, Point Grey and South Vancouver (the latter two communities did not join the city until 1929).

PHOTO SOURCE: BC HYDRO: A01116

GRANVILLE BRIDGE GALA – Much-decorated observation car 124 leads a southbound procession of streetcars on Granville Bridge in an opening ceremony on Labour Day, September 6, 1909. The gala event marked the opening of the new bridge across False Creek, which replaced an obsolete, near-condemned crossing. Earl Grey, Canada's governor general, stands directly behind the car's headlight, with Lady Grey, Vancouver's mayor C. S. Douglas, motorman R. Piper, and conductor J. McSavaney to his left. At far left is the head of the contracting firm that built the bridge, W. Armstrong.

PHOTO SOURCE: BC HYDRO: A0103

With seven shows a day and non-stop humour, Lyons soon became the tour's biggest draw. His mugging with a megaphone often brought repeat customers for the 50-cent tour, where they could appreciate homemade quips like "We are now passing Petticoat Lane. Just inside the outskirts" or "Our first observation car: the baby carriage."[49] The tours took one of two main routes from downtown, either running out to 41st and Dunbar and back, or heading to 10th and Crown, then to English Bay and back. Each trip usually racked up around 18 miles (30 kilometres); if the wind got too chilly along the way, passengers wrapped themselves in blankets supplied by Hudson's Bay.

At the end of the tour, passengers could buy a "surprise" group photo, thanks to route manoeuvring and some ingenuity by lensman Harry Bullen. (Bullen came to Vancouver in 1907 to act as B.C. Electric's official photographer.) The car would stop a block from the Carrall Street station, supposedly to let passengers admire the architecture of the New Dodson Hotel. Meanwhile, Bullen took the picture from the second-storey window of his hotel room, which he had rented for the season, and counted the number of families on board to estimate how many photos he would sell. As the obser-

CRUISE WITH A VIEW – Sightseeing tours in an open-air observation car began in Vancouver in 1909. Car 124 was one of two (123, 124) built by B.C. Electric and patterned after a similar Montreal vehicle. Dick Gardner and Teddy Lyons, especially the latter, were renowned as observation car raconteur-guides. Cars 123 and 124 ran their last trips in 1950; 124 was scrapped on February 14, 1951.

PHOTO SOURCE: CMBC: SO-2

CREWS ON A CRUISE – Conductors, motormen, officials and Prior Street barn crew pose with newly arrived observation car 124 in 1909.

PHOTO SOURCE: HARRY BULLEN PHOTO, VPL: SO-I

vation car continued, he developed and printed the pictures. Then he rode his bicycle to Granville and Robson and deposited the photos in a box at the rear of the passing vehicle, as it finished its trip. The conductor took out the photos to sell while Bullen pedalled his bike back to the hotel to prepare for the next tour. [50]

Car 124 launched its first showy display in Vancouver on September 6, 1909, to celebrate the opening of the new Granville Street Bridge. Canada's Governor General, His Excellency Earl Grey, and Lady Grey rode the decorated car along with local dignitaries. The car proved highly popular from its first day of service.

Car 124 was one of two cars built in B.C. Electric's New Westminster shops, based on designs purchased from the Montreal Tramway Company. The other, car 123, went to Victoria, but after a ho-hum stint there, joined its sister in Vancouver in 1919.

The first-ever sightseeing car to grace Vancouver streets operated in 1903 and 1904. This ordinary streetcar, nicknamed the "toast rack" due to its open sides, gave tours from downtown (today's Gastown) to Stanley Park for 25 cents.

A KITSILANO CRUISE – The Fourth Avenue streetcar line was in service as far west as Vine Street by October 1909, a few months after this photo was taken. This Fourth Avenue view near Waterloo Street looks east to Blenheim, as a mostly Italian work gang extends the line to its final terminus, Alma Street.

PHOTO SOURCE: CVA 7-78

Stanley Park: "Improved aesthetics" or "lunch baskets and bottled beer"?

Money and power defined the contentious issue of transporting people to and from, and possibly within, Vancouver's "recreational jewel" of Stanley Park by the late 1800s.

By 1909, access to the park was equitable enough. That year, a survey of 33,000 visitors to the park showed that most (30,500) arrived on foot, having travelled to and from the park by streetcar. The rest used (in rounded numbers): horse and buggy (1,100), bicycle (600), saddled horse (400) and automobile (400). [51]

A streetcar ride to the park for a day outing, picnic or swim was a major family excursion and social event. Vancouver resident Ralph Shaw recalls at age 95: "We used to board the streetcar and travel along Broadway to Granville, down Granville to Davie, down Davie to English Bay, then walk to Second Beach for our family picnic." His family repeated this trip from Mount Pleasant two or three times each summer and saw it as a highlight of the season.

Band concerts at Stanley Park were popular entertainment, especially for the city's gentry. B.C. Electric sponsored concerts in the park and ran newspaper ads about upcoming ones; it reminded readers that they could take the Robson or Pender streetcar directly to the park entrance.

Nevertheless, by 1910, many Vancouverites wanted greater access to Stanley Park. The issue of park-related transit grew into a city-wide debate that polarized tourists and the West End gentry against Vancouver's lower-middle class and working class. A private operator issued a proposal in August that year to run streetcars around the circumference of Stanley Park. This pitted the purists who sought a natural, untrammelled park against those who wanted greater populist access. The debate gained momentum from the City Beautiful movement, a popular concept spreading across North America that focussed on "the need to improve the aesthetic qualities of urban places." Romantics decried the thought of streetcars carrying "thou-

VETERAN CONDUCTOR – Charles Woodcock started with B.C. Electric in May 1909 as conductor No. 112. He served 23 years with the street railway company and passed away on June 7, 1932.

PHOTO CREDIT: HEATHER CONN (FROM HE COLLECTION)

DOUBLE-TRACKED EXTENSION – This new Fourth Avenue streetcar line, completed in late October 1909, was a strong sign of the times; it was double tracked from its inception, with the expectation that transit service in the area would be heavily used. This was a departure from the typical single-tracking of new lines into uninhabited regions. J. Quiney's sign and the corner street light suggest that habitation will soon follow.

PHOTO SOURCE: CVA 7-79

sands of people with lunch baskets and bottled beer into the park's recesses."[52] Reformists, some of whom wanted a sports stadium built at the park entrance, petitioned the city to put the streetcar proposal to a vote.

In a January 1912 plebiscite, Vancouver's lower-income east and southeast wards marginally approved a proposal, a different version from the one made two years earlier, for a municipally owned streetcar service in Stanley Park. However, wealthy West End voters massively opposed the plan, and it was defeated. Observers charged that the park board discriminated in its treatment of various transportation modes. It allowed the buggies and cars of wealthy residents to reach the "far corners" of Stanley Park, while denying "plain every-day people" a public transit service that would take them to the park's remoter areas, away from the crowds at the park entrance.[53]

Accidents: "Lakeview disaster" city's worst transit tragedy

LAKEVIEW FATALITY – The 1909 "Lakeview disaster" killed 15 people, including motorman G. Thorburn, pictured here, and conductor Harris.

PHOTO SOURCE: HEATHER CONN (BC HYDRO INFORMATION SERVICES, SPECIAL COLLECTIONS)

Accident reports in Vancouver's early transit days list a litany of hazards, from crazed livestock loose on the track to the occasional robbery or assault. Some over-eager passengers, too impatient to wait until a streetcar or interurban came to a complete stop, injured themselves or even died when they leaped off a moving vehicle. Poorly maintained track or a dilapidated Granville Bridge could threaten passenger safety, and a boys' prank resulted in passenger deaths.

With challenges from equipment, weather, runaway animals and criminal behaviour, early transit operations resulted in considerable fatalities by today's standards. In one incident on December 6, 1903, thick fog caused the collision of streetcars 34 and 38 at noon on the south end of the Main Street Bridge; two men received serious injuries. In another case, some boys released the brakes on a massive steel bunker (heavily loaded rail car) parked on a spur line off the steep track on Main Street south from 59th Avenue; the bunker broke loose, plummeted down the track and

WHEN BRAKES FAIL – No fatalities occurred in a North Vancouver mishap when streetcar 62 swept past the end of its tracks at the Lonsdale ferry wharf and wound up in the drink on August 12, 1909. The vehicle's brakes reportedly failed, although no proof remained in an era that predated accident investigations; B.C. Electric ordered the car burned to scrap at the water's edge that night.

This view looks west at the foot of Lonsdale Avenue. Streetcar 62 was built by B.C. Electric in New Westminster in 1904.

PHOTO SOURCE: CMBC: SS-00-5

FRONT-END FENDER-BENDER – This streetcar, one of 10 numbered 150 to 159, has taken a considerable beating in an unrecorded altercation and location. This mishap likely occurred soon after the vehicle arrived in 1908 from New Jersey builder John Stephenson Company. Such a degree of damage was unusual, given the size and quantity of competing street traffic at the time.

PHOTO SOURCE: BC HYDRO: A0019

ONLY ONE YEAR OLD – Interurban car "Sumas," built in 1907 by B.C. Electric, stops momentarily at Epworth, shortly to be renamed Lakeview (Victoria Drive crossing). The vehicle is on the Central Park line on its way to New Westminster in 1908.

A year later, this car was wrecked in what was known as "the Lakeview disaster," the worst accident in the long history of the B.C. Electric Railway, in which 15 people died. This occurred not 100 yards east of this point, when the car was bound for New Westminster.

"Sumas" was rebuilt to passenger/mail interurban car 1501, and in 1928, to passenger interurban 1216. The car's 50-year life span ended when it was scrapped by burning at the Kitsilano shops in September 1957.

PHOTO SOURCE: CVA 330-12

collided with an upcoming streetcar, killing many passengers and destroying the streetcar.[54]

Not all transit accidents ended in tragedy. In 1909, when the brakes failed on North Vancouver car 62, it hurtled off the track at the end of Lonsdale, prompting motorman John Kelly and two passengers to jump to safety. As the vehicle flew to the edge of the wharf, conductor Jones convinced the rest of the passengers, including the wife of North Vancouver's mayor, to remain on board. When the car plunged into Burrard Inlet with all inside, surprisingly, no one was injured. The only reported mishap was Kelly's broken leg.

In another incident, a runaway streetcar had only one occupant, an elderly Chinese man. As his vehicle lurched out of control down Main Street, he managed to hang on to a shoulder strap and merely swayed his way to safety, shaken but unhurt.

The worst public transit accident in Vancouver's early history, known as "the Lakeview disaster," occurred in the early morning of November 10, 1909. Fourteen people died immediately, and one later, when a load of timbers shot off a runaway flat car, "rushing cityward with tremendous momentum," and demolished eastbound interurban car "Sumas" just after it left Lakeview station at Victoria Drive.

The car's remaining nine passengers were seriously injured. "No one living in Cedar Cottage at that time has forgotten the accident," recorded a local school publication almost 60 years later. "They remember that the roof of the car was sheared right off, that women were turned back from the dreadful scene, and that many people in Cedar Cottage lost relatives or friends." [55] Criminal charges brought against the vehicle's crew were dropped. B.C. Electric voluntarily gave $135,000 to the families of the deceased and to those injured.

The tragedy spurred the public, led by the Trades and Labor Council, to seek greater supervision of interurban lines. In 1911, the provincial legislature passed the Tramways Inspection Act, which introduced British Columbia's first-ever regulations regarding transit service and safety. The government appointed an "extremely conscientious" inspector, William Rae, who rejected any freight or passenger cars he deemed unfit for service; he also paid close attention to overcrowding of streetcars.

Despite the efforts of many diligent staff, the number of transit-related deaths in these early years was high. A provincial Department of Railways report, published in 1917, lists 29 deaths on B.C. Electric's entire transit system from 1911 to 1915 inclusive; this includes both Vancouver and Victoria regions. Of these, six were employees. [56]

"Juggernauts traverse our streets with no protection whatsoever"

The deaths of three Vancouver streetcar passengers in late 1907 spawned an outcry for changes in local transit regulations and safety features.

Safety rules introduced in 1911

The B.C. attorney general ordered regulatory changes in 1911 to end overcrowding on public vehicles and to increase safety in the event of a collision. Changes included the following:

- Standees were no longer allowed on interurban cars between Vancouver and Chilliwack and New Westminster; the number of passengers would be limited to the tram's seating capacity. This resulted in the compulsory use of multi-car trains, which provided more combined passenger space.

- A separate compartment for mail and baggage was required on interurbans; this would eliminate the practice of piling mail and luggage onto unoccupied seats.

- Passengers could no longer ride the bumpers of outside steps of a streetcar or interurban. (Streetcars later replaced wooden exterior ledges with sloped, beveled tin bumpers that eliminated room or support for standing passengers.)

- No one could operate a public vehicle without first taking an exam and a sight and hearing test.

- Streetcars had to display a "Car Full" sign and have a gate to keep their platform inaccessible to the public when there was no more room for passengers. (A car was to be deemed full when all seats were occupied with one standee for every four square feet of standing room.) "This system is expected to do away with accidents caused by impatient people jumping on or off the platform while the car is in motion," reported *The Vancouver Sun* on August 10, 1912.

An editorial cartoon shows a man fleeing the maw of a streetcar. The caption reads: "This Goblin needs muzzling." (B.C. Saturday Sunset, November 9, 1907)

1910

The fast pace of progress in early Vancouver did not impress all its residents. Artist Emily Carr, who lived in the city from 1905 to 1910, wrote of this period:

Vancouver was . . . growing hard. Almost every day you saw more of her forest being pushed back, half-cleared, waiting to be drained and built upon – mile upon mile of charred stumps and boggy skunk-cabbage swamp, root-holes filled with brown stagnant water, reflecting blue sky by day, rasping with frog croaks by night, fireweed . . . loveliness trying to hide the hideous transition from wild to tamed land. [57]

- Vancouver population is 93,700.
- Premier Richard McBride drives the last spike on B.C. Electric's Chilliwack interurban line on October 3. The 63.8-mile (102.7-kilometre) line is the longest interurban railway line ever built in Canada; regular service begins the next day.
- Vancouver's transit system carries 122,455 passengers on August 22: a record for a single day.
- B.C. Electric cannot keep up with the demand for more vehicles; the company makes an unprecedented commitment for 122 new cars in the next year, including 50 for Vancouver alone. The company cannot build them all at its New Westminster shops, which are running to capacity, and places orders with other builders.
- A man in Surrey is fined $10 for speeding in his 1907 Marion automobile on April 20. He was travelling at 12 miles per hour (19.3 kilometres per hour).
- Car dealer Henry ("Harry") Hooper makes a record automobile trip from Chilliwack to New Westminster in two hours and ten minutes.
- During this year, the complete B.C. Electric system, including Victoria, carries almost 40 million riders (up 10 million over the previous year) on 200 streetcars and interurbans; 41,142 tons of freight are hauled.

A coroner's jury and the media blasted the city's "defective" law of stopping streetcars on the "far side" of an intersection. They urged that, instead, passengers should disembark on the "near side," before crossing the intersecting street, allowing for a safer and more visible exit, away from traffic flow.

"Not only should the cars stop on the near side, in the interests of public safety, but they should be equipped with a fender, and guards that will prevent a body from falling beneath the wheels," charged a November 2, 1907, editorial in *B.C. Saturday Sunset*. "Had these appliances been in use on the B.C. Electric Railway cars in this city, it is probable that the three recent victims of the cars would today be alive." (Those in favour of the "far side" regulation argued that it enabled passengers to board and disembark on dry ground; whereas if a streetcar stopped on the near side, passengers would have to "descend into mud.")

The editorial called Vancouver's outdated far-side streetcar system a "deadly fallacy" and noted that almost every other Canadian city had converted to the near-side practice. In Montreal, the old system had killed and maimed so many people that the railway company there was forced to change the regulation. The editorial writer described how he and a friend narrowly escaped getting run down in that city under the far-side system, whereupon his friend remarked: "That system is the right way to kill people." The editorial continued: "We allow juggernauts to traverse our streets amid throngs of people with no protection whatsoever except the constant vigilance of the motorman."

Many new residents in Vancouver's growing city were unfamiliar with the antiquated far-side system, resulting in embarrassment, inconvenience and public endangerment, the writer noted. Similarly, he charged that Vancouver's streetcars were obsolete since they opened at only one end, limiting the time and convenience of passengers boarding and disembarking. He favoured a two-door system,

NO BRIDGE TO RIVAL THIS – No previous transportation infrastructure in Vancouver's history could equal the impressive Granville Bridge, which opened on September 6, 1909. Governor General Earl Grey officially unveiled the bridge, a vital link to the fast-developing western side of the city. This deluxe new bridge replaced one built in 1889.

In the middle of the bridge is one of the new double-trucked streetcars, built in New Westminster. In the distance is the 1902-built Kitsilano trestle, which carried B.C. Electric's Steveston interurban line.

STATE-OF-THE-ART SERVICE – One of the "name" interurbans, built in New Westminster by B.C. Electric, passes just east of Cedar Cottage on the Central Park line in 1908. This elegant vehicle was considered the best of its kind at the time. Double-track construction is underway next to the single-track line on which the interurban is operating; this will allow for increased service on the same route. The narrow-gauge tracks are used to remove rubble from widening of the right-of-way.

NO CALL FOR CARS – This westward view of Hastings Street from Richards Street in 1910 reveals that automobiles were rare and even pedestrians were scarce. Perhaps that's why the streetcar's safety fender is up rather than down; it's not needed here to fend off stumbling passersby.

PHOTO SOURCE: CVA: STR P. 66

FADING GLORY – Cordova Street was already losing its draw for people by 1909, the year of this photo. Previously, it had shared status with Granville and Hastings as the most popular downtown destination streets. In this eastward view along Hastings, from just west of Carrall Street, both commercial and pedestrian traffic is plentiful.

The streetcar in the foreground will turn to the right at the top of the hill onto Main Street and make its way south to Broadway and the Fairview district. At the streetcar's front end, additional tracks are visible; these connected Canadian Pacific Railway's waterfront terminal tracks with its False Creek yard and roundhouse. This hazardous and disruptive connection remained until the C.P.R. inaugurated a tunnel under downtown in 1932. Today, SkyTrain uses the same tunnel.

PHOTO SOURCE: CVA: STR P. 24 N. 98

BUILT-IN SPRINKLER SYSTEM – This sprinkler car, which did not carry passengers, served as a street-cleaner before paved roads and rubber-tired traffic came along. It sprays at the west end of Georgia Street near Stanley Park in 1910, as per a contract between B.C. Electric and Vancouver's civic government. Photos that show the sprinklers in action are extremely rare.

Car 550, built in 1905 by B.C. Electric, was originally numbered 188, and would finish its working life numbered S.50.

PHOTO SOURCE: CMBC: IF-40-1

COMING FROM THE MOUNTAIN – During May of 1910, the inaugural month of streetcar service on North Vancouver's Lynn Valley line, either car 34 or 36 poses on the pile and timber trestle on Lynn Valley Road over Hastings Creek, just east of today's Mountain Highway crossing. New suburbs were in the process of creation.

PHOTO SOURCE: NVMA: 8469

NOT A COFFEE MUG – "Coffee can" fare collectors, like this original one donated to BC Hydro, were used on Vancouver streetcars from 1890 to 1909.

PHOTO CREDIT: HEATHER CONN
(BC HYDRO INFORMATION SERVICES,
SPECIAL COLLECTIONS)

which would take half the time to empty and fill a streetcar. He concluded: "No modern system of street railway is equipped with cars open only at one end."

After much criticism, Vancouver finally adopted the nearside custom of stopping for passengers before crossing a street. The city introduced the so-called "nearside" car, number 501, in December of 1912. This vehicle, unique at the time, had no rear platform so passengers entered and exited at the front. The front platform was enlarged to provide room for both the motorman and the conductor. The motorman controlled both the entrance and exit doors while the conductor controlled the rear emergency door.

AT ITS COSMOPOLITAN BEST – In this northward view along Granville Street from Pender Street, the nearly new post office (today's Sinclair Centre) stands on the left. The Canadian Pacific Railway terminal is in the centre and the Bank of Commerce (today's Birks) is on the right.

Two double-trucked streetcars, newly built, are at their Hastings Street stop. Cars 200 to 229 featured frosted-glass windows and the interior overhead light bulbs bore B.C. Electric's etched initials, B.C.E.R.

PHOTO SOURCE: CVA: STR P. 302 N. 255

PAY-AS-YOU-ENTER DAYS – Car 178, built by B.C. Electric in New Westminster in 1910, reflects a new fare policy introduced the previous year: pay-as-you-enter. Before 1909, a conductor walked the length of the streetcar and collected fares; this could involve jostling through a crowd of standees or leaning out to those who hung precariously off the rear of the vehicle.

One old-timer remembered: "[If] the tram was full, say after the men got off work, they could ride on the running boards on the outside of the car, paying their nickel fare into the leather cup that was handed out by the conductor and passed from passenger to passenger till it reached the back of the tram." [58] A July 1932 issue of the *The B.C. Electric Employees' Magazine* recounts: "Remember the memory tests in the collection of fares?...The crowd boarded and the conductor went after fares later, sometimes considerably later."

This method of collection lasted little more than two decades, doomed by the necessity of larger streetcars. The introduction of B.C. Electric's first P.A.Y.E. (pay-as-you-enter) street-cars on August 29, 1909, signalled the end of the "coffee can" collection service. (The P.A.Y.E. designation was used on streetcars throughout Canada and the United States.)

In this photo, a leading-edge car stands at 4th Avenue and Alma Street. A semi-convertible streetcar, its windows retreat into its Narragansett-style curved sides. (This New England style allowed windows to slide into roof pockets, making the whole window disappear. On a regular streetcar, half the window went up, the other half remained stationary.) The two-person crew reveals the tools of its trade: the motorman's watch and the conductor's coin holder.

PHOTO SOURCE: CMBC: SC-10-13

Sporting Events: Avid fans take public transit to games

"Lacrosse specials": trains transported thousands to each game

Nothing stirred the fervour of local sports fans more than watching their beloved lacrosse teams in the early 1900s. Lacrosse was hugely popular back then – much more so than hockey. Lacrosse games between rival Vancouver and New Westminster teams drew crowds of 15,000 to 20,000 rowdy fans who needed transportation to and from

OUR NATIONAL SPORT – Lacrosse dominated all other sports in B.C.'s major centres for the first 40 years of the twentieth century. B.C. Electric's streetcars and interurbans, and their crews, truly worked overtime to transport fans to and from the games.

Action shots of games in the earlier part of the century are rare. In this 1912 photo, Canada's most celebrated lacrosse team, the New Westminster Salmonbellies, defends its goal from a shot by Vancouver's number 9, Bones Allen. Others, from left, are umpire Harry Godfrey, goalkeeper Johnny Howard, Bun Clarke and Hugh Gifford.

PHOTO SOURCE: CVA: SP. P. 71 N. 46

Monster Lacrosse Match

On Brockton Point Grounds

DOMINION DAY
Wednesday, July 1st, 1903

VANCOUVER VS. VICTORIA

Both teams are playing great lacrosse this year and a hotly contested match may be looked for.

The Victorians will put up a hard fight to lower Vancouver's standard, but they'll have their hands full every minute of the time. If you don't believe so, go out and see the game. It will be fast and furious.

Game called at 3 p.m.

The full Military Band under the leadership of Mr. F. Highfield will be in attendance.

The Street Cars Run Direct to the Park.
Special car service for this event.

Championship
Lacrosse Match
Saturday, July 13

Queen's Park Grounds, New Westminster

Vancouver vs. New Westminster

The Vancouver team has been considerably strengthened since last meeting the New Westminster team, and expects to win from the mighty men by the Fraser. A splendid exhibition of Canada's national game is assured whoever wins.

SPECIAL CAR SERVICE

Special cars will leave the ram Office direct for Queen's Park at short intervals, commencing at 1 p.m.

Fare 50c. Return

games.[59] In New Westminster, city businesses closed on the day of a major match. (The New Westminster Salmonbellies, one of Canada's best teams in lacrosse history, won the Minto Cup for the Canadian championship every year from 1908 to 1914, except in 1911, when Vancouver won.)

B.C. Electric responded to local sports fever with "lacrosse specials": interurban trains, used only for championship matches, which ran at short intervals. For a 50-cent return fare, fans travelled from downtown Vancouver to Queen's Park in New Westminster on the Central Park line, and vice-versa. *The Columbian* reported during the 1910 Minto Cup match between the Salmonbellies and Montreal: "The B.C.E.R. has at its disposal today, 36 cars, the largest number ever run between this city and Vancouver . . . three specials have been running to and from the Park every half hour."[60] The company advertised upcoming big matches in newspaper notices, promoting its role in transporting fans.

Before the interurban line opened in 1891, most fans took a C.P.R. train to games; the railway ran lacrosse trains to Port Moody and then along a secondary line to New Westminster. Riders switched to transit when it became available because it offered cheaper, faster and more direct service.

A QUICK JAUNT TO THE CLUB – The Vancouver Lawn Tennis Club flourishes in 1905 in the West End, Vancouver's choicest residential area. Even for its upper-crust members, a streetcar is the means of transportation. The club is on a streetcar line, as one would expect, on Denman Street's east side between Barclay and Nelson streets. The clubhouse is partly visible to the left.

The club would stay at this location for another decade before moving to 16th Avenue and Fir Street, the northern edge of Shaughnessy Heights, Vancouver's ultimate high-priced residential development. Even in this ritzy neighbourhood, the club stood only a short block away from streetcar service on Granville Street.

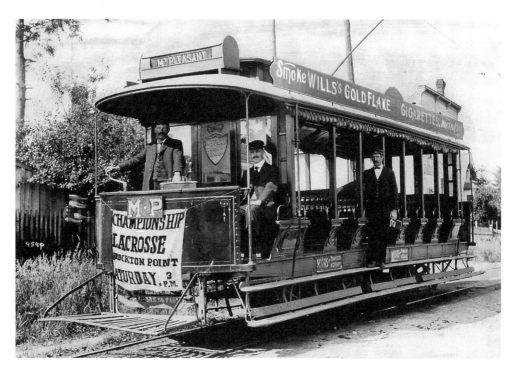

SPORTS FANS & FARES – With front banners promoting upcoming games, Vancouver's early streetcars advertise themselves as vehicles that cater to sports fans. This 1903 photo shows car 23, an open-air streetcar, at Main and 16th on the Mount Pleasant route, with motorman John Paxman and conductors A.B. Greer and J. Jeffers.

PHOTO SOURCE: CMBC: SC-00-2

ON THE GO TO A GAME – The "Arena Hockey" sign on car 172, photographed here in 1910, makes its destination clear. (Five years later, the Vancouver Millionaires hockey team would win the Stanley Cup.) This car operates as a pay-as-you-enter vehicle. The motorman poses on the front step beside the conductor.

PHOTO SOURCE: CMBC: SC-10-2

WORLD'S FIRST DOME CARS – A Dick-Kerr locomotive in 1910 pulls a group of C.P.R. coaches, including three Rocky Mountain observation cars (they were the world's first dome cars and remarkable for their time). The train is headed from Vancouver to Minoru Park horse-racing track on B.C. Electric's interurban line to Steveston. (It's Good Friday and many citizens complained to the local press that gambling on a religious day was sinful.)

This locomotive is one of B.C. Electric's first large ones, numbered 911, 912 and 913, used on the new Chilliwack interurban line. (They were later renumbered 990, 991 and 992.) B.C. Electric was based in London, England until 1928, so it came as no surprise that these first locomotives were ordered from the Dick-Kerr Company in Britain.

PHOTO SOURCE: GEORGE E. TIMMS PHOTO, VPL 7184

Early streetcars also offered direct service to Stanley Park, where lacrosse games were held at Brockton Point; the vehicles promoted the matches with banners on their front bumper.

Initially, B.C. Electric used five or six extra streetcars to take fans to lacrosse matches. But by 1906, Saturday games were drawing up to 10,000 spectators. The company responded with inventive flair: it converted open flat-bed rail cars into "lacrosse trains." More than 100 spectators, mostly male, could squeeze onto rows of bench seats in each car, which were fenced with three-foot-high (one-metre) railing on all sides. These cars were coupled to an electric locomotive.

The wild spectator rides remained popular for years, even after more interurbans became available. The special trains and interurbans served fans in both directions; they brought crowds to Vancouver, with streetcar transfers to Stanley Park, or arrived directly onto Exhibition Grounds in New Westminster, where the siding was lengthened to allow room for the extra interurban cars to park and wait for the return trip to Vancouver.

A NOTABLE NEWCOMER – Newly acquired interurban car 401 attracts considerable interest in the late summer of 1910 at Brighouse on Lulu Island. Built by American Car Company, this handsome vehicle has recently arrived for service on B.C. Electric's soon-to-be-opened New Westminster–Chilliwack line. Car 401 would be renumbered to 1400 in 1913, and ultimately to car 1321 in 1942; it continued operating until B.C. Electric scrapped it in 1954.

PHOTO SOURCE: CVA: TRANS P. 146 N. 94

Today, one observer surmises that the cheap, efficient interurban service to and from lacrosse games in the Lower Mainland contributed to the success of both the local leagues and the national game before the First World War. In her words: "Without the extraordinary number of spectators generated by those lacrosse specials, the great days of the New Westminster and Vancouver lacrosse rivalry might never have materialized." [61]

Horse racing: fans ride world's first railway dome cars

Thoroughbred horse racing at Minoru Park (later Brighouse in today's city of Richmond) emerged as another popular destination for interurban passengers, who wore their Sunday best on their way to bet and socialize. Seven thousand spectators attended races at this track when it opened on August 21, 1909. B.C. Electric's Steveston interurban line provided direct service from Granville Station to Minoru Park and back again on a 20-mile (32-kilometre) round trip; the line's $1.25 return fare even included entry to the track.

Only a few yards away from the B.C. Electric main line, the track offered a special interurban loop with a spur line to the back of the grandstand; the interurbans could

conveniently offload passengers, then wait in the siding for fans to return at the end of the day. (This practice was repeated successfully in 1914, when another racetrack, Lansdowne Park, opened.) Freight trains could also unload horses and hay at the same spot.

From the time Minoru Park opened, the racetrack was a social magnet, and B.C. Electric scrambled to provide service. More than half the spectators arrived by interurbans, prompting the largest-ever ridership increase on the Steveston line. B.C. Electric offered non-stop race specials with extra interurbans and even added Vancouver streetcars to the line to accommodate passenger overflow. (These streetcar trips were no longer needed by 1910, since many additional new interurbans were in service.)

To handle its high-volume racetrack ridership, B.C. Electric decided to duplicate the success of its lacrosse trains. It poured racing fans into 10 former C.P.R. flat cars, outfitted with wooden seats, and pulled them behind an electric locomotive. Racetrack enthusiasts also made their way in style on the interurban line, thanks to some deluxe transportation loaned from the C.P.R.: several luxurious passenger coaches and off-duty Rocky Mountain observation cars, the world's first railway dome cars.

Other novelty sporting excursions meant extra trips and lucrative business for B.C. Electric. When the first airplane flight in western Canada left from Minoru Park on

CEDAR COTTAGE CAR — Vancouver's first transit employees appear with streetcar 150 in this photo, taken at Cedar Cottage in 1910. The streetcar is only two years old. D. McLean served as motorman No. 1, with J. J. Jeffers as conductor No. 2. The third figure is a student motorman undergoing training on the line. The two boys remain unidentified.

A Scottish native, McLean started in transit as a blacksmith in B.C. Electric's shops in 1893,

earning $2.50 a day; during slack times, he put in labour on the streetcar tracks. Sometimes he worked at the forge in the morning and took out a streetcar for the evening rush. At the time, city transit service needed 10 streetcars to cope with evening rush hour, according to the January 1920 issue of *The B.C. Electric Employees' Magazine*.

PHOTO SOURCE: BC HYDRO:
THE B.C. ELECTRIC EMPLOYEES' MAGAZINE,
JANUARY 1920, P. 9

1911

- The 115 men of the car shops work doggedly throughout August to finish 25 steel-frame, single-end streetcars for Vancouver and to finish converting the older interurban cars to multiple-unit operation.
- B.C. Electric builds a new head office in downtown Vancouver.
- Vancouver starts "owl" car service, running from midnight until 3:20 a.m., which costs a double fare.
- The Burnaby Lake line, B.C. Electric's third interurban line, opens for regular service on June 12, 1911, sparking "a major real estate boom....[but] much of the land immediately adjacent to the lake was bog. Few people actually built homes near Burnaby Lake. The company tried to arrange time tables to suit workingmen but the district did not attract settlers." [63] The line's short, very steep grades at either end made it difficult for freight operations.
- May is B.C. Electric's highest streetcar ridership month ever in Vancouver, with almost 3.5 million passengers.
- The 1911 Dominion government census gives these population figures: Vancouver 108,597; South Vancouver 16,126; Point Grey 4,320; and North Vancouver 8,196. Vancouver now included Hastings townsite and District Lot 301.

Rolling stock a laughing stock

Vancouver's early streetcars did not impress all visitors. One immigrant, newly arrived from Belfast in 1911, broke up laughing at her first sight of one.

"That's the funniest-looking thing I've ever seen," Eleanor Quayle reportedly said, according to grandson Ted Gardner, a retired streetcar repairer. She was gazing at single-truck car 51 as if it had crawled out of some prehistoric swamp.

"She thought the first streetcars were ridiculous and rough riding with their wooden spindle seats," said Gardner. "She was used to double-decker buses in Dublin that had plush seats."

Despite the vehicles' lack of style, Ted's grandmother rode Vancouver's streetcars until her death several years later.

March 25, 1910, the company used eight extra cars to bring 3,500 people to the site. They saw Californian Charles K. Hamilton lift off in his Curtiss-type pusher biplane, some later claiming that he flew 55 miles per hour (88.5 kilometres per hour). Similarly, crowds thronged to Minoru Park in the late summer of 1912 to see car racer Barney Oldfield appear as a special feature at the horse races.

Baseball: B.C. Electric defies the law to transport baseball fans

From providing illegal passenger trips to financial support, B.C. Electric was a major player on the local baseball scene. The company paid for grandstands at a new baseball park in Vancouver at Ninth Avenue (now Broadway) and Heather Street in 1903, and ran special streetcar service to the games.

B.C. Electric defied the law in 1915 by operating regular Sunday baseball excursions on its Fraser Valley interurban line to Huntington, where fans disembarked and walked across the border to games in Sumas, Washington. Thanks to public transit, they enjoyed "a delightful half day through the South Fraser Valley" to watch two of the coast's top amateur teams, the Sumas team and B.C. Electric's own New Westminster team.

Since these trips violated the Lord's Day Act, a petition went before B.C. Attorney General W. J. Bowser, requesting that the excursions be discontinued. He rejected the request and, in his response, supported the initiative for expanded recreational opportunities: "[W]hile . . . I entirely disapprove of baseball games on Sunday . . . I do not feel that I would be justified in going to the extent of granting a fiat to interfere with the opportunity of those who have no other day to travel, taking advantage of cheap excursions to get away from our congested centers and go into the country on the Lord's Day." [62]

Without interurbans, and with virtually no alternative transportation, thousands of sports enthusiasts would never have watched

STREETCAR AT A SIDING – This streetcar stands next to labour crews constructing a siding at Willingdon (formerly Queens) Avenue in Burnaby around early 1914. This track work formed part of the only streetcar line built from Vancouver to Burnaby; it proceeded east on Hastings Street from Boundary Road to Ellesmere Avenue for about two miles (3.2 kilometres). The line opened on December 22, 1913, and remained single-tracked for the life of its operation.

PHOTO SOURCE: CVA: 359-12

HERITAGE BUILDING – This artist's rendering, done in 1911, depicts a magnificent stone building that still stands today, enlarged and modified, at Carrall and Hastings: the former B.C. Electric head office and depot. It served as Vancouver's interurban depot for New Westminster- and Chilliwack-bound riders, beginning August 6, 1912.

Designed by architects Somervell and Putnam, the five-storey building cost $420,000 to construct; an imposing and massive structure at the time, it publicly symbolized the power and status of B.C. Electric.

The one track off Hastings Street split into two as it entered the depot, while another track from Hastings, essentially for freight movements, found room between the west side of the new structure and C.P.R.'s line between the waterfront and False Creek. (A tunnel under downtown would replace this line in 1932.)

PHOTO SOURCE: BC HYDRO: A0155

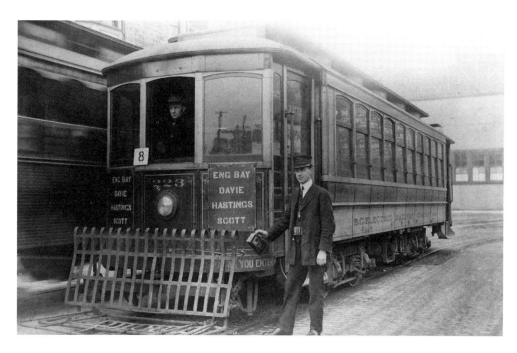

A NEAR-NEW NOVELTY – Car 223 appears almost new in this photo, following its arrival from Philadelphia in 1911. It was one of 30 cars, numbered 200 to 229, built by Brill in this eastern U.S. city.

Shown here with the motorman and conductor, this streetcar is on scheduled run number 8 in Vancouver. The destination Scott Street, which appears on the front of the car, refers to today's Fraser Street from Kingsway south to 5th Avenue.

PHOTO SOURCE: VPL: SC-10-5

CAR BARN STAFF — It took skilled men to keep Vancouver's streetcars operational every day, yet these employees often remained anonymous. This 1912 photo, taken of the staff at Mount Pleasant car barn at 13th Avenue and Main Street, gives the unsung heroes their due.

From left, inside the car: F. Williams, R. Richards, T. Condell, W. Shankster, R. Hutchcroft, F. Wheatley, C. Gray, F. Styles, W. Neilson, G. Davidson,

W. Hughes. Outside the car: J. McAllister, J. Pugsley, D. Gordon, J. Kerr, J. Meikle, D. Wylie, J. Pounds, J. Jones, F. Thomas, W. Grant, A. Viner, A. Jelly, W. Waybourne, J. Dew, H. Barrett, B. Cave, A. Juggins, T. De Roche.

PHOTO SOURCE: BC HYDRO:
THE B.C. ELECTRIC EMPLOYEES' MAGAZINE,
OCTOBER 1922, P. 17

their favourite teams or seen championship matches. Public transit provided the only link, and an affordable one at that, between city-dwellers and popular recreational events and facilities during the region's developing years.

Special Events: "All traffic on the line halted" for royal visits

> When His Royal Highness arrives on September 18 he will find a bustling city, cosmopolitan in its aspect, but with the same common spirit of faith urging its citizens to carry on the work laid down on the broad foundations of 1890.
>
> ***The Daily Province,*** **September 18, 1912**

Visits by royalty and celebrities to early Vancouver brought flocks of fans streaming to streetcars and interurbans. Similarly, holiday celebrations and opening ceremonies, whether for a new bridge or the city's first public exhibition, brought transit vehicles out in full force. Streetcars whisked hundreds and sometimes thousands of people to and from special events in a single day. Usually led by an observation car, streetcars often formed a fleet of parade vehicles, themselves a much-decorated part of the spectacle.

In those days, even funerals were grand affairs, and most Vancouver residents used a special streetcar line that travelled to Mountain View Cemetery. (The city's first cemetery-line streetcar ran on August 20, 1904, so that members of the Street Railwaymen's Union could attend a funeral; the 1.59-mile (2.6-kilometre) line began 20-minute regular service on September 16.) However, some passengers objected to the car's destination sign. In 1908, Fairview residents voiced their feelings about riding a streetcar named "cemetery"; spurred by a petition started by Reverend Ebenezer Robson, the name was scrapped and replaced with the more evocative "Mountain View," the name of the cemetery. [64]

A new Granville Bridge opened on September 6, 1909 – a long-overdue replacement for the city's original decrepit, near-condemned bridge. In line with the times, the city hosted the event with much fanfare. Earl Grey, Canada's governor general, and Mayor C.S. Douglas were among the dignitaries who rode in observation car 124 over the bridge and back to the Hotel Vancouver.

A CITY POISED FOR EXPANSION – This view, towards the northeast, shows the corner of Granville and Pender streets in 1911. The streetcar will turn onto the track in the foreground as it makes its way to Stanley Park. Its eastern terminus is Hastings Park, the site of the Vancouver Exhibition, on a route via Powell and McGill streets to Renfrew Street.

The one-storey buildings across the street will be razed in a matter of months to make way for the Rogers Building, as Vancouver gloriously remakes itself during the exciting second decade of the twentieth century.

PHOTO SOURCE: CVA: BU P. 526.1 N. 482

B.C. Electric officials had cancelled streetcar service across the old rickety bridge, fearing its potential collapse. With the resumption of Fairview service, development of the west side of Vancouver and Point Grey would begin in earnest.

Streetcars provided access to another gala event in Vancouver – the city's first exhibition, which ran from August 16 to 21 at Hastings Park in 1910. Thousands piled onto streetcars to see Prime Minister Sir Wilfrid Laurier open the exhibition.

For a similar grand occasion, New Westminster's Empire Day celebration on May 24, 1911, B.C. Electric transported about 12,000 people to Queen's Park. Thirty-two extra cars were used: nine large interurbans; seven of the large, newer, double-trucked streetcars (briefly called "suburbans"); eight city cars and eight flat cars, besides the usual schedule. Only 15 minutes were lost on the entire day's schedule on the interurban line from Vancouver. (A special track along 4th Avenue, which led to Queen's Park, was used only for such special events and lacrosse games.)

Pole 1

BRIDGE TO THE FUTURE – Streetcars in 1909 still speed along the original Granville Bridge, built in 1889, in this view looking south. The new Granville Bridge in the background is almost ready to open.

PHOTO SOURCE: CVA: BR P. 13

A ROYAL WELCOME – The visit to Vancouver in September 1912 by Canada's governor general and his wife, the Duke and Duchess of Connaught, sparked celebrations across the city.

This monolithic arch was made for the occasion. It straddles Hastings Street in this view to the west, from Seymour Street. A few automobiles venture into streetcar territory, a harbinger of things to come.

PHOTO SOURCE: BC HYDRO: A0743

The biggest spectacle to hit Vancouver in these glory years was the 1912 visit of Canada's governor general, the Duke of Connaught, with the Duchess of Connaught and their daughter Princess Patricia. The couple had first visited Vancouver in 1890 and must have been surprised at the city's changes upon their return. To honour the occasion, B.C. Electric bedecked its head office with strings of lights, giving the building the look of a jewelled layer cake.

Transit workers remodelled and specially decorated interurban car 1304 as a cozy, private retreat or sitting room. They removed the car's seats and partitions and replaced them with plush lounge chairs and sofas in cream and green, trimmed by fancy white curtains and carpeting. On the outside, there was a new paint job with two royal coats of arms on each side; the name "Connaught" and the company's name were lettered in gold on both sides. (After the royal visit, car 1304 went back into regular service, with

A CORONATION CELEBRATION – A north-bound Robson streetcar seems marooned in a sea of humanity at Granville and Georgia streets, where Vancouverites throng to celebrate the coronation of King George V in London's Westminster Abbey on June 22, 1911.

The C.P.R.'s chateau-style railway terminus, soon to be replaced by an even larger structure, towers imposingly at the foot of Granville. At this time, Vancouver was only 25 years old.

PHOTO SOURCE: CVA: 99-159

A SIGNIFICANT MILESTONE – Crowds throng around observation car 124 on opening day of the new Granville Bridge. The observation car, built only two months earlier in B.C. Electric's New Westminster shops, has stopped to let Canada's governor general Earl Grey direct the official opening ceremonies. Streetcars trail behind, carrying dignitaries.

PHOTO SOURCE: CVA: BR N. 37.2

seats and partitions reinstated. Today, it is the only remaining Fraser Valley interurban and is located in a museum in the tiny village of Brooks, Oregon.)

A local newspaper gave details of the Duke's journey from the Hastings and Carrall depot to New Westminster over the Central Park interurban line on September 21, 1912 (the Duchess stayed in Vancouver). The car left downtown at 10:45 a.m.:

All traffic on the line had been halted at 10:30 a.m., all spurs and sidings had been spiked, and a pilot car with police officials ran five minutes ahead. Thousands of people gathered along the route to catch a glimpse and wave. From Edmonds, the party proceeded via the Twelfth Street routing into New Westminster, where an honour guard of 100 members of the 104th Regiment and its band welcomed the royal party. Continuing their tour by automobile, the Duke and his entourage visited, among other sights, the huge mill at Fraser Mills. The return trip to Vancouver, with motorman Freure and conductor Grimmer still on duty, was taken on the Lulu Island branch via Eburne.[65]

Two days earlier, the Duke and Duchess had officially opened the Connaught (previously Cambie) Bridge, which replaced an obsolete one built in 1892. (Despite its official name, locals never called the bridge "Connaught," preferring Cambie Street Bridge.)

CROWDS CRAM IN – The opening of the first Vancouver Exhibition on August 15, 1910 would have been a bust without this Powell Street streetcar line. The extension of the line beyond Nanaimo Street via McGill to Renfrew in May 1910 made it possible for streetcars to access this show in its relatively remote location at Hastings Park.

Many people, some clinging to a narrow rear bumper, squeeze onto rows of packed streetcars to attend the exhibition. (The extravaganza was a precursor to the Pacific National Exhibition.) This view looks south on Renfrew Street. The streetcars have just turned southward onto Renfrew from McGill Street. The streetcar at far right, which is looping onto Eton Street, displays an older paint job with a cream-coloured panel. In the right background is the exhibition's centrepiece, the Industrial Building, demolished in 1936. It was situated just south of today's Pacific Coliseum. The grandstand at the far left stands close to the site of today's racetrack.

PHOTO SOURCE: CVA 7-106

A DECORATED DEPOT – Only a year old, B.C. Electric's magnificent interurban depot in New Westminster marks the imminent arrival of the Duke of Connaught and his party aboard a specially refurbished interurban car on September 21, 1912.

This station, at the southeast corner of 8th and Columbia streets, had three tracks running through it. The structure was the hub for six of the company's interurban lines: Burnaby Lake, Central Park, Chilliwack, Fraser Mills, Marpole and Queensborough.

PHOTO SOURCE: CVA: L9N 943

UNDER THE ARCHES – Decorative arches, built by community groups or ethnic societies, were commonly constructed to mark a visit by a royal family member. These temporary structures spanned the full width of a street.

Here, streetcars approach an arch erected across Granville Street just south of Dunsmuir by the Progress Club – "Promoting Provincial Progress." This arch, along with nine others, hon-ours the September 1912 visit of the Duke and Duchess of Connaught.

The arch frames the post office at Hastings Street and the chateau-like C.P.R. station one block farther. The station, draped with flags and garlands, bears a sign that reads: GOD BLESS OUR KING ON WHOSE EMPIRE THE SUN NEVER SETS. [66]

PHOTO SOURCE: CVA 323-11

AN INAUGURAL RUN – B.C. Premier Richard McBride and the province's lieutenant-governor, Thomas Paterson, join B.C. Electric and municipal officials on the rainy morning of October 3, 1910, before the ceremonial first run to Chilliwack on the new interurban line. They have reason to be proud: the 64-mile (102.7-kilometre) line was Canada's longest interurban route; it cost $3.5 million to build and used no govern-ment assistance. This special occasion, which put B.C. on the map in many ways, warranted a formal program for guests with opening ceremonies, a luncheon and toast to the King. Chilliwack had a population of 1,500 at the time.

The train consisted of the following jade green cars, from left: 403 (later 1401), 402 (later 1301), and lead car 300 (later 1700).

PHOTO SOURCE: CMBC: ICR-03

A CREDIT TO CONSTRUCTION – The men of B.C. Electric's car-building shops in New Westminster built almost 200 vehicles between 1903 and 1914, the life span of these shops. Pictured here in 1912, the shop crew receives much-deserved recognition during the heyday of streetcar and interurban operations.

PHOTO SOURCE: BC HYDRO: A0778

A TRAM TAKES FIVE – This station, shown in an eastward view in 1912, served as the Vancouver terminus of the interurban line through Marpole to Steveston from its inception in 1905 until 1914. Granville Bridge, built in 1909, is in the background; a staircase from the bridge to ground level provides access to the station.

Interurban car 1203 was the first such vehicle constructed by B.C. Electric's own shop in New Westminster in March 1903.

PHOTO SOURCE: BC HYDRO: A0726

Robbers and Rogues Add Danger to the Ride:
"He called me a vile name under his breath"

Passage on an early public transit vehicle could sometimes be a hair-raising experience. A petty criminal might sit next to a sedate matron or a drunk and disorderly dock worker could harass a shy woman. A conductor did his best to ensure the safety of his passengers and minimize fare fraud or other crimes, but as a one-man security force, he didn't always succeed.

The simple act of fare collection resulted in fisticuffs for conductor Ted Roberts on May 27, 1912. After a passenger on interurban car 1212 refused to pay his fare between Edmonds and Highland stations, Roberts filed this report:

He called me a vile name under his breath, a name I would not take from anyone. I grabbed him and started for the door. He broke my hold and I got a better one. The car came to a stop and we both went through the door in the smoker, breaking it

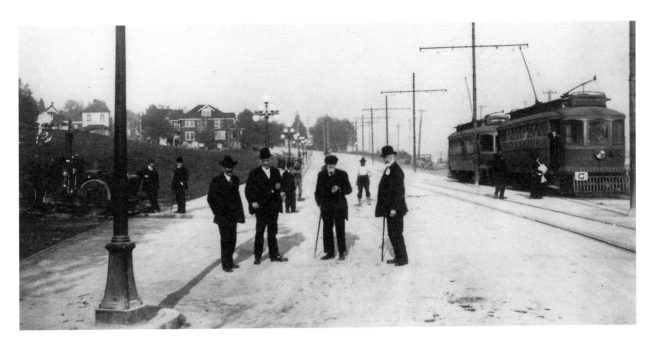

OVERNIGHT MODERNIZATION – Streetcars 100 and 102, clearly on show here in December 1912, have just gone into service in New Westminster, transforming the city's transit system overnight. The two-person, double-ended streetcars were two of a set of 12 built by B.C. Electric at the company's local shops for New Westminster service. It's possible that the stately gentlemen in this eastward view, which shows Columbia Street at Albert Crescent, are B.C. Electric officials.

PHOTO SOURCE: CMBC: SS-10-2

1912

- More than 60 per cent of B.C.'s population lives within B.C. Electric's territory.

- The B.C. Minister of Railways publishes a regulation regarding streetcar operation, stating that "on business streets of a City, speed must not exceed twelve (12) miles per hour, and on other streets eighteen (18) miles per hour."

- B.C. Electric announces on March 27 a $250,000 contract to the St. Louis Car Company for 22 passenger interurban cars (later increased to 28) and two baggage-express cars, the largest interurban car order it will ever make.

- One-hundred-and-forty streetcars operate in Vancouver during weekday rush hour.

- A five-cent settlers' rate is introduced on September 17 on the Point Grey streetcar lines.

- To meet its need for more vehicles as soon as possible, on November 26 B.C. Electric places a $500,000 order for 65 streetcars (later reduced to 40) with the eastern Canadian firm Preston Car & Coach Company.

- With a growing proliferation of line extensions and routes, more distinct and visible destination signs appear on Vancouver streetcars; for example, a rectangle with diagonal red-and-white lines signifies Grandview, a red ball on white indicates Hastings East, and a green-and-white diagonal sign means Stanley Park.

- The first on-board signal buzzers are installed for passenger use on December 22.

- Burnaby's population hits 15,000, an increase of more than 14,000 in four years, thanks to a real estate explosion.

- B.C. Electric discusses the use of motor buses for the first time.

and cutting my hand. I looked to see if he was cut as his head went through the glass. He then told me he would pay. He handed me 50 cents and I rung 25 cents for fare and 25 cents for glass. He got off at the next station. [67]

Three days earlier, conductor Joseph Smith had ordered three men off his streetcar as it left Carrall Street; they did not go quietly. "One of them used very bad language which I would not mention in a report," he states. Another pulled the streetcar's trolley off the wire as the vehicle started up. The last man grabbed Smith's leg and tried to pull him down. The men were arrested and fined $20 plus costs. [68]

While driving his streetcar along Hastings East in January 1912, motorman John Matthews learned that an automobile stopped on the tracks, apparently broken down, was not what it appeared to be. He reported:

Immediately after I stopped, a Man with his face completely Masked rushed to the front pointing a Rifle at me threatening to shoot if I moved one inch. Another rushed in at the rear with a Revolver in each hand threatening to do the same. We could see it was useless to give any resistance, so we had to leave the platform to the Street.

The Conductor was the first to get searched. They took the Cash Box and all his pocket money, I cannot say how much he had, then my turn came. About five Dollars they had off me. They took my traveling badge No. 50. I had it in a small leather case. We were then marched up to the rear platform of the Car and told to stop there or else they would shoot if we moved.

I then heard the Motor Car in motion. Thinking they had gone I made to go to the front intending to rush after. They fired on us. The second shot hit Conductor Baker on the top of his scalp. Four shots was fired. As soon as they cleared out I discovered they had robbed the Car of its Controller handle and also air handle, entirely paralyzing the Car from being moved. There was only one Lady Passenger in the Car at the time who attended to the conductor until I ran up to the Switch where the other Car was waiting her crossing. We made all haste to get the Wounded Man to Hospital. [69]

NON-STOP PROGRESS — Kerrisdale is just beginning to come alive in 1912. This image signifies a phenomenal amount of street railway growth. B.C. Electric's Vancouver-to-Steveston interurban line, recently double-tracked for faster, improved service, crosses in the foreground. A new platform and station have just been completed for northbound passengers on the added track. In the background, one of the company's new, large, double-trucked streetcars waits on 41st Avenue and West Boulevard in this westward view. The streetcar track between this connection with the interurban and Dunbar Street also opened in 1912.

PHOTO SOURCE: BC HYDRO: A0171

The September 18, 1912, edition of *The Province* reported two separate thefts aboard interurban cars. In one case, two pickpockets on a Central Park car accosted a wealthy rancher and blocked his exit at Main Street; they robbed him of cash, cheques and valuable papers. In another, a pickpocket robbed a Cedar Cottage resident of a purse containing $35.

In the following year, two masked robbers held up an interurban car on June 11 during its 9:30 p.m. run from Eburne (Marpole) to New Westminster. The men boarded the car with guns drawn and robbed 13 passengers, the motorman and conductor of $50 and a gold watch. After each thief backed away to an opposite end of the car, the crime duo jumped off into the underbrush and disappeared. Motorman Barnes is said to have made record time to New Westminster to notify authorities. B.C. Electric offered $250 for information leading to the men's arrest.

Outdoor Leisure: Passengers with feathers and fur ride in the baggage car

Thanks in part to public transit, outdoor leisure became a big part of Vancouver life in the early 1900s. Tourists and residents could board a streetcar or tram and easily get to a spectacular natural setting, from the North Shore mountains to parks and beaches outside the city. People could climb aboard an interurban and head to Burnaby Lake for ice skating. Hunters could put their dogs in the baggage car and head to the Fraser Valley, where there was plenty of game. Similarly, the interurban line provided access to lakes and rivers with excellent fishing. Annual picnics were a popular event for schools and businesses. Cycling clubs and informal hiking groups used the interurbans to seek out new terrain for their regular excursions; cyclists paid extra to store their "wheel" on the interurban.

With hunting and fishing gaining favour as male pastimes, Vancouver shops began to advertise camping gear by 1906. Meanwhile, the North Shore mountains were

SOUTH VANCOUVER NICHE – Two forms of transportation compete in this view that looks north on Fraser Street from 26th Avenue in 1912. The approaching streetcar was by far the most affordable choice and, in those days, proved more reliable, safe and comfortable than a car. The shops and businesses shown here, including City Heights Post Office on the right at 4122 Fraser Street, quickly appeared after the building of the streetcar line in 1909. This area was a key community within the municipality of South Vancouver, which did not become part of Vancouver until January 1, 1929.

PHOTO SOURCE: CVA: S9N 1017

attracting Vancouverites keen on hiking and skiing. Grouse Mountain, Lynn Valley and other destinations were easily accessible by streetcar.

B.C. Electric made its services more attractive to sports enthusiasts returning from the Fraser Valley by allowing them to board between interurban stations, as long as the conductor knew the time and day ahead of time. This made camping, and the loading of hunting dogs, fish or game, far more convenient. By 1920, the company published an eight-page pamphlet, *Fishing and Shooting along the BC Electric*, which included maps, descriptions of rivers, good fishing and hunting locations, dates of hunting seasons, and the best stations for disembarking.

B.C. Electric even offered services to a more obscure group of outdoor fanciers: pigeon racers. With their specialty birds stored in the baggage car, they could ride from the Lower Mainland to the Fraser Valley and stop at a predetermined station along the way to release their birds.

A September 13, 1912 newspaper ad promotes transit use to reach recreational activities.

NOTES

[1]   *B.C. Saturday Sunset*, Sept. 25, 1909, pp. 4–9.

[2]   Roy, "The British Columbia Electric Railway Company, 1897–1928," p. 92.

[3]   B.C. Electric Railway Company, Petitions, Box 158, Nov. 3, 1905.

[4]   Taylor, *The Automobile Saga of British Columbia*, p. 56.

[5]   BC Hydro Power Pioneers, *Gaslights to Gigawatts*, p. 27.

[6]   Yee, *Saltwater City*, p. 24.

[7]   McDonald, *Making Vancouver*, p. 115.

[8]   BC Hydro Power Pioneers, *Gaslights to Gigawatts*, p. 18.

[9]   *The Family Post*, April 5, 1952, p. 1.

[10] McGeachie, *Bygones of Burnaby*, p. 21.

[11] Takata, *Nikkei Legacy – The Story of Japanese Canadians from Settlement to Today*, p. 37.

[12] Adachi, *The Enemy That Never Was*, p. 27.

[13] Interview with Jim Wong-Chu, Jan. 14, 2002.

[14] Takata, *Nikkei Legacy*, p. 23.

[15] *Family Post*, March 20, 1952.

[16] Browne, "I remember . . . The trams rocking, rattling, rolling," *The Vancouver Sun*, Nov. 12, 1971, 3A.

[17] Browne, "Happier days on the trams," *The Vancouver Sun*, April 8, 1978, p. 6.

[18] "Down memory lane on a streetcar," *The Province*, April 10, 1992, p. A48.

[19] *Sunset Smorgasbord*, Aug./Sept. 1974, p. 6, cited in Celine Rich, ed., *Collected Memories*, p. 41.

[20] Jan. 3 1905 petition to J. Buntzen, BCER, Petitions, Box 158.

[21] Jan. 6, 1905 letter by J. Buntzen, BCER, Petitions, Box 158.

[22] Ewert, *The Perfect Little Streetcar System*, p. 6.

[23] Ewert, *Streetcar System*, p. 7.

[24] Ewert, *Streetcar System*, p. 29.

[25] *The Province*, Jan. 8, 1901, p. 1.

[26] BC Hydro Power Pioneers, *Gaslights to Gigawatts*, p. 26.

[27] "Down memory lane on a streetcar," *The Province*, April 10, 1992, A48.

[28] BCER, Petitions.

[29] Aug. 23, 1907 letter from R. H. Sperling, BCER, Petitions, Box 158-11.

[30] BC Hydro Power Pioneers, *Gaslights to Gigawatts*, p. 28.

[31] Nicol, *Vancouver*, p. 124.

[32] McGeachie, *Bygones of Burnaby*, p. 23.

[33] Oct. 24, 1911 petition to the B.C. Electric Railway general manager of freight dept from managers of local stores, BCER records, Petitions, Box 158-15.

[34] *The B.C. Electric Employees' Magazine*, July 1932, p. 17.

[35] "1909 Land Rush," *Collected Memories*, p. 126.

[36] *The Daily Province*, Sept. 9, 1909, p. 13.

[37] *Saturday Sunset*, Aug. 24, 1907, p. 16.

[38] "A Walk Along English Bay with Peggy Imredy, VHS field trip," June 25, 1977, Vancouver Historical Society newsletter, Sept. 1977, p. 5.

[39] *The Daily Province*, Sept. 1, 1909, p. 13.

[40] *The Daily Province*, Sept. 1, 1909, p. 17.

[41] Roy, "Electric Railway," p. 96.

42   Morley, *Vancouver – From Milltown to Metropolis*, p. 121.

43   Nov. 27, 1907 letter from The Hastings Street East Property Owners Association to Maurice R. Gifford, BCER Company files, Petitions.

44   1907 petition from residents and property owners of South Vancouver to B.C. Electric Railway Company, B.C. Electric Railway Company files, Petitions.

45   *The B.C. Electric Employees' Magazine*, Dec. 1925, p. 11.

46   *The B.C. Electric Employees' Magazine*, Dec. 1925, p. 11.

47   Preliminary report on electric railway project for Municipality of Point Grey by Cleveland & Dutcher, engineers, 1908, p. 8.

48   Light, "The Candid Camera Streetcar," *Westworld*, September 1981, p. 68.

49   Lyons, *Jokes by Teddy Lyons*, c. 1935.

50   Scullion and Thirkell, "Pedalling Photog Peddled Pictures to Passengers," *Vancouver Sun*, Aug. 5, 1995, p. D6.

51   Roy, *Vancouver: An Illustrated History*, p. 32.

52   McDonald, *Making Vancouver: Class, Status, and Social Boundaries, 1863–1913*, p. 172.

53   McDonald, *Making Vancouver*, p.174–5.

54   *Sunset Smorgasbord*, Aug./Sept. 1974, cited in *Collected Memories*, p. 35.

55   Reid and Lysell, eds., *The Days Before Yesterday in Cedar Cottage*, p. 35.

56   *Report of the Department of Railways of the Province of British Columbia, from 1911 to December 31st, 1916*, p. D 43.

57   Emily Carr, "Vancouver," *The Emily Carr Omnibus*, p. 425.

58   Interview with Fred Browsword by Murray Chapniss, *The Revue*, Feb. 13, 1991, cited in *Collected Memories*, p. 35.

59   Schrodt, "Taking the Tram: Travelling to Sport and Recreation Activities on Greater Vancouver's Interurban Railway – 1890s to 1920s," *Canadian Journal of History of Sports*, May 1988, p. 54.

60   Schrodt, "Taking the Tram," p. 55.

61   Schrodt, "Taking the Tram," p. 59.

62   Schrodt, "Taking the Tram," p. 58.

63   Roy, "Electric Railway," p. 126.

64   *Vancouver, The Golden Years 1900–1910*, p. 10.

65   "The City of Vancouver as His Royal Highness Saw It Twenty-two Years Ago," *The Daily Province*, Sept. 21, 1912, p. 15.

66   Harding, "Fanciful arches were temporary tributes," *The Vancouver Sun*, Dec. 15, 2001, p. F5.

67   B.C. Electric Railway records, Accidents file 146-4, Box 146.

68   May 24, 1912 incident, Accidents file 146-4, Box 146.

69   BC Hydro Power Pioneers, *Gaslights to Gigawatts*, p. 27.

1913-1915

The Future Beckons
1913 – 1915

A UNIQUE STREETCAR LINE — Even as the automobile gained popularity, the opening of the only streetcar line from Vancouver to Burnaby prompted fanfare and heavy patronage on December 22, 1913. B.C. Electric constructed the 10,000-foot (3,048-metre) Hastings Extension line on Hastings Street from Boundary Road to Ellesmere Avenue, the southern edge of Capitol Hill.

Car 305, double-trucked and double-ended, was built by J.G. Brill of Philadelphia in 1912.

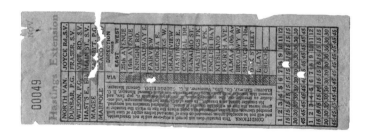

Cars and Jitneys Around the Corner

The shrewdest of railwaymen could not have predicted that the solid and capable trolley [streetcar], or the sleek and efficient interurban, would ever be just a memory. No one could imagine anything that could challenge the trolley's established place in the life of cities.

Sarah Riedman,
Clang! Clang! The Story of Trolleys

"Rails-to-rubber" transformation awaits

Public transit was well established in the Vancouver region by early 1913. B.C. Electric was in an enviable position: it maintained satisfactory relationships with both the municipal and provincial governments, it had no financial worries, the street railway and interurban system was practically complete, and its hydroelectric power system was well entrenched.

Later that year, however, the company's balance of power shifted dramatically. An ominous note was sounded in September, when the revised streetcar schedule showed less frequent service and higher fares. Ridership had fallen from the same month the previous year. In North Vancouver, ridership for the week ending September 27 dropped 12,577 from the same week in 1912, even though operating mileage fell by only two per cent.[1]

Vancouverites now had survival on their minds. Growing unemployment in B.C., combined with escalating conflicts in the Balkans, left many fearful and insecure. They did not want to pay more for public transportation and considered street railways a lesser priority. Most had lost confidence in the area's economy. The boom of 1896 to 1912 was over.

1913

- Vancouver streetcar fares are eight tickets for 25 cents in May.
- The recently paved Vancouver Road is renamed Kingsway in September and opens with a parade of automobiles and fanfare.
- The Pacific Highway opens on July 12, running from the Fraser River bridge to the U.S. border.
- A subscription to one of Vancouver's newspapers comes with the bonus of a building lot in White Rock.
- Coast Salish natives of the Kitsilano reserve sell their 71.6 acres (29 hectares) to the B.C. Government for $218,750. The land is valued at $2 million after it is divided into residential lots.

As a symbol of the changing times, a new streetcar line in South Vancouver – a section on 41st Avenue between Granville and Main streets – was built in 1913 but no vehicles ever ran on it. Discussions were held to extend the line eastward to Victoria Drive the following year, but that never happened.

That same year, the hobble skirt car, a deluxe import used in New York City, did not catch on when it arrived in Vancouver. Initially, the vehicle was received with great fanfare and its sophisticated lines and unique design symbolized how far public transit had come from its simple roots. But Vancouverites voted with their feet – they did not ride this stylish vehicle for long.

By the end of June 1913 the financial state of street railways was crumbling. The company's profit of $342,671 was a bleak $3,454 gain over its profit from five years earlier, even though it had done three million dollars more business in 1913. Meanwhile, the corporation's capital investment soared to $43.5 million in 1913 compared to $12 million in 1908.[2]

In the fall of 1913, after decades of wrangling with the city of Vancouver over franchise rights and right-of-ways, the street railway company announced that it might consider selling its Vancouver transit system to the city. Gone were its long-held popularity and power; moreover, there was growing competition from automobiles.

Not surprisingly, the number of passengers on Vancouver's street railway system dropped the following year. B.C. Electric's Johannes Buntzen felt increasingly victimized by the city's bureaucratic red tape. He complained that most city council members were "faddists or demagogues whose only object was to pander to the anti-corporation and anti-monopoly ideas."[3] Meanwhile, the last of the three Connaught interurban cars was put into service on May 1, 1914, marking an end to the artistry and craftsmanship of the New Westminster car shops.

Another major threat, jitneys or private fare cars, appeared in Vancouver in November 1914. They cruised streetcar lines, snatched up waiting passengers and rushed them to their destinations in less time than the streetcars. A spin in a jitney was the first time in an automobile for many passengers, and their first ride in a rubber-tired public transportation vehicle.

In November of the following year, Vancouver's public transit system suffered a sad and unprecedented blow: its first shutdown of operations. It closed a one-car shuttle line on Commercial Drive between Powell and Venables due to a lack of passengers. That same year, Vancouver citizens sought a reduction in public utility and fuel charges and persuaded city council to investigate the matter by appointing a special committee.

In Burnaby, realtors had focussed a large development scheme around the Burnaby Lake interurban line, expecting an influx of settlers and property sales, but this plan collapsed after the start of the First World War.

A SWEEP THROUGH SOUTH VANCOUVER – This 1914 view looks directly north along Main Street. A recently completed streetcar line extension curves to the west. It then swings east in the lower right corner of the photo to connect with B.C. Electric's five-year-old, Marpole–New Westminster interurban line.

This sweeping curve allowed freight trains to access Main Street, particularly to service the quarry at Little Mountain off 33rd Avenue. Marine Drive crosses Main Street at the foot of the distant hill.

PHOTO SOURCE: CVA: STR. P. 230 N. 277

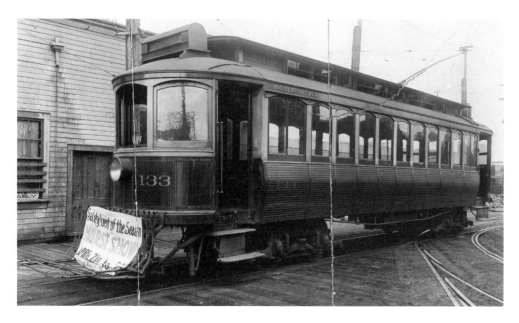

STILL-LIFE PORTRAIT – Streetcar 133 appears here four years after it was built in B.C. Electric's shop in New Westminster in 1909. Passengers entered at the rear of the car and exited at the front. Left-hand drive would prevail until January 1, 1922, when all vehicular traffic switched to the right side of the road. Car 133 provided unbroken daily service for 38 more years.

PHOTO SOURCE: BC HYDRO: A0012

A WELCOME ADDITION – By 1913, Vancouver's Main Street car barn was far too small to handle all the streetcars in service. A construction team rebuilt a section of the barn, which took up an entire block west to Quebec Street between 13th and 14th avenues. The section's southern half, originally open-roofed, was enclosed, enabling streetcars to park on the roof, which was structured to contain nine tracks and was accessed via 13th Avenue and Quebec Street. Off Main Street, 20 tracks of enclosed barn space were available.

In this 1913 view west from Main Street, the new concrete reinforced structure on the southern half of the block is under construction.

PHOTO SOURCE: BC HYDRO: AO165/46

By this time, street railway executives knew that their dominion over transportation had changed forever. For the first time, they discussed a new form of public transit, the motorized bus, which would threaten and ultimately replace their streetcars and interurbans.

Still a crude invention, the bus appeared to symbolize the changing face of public ridership. To have denied its future path would have meant suicide, yet transit innovators remained cautious. They viewed the bus similarly to how others had seen electric-powered streetcars 25 years earlier: this trend would involve risk and possibly tremendous error, yet it could have great advantages over previous methods.

Not from the far side

Another experimental New York streetcar accompanied the hobble skirt car when it arrived in Vancouver in 1913: the near-side car. (The name refers to the practice of letting passengers off "near," or before crossing an intersection, rather than after.) The late Ted Gardner, a transit vehicle mechanic at the time, remembered working on this streetcar at the Prior Street car barns. "It was a good running car," he said, noting that it had General Electric 67 motors. "The front had a very large vestibule with a smaller vestibule at the back." Although this special streetcar operated as a regular vehicle in Vancouver, Ted said that he only saw it once and little is known of it.

Without realizing it, street railway officials were launching yet another revolution in public transit – a far-reaching transformation of local roadways that became known as the "rails-to-rubber" campaign more than three decades later. This switch to buses for daily travel competed with the rising power of the automobile; it lay the groundwork for modern efforts to entice people out of their cars, particularly single-occupancy vehicles, and choose public transportation for commuting, instead.

Despite looming changes, streetcars and interurbans between 1913 and 1915 remained a catalyst for socializing and community-building: some chivalrous conductors escorted female passengers home at night between stops; streetcars delivered bundles of daily newspapers to streetcorner news boys; vehicles delivered prescriptions from pharmacists; young couples on a date could flirt and travel to trysts without a chaperone; and conductors chatted with passengers and brought groceries to at-home housewives. Friendliness, warmth and camaraderie between staff and passengers of streetcars and interurbans seemed to dominate, despite a depression, ever-increasing competition for dwindling fares and a large drop in transit popularity.

Today, such informal, folksy connections seem like a lost art in our impersonal, high-speed world of daily urban travel. One observer commented about Vancouver's bus system in the late 1970s: "Camaraderie between operator and passengers is sadly lacking. Everyone seems insulated against his fellow being. Glumness prevails. We seem to be suffering from New Yorkitis – a dreadful disease."[4]

By 1913 to 1915, the sizzle of the previous two decades had disappeared and everything – jobs, businesses, homes, families, transportation methods, street railway vehicles – was threatened. Survival, rather than huge success, shaped decisions for the future. The razzle-dazzle was over – it was time to regroup and recover.

Vancouver's Hobble Skirt Car: "It will prove one of the greatest enemies of the limousine and taxicab"

In the city's early days, when less than a handful of rough, open-air streetcars teetered along utilitarian tracks, a sleek, low-floor vehicle designed and built to accommodate women's fashion would have seemed loony. But within about two decades, the glamorous "hobble skirt car" with low-slung lines did indeed appear on Vancouver streets. Critics could argue it was all style, no substance, but this trendy piece of equipment symbolized the quick transformation of the city and its public transit. Fuelled by visions of grandeur, pre-war Vancouver demanded more than bare functionality in its buildings, and also required public vehicles to be top of the line.

The city introduced its first "stepless" car on March 18, 1913. Known as a "dragon" in California and a "public welfare" car in New York, it cleared the rails by a mere seven inches (18 cm). Women who wore long, constrictive hobble skirts, which limited their stride to only 12 inches (30 centimetres), could easily board

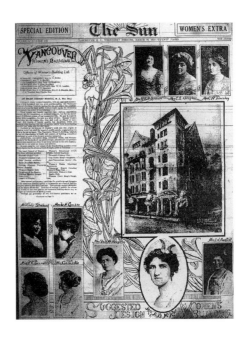

BARE CALVES AND ALL – A woman boards an open-air street-car in the U.S. in 1913, the same year that the hobble skirt car appeared in Vancouver. This flashing of bare legs was considered risqué for the times.

PHOTO SOURCE: LC 230516

The plight of lady passengers

Women rarely appear in transit-related photos or documents from Vancouver's glory years, even though they rode streetcars and interurbans every day. But they do receive mention as "lady passengers" in a B.C. government report on transit-related accidents between 1911 and 1915, where various women are impatient or headstrong, stride on and off still-moving vehicles, suffer nervous shock, have their dress torn, or receive cuts and scratches, bruises, sprains and other minor injuries.

A few wind up with broken ribs or end up unconscious after falling from a streetcar or interurban. One unfortunate woman has a miscarriage after a fall while boarding. Another emerges unscathed but with a lost purse and earrings following a 1911 collision between interurbans 1007 and 1011. Another female passenger in the same accident is reportedly shaken up and has her umbrella broken.[8]

Yet another woman saves the day with her hairpin, as reported in a separate incident around 1913. The only passenger riding on the Oak Street line, she provides assistance when the vehicle loses electrical current and stops. One account states: "Acceding to the motorman's request, she graciously surrendered her hairpin, and with its help, the car regained its spark and proceeded without further mishap to its destination."[9]

the car. Fashionable females no longer had to suffer torn seams or the impropriety of hoisted hems. They could board "without trepidation, a stepladder and a screen . . . [and] without the fear of a hundred curious eyes," announced the March 19, 1913, edition of *The Vancouver Sun*.

Car 500 made its "delightful" trial trip a day earlier. More than two dozen prominent women in furs and finery joined dignitaries such as B.C. Electric general manager R.H. Sperling and his wife on the "lady's street car." It left the Carrall Street interurban station for an afternoon outing and travelled over the Fairview line to English Bay, with passengers treated to "dainty tea and ices" on the return trip. *The Vancouver Sun* reported on March 19, 1913: "[T]he unanimous opinion of all those aboard was that the car is here to stay and that it will prove one of the greatest enemies of the limousine and taxicab, which came into such vogue when the tight skirt was decreed."

The hobble skirt car came into service the same day as another marketing triumph – the first women's edition of *The Vancouver Sun*. Two hundred genteel matrons peddled thousands of copies of the special issue on street corners and rode "bannered automobiles" to promote its sales. The "Women's Extra," written, edited and distributed by women, sold out in three hours and had a successful second printing the same day. As a fundraiser for construction of a downtown "women's building," this neophyte news section "was a success unprecedented in the work of club women in Canada," reported *The Vancouver Sun* on March 20, 1913.

Sadly, the hobble skirt car did not prove popular in Vancouver; it operated for only a few months, with chief motorman Sam Wilcockson often at the controls, mostly on the Fairview belt line. Passengers found its single middle door confusing and "a nuisance"; they were used to the convenience of a single-door front entry and double-door rear exit. While in operation, the car frequently lurched off the track due to its low centre construction.

SLEEK AND STEPLESS – Vancouver's hobble skirt streetcar, shown here in 1913, echoed transit and fashion trends in New York City. Despite its advanced styling, the car never caught on anywhere in North America.

A STAB AT SOPHISTICATION – Vancouver's society women pose with the city's only hobble skirt, or stepless, car on the day of its trial run, March 18, 1913.

An artist's drawing of a fashionable hobble skirt in a March 12, 1913 Vancouver newspaper.

WOMEN BEHIND THE SCENES – Female switchboard operators staff a new telephone system at B.C. Electric's head office at Carrall and Hastings streets in 1914. Women in Vancouver did not gain recognition or public involvement as transit employees until almost three decades later when B.C. Electric's Guides appeared in July 1943. These women sold tickets and provided rider information before passengers boarded streetcars. Eleven women started work as on-board "conductorettes" on October 12, 1943, replacing male employees then needed overseas. Canada's Selective Service Board ruled that only women would serve as conductors and only men over 45 as motormen. After the end of the Second World War, however, many conductorettes lost their jobs to returning servicemen.

PHOTO SOURCE: CVA: L9N 946

COMING IN TO CEDAR COTTAGE – An interurban coach, bound for New Westminster, slows to a stop at Cedar Cottage station at Commercial Drive and Findlay Street in 1913. Notice the attractive detailing visible in the construction of the station shelter.

The neighbourhood of Cedar Cottage, especially north on Commercial Drive from this point, had a delightful small-town ambience. It formed an important commercial stop along the Vancouver–New Westminster interurban line.

PHOTO SOURCE: GEORGE E. TIMMS PHOTO, VPL 7383

Adam plays escort in the eve

Female passengers on Burnaby's one streetcar line from Vancouver received the added bonus of an informal door-to-door escort.

A conductor known as Adam, who worked the late-night run for many years after 1913, gave his solo female passengers extra-gallant attention. When a woman got to her stop, he would park the streetcar, get off the vehicle and escort her to the door of her home. Presumably, he still managed to keep to his schedule.

In those days, running time for the Hastings Street car, which operated from Boundary to Ellesmere, was nine minutes one way. The streetcar left each terminal every 24 minutes from 6 to 10 a.m. and then every half-hour until midnight. This trip saved a lot of walking for North Burnaby residents.

But road conditions at the time weren't the best. Hastings Street wasn't graded and the streetcar tracks had to be laid below street level at one section. When the streetcar reached this point, it looked as if it were about to go underground. [10]

A PEAK TIME – About a dozen jitneys, or private taxis, compete with streetcars for customers on Hastings Street in 1914, a harbinger of things to come. Public transportation is soon to face a huge slump in ridership due to the growing popularity of automobiles and private bus and taxi service. This view looks east from the third floor of B.C. Electric's head office building and interurban terminus at Carrall Street.

PHOTO SOURCE: CMBC: SS-10-6

This bouquet got the boot

Two young women, newly arrived from Dublin around 1913, got off at the end of the 4th Avenue line at Alma Street, where tall trees surrounded the tracks. At the time, this area featured little more than swampy bush and a nearby creek.

The novelty of wild surroundings enthralled one of the women. She pointed to some yellow flowers with broad leaves and exclaimed to her friend: "Look at these beautiful flowers. Let's pick a bouquet."

The women eagerly gathered a large cluster of the distinctive flowers and brought them on board the streetcar on their way home. Within seconds, the conductor yelled at them: "Get those things out of here. They're stinking up the car." The women reluctantly heaved the flowers out the back end of the streetcar.

Ted Gardner grinned and laughed in the telling of this family tale: the women were his grandmother Adeline and her friend Isma — they had unwittingly picked an armful of skunk cabbage. [11]

"It turned out to be such a fizzle," said retired car repairer Ted Gardner in 2002. "It was underpowered and useless. It only had two motors and four axles with small wheels. The other streetcars had four motors with eight large wheels." The hobble skirt car got stuck going up from 1st and Main to Kingsway and Main, says Gardner, and it couldn't negotiate the hill up to Granville. By contrast, Fairview streetcars 260 to 274 "just walked up the hill with a standing haul," using their four 38-horsepower motors.

The one-of-a-kind qualities of car 500 ultimately proved too costly and inconvenient to maintain; the vehicle, built by J.G. Brill of Philadelphia, did not share interchangeable parts with the rest of the fleet and many of its mechanisms were reportedly hard to get at to repair. Besides, at a time when the average streetcar cost $8,000, the hobble skirt car came in at $15,704. (Gardner recalled one expensive feature of car 500 and 501: the leather straps used for standing passengers had ivory on them.) The car was withdrawn from service, its motors taken out, and the body sold for a mere $50 in 1939.[5]

However, the car's novel steel construction and 51 seats (most wooden streetcars of the day had 36 to 42 seats) seemed ahead of its time. New York Railways Company, which developed the car in 1912, decided that all new cars for its system would be stepless by the end of that year. Within a few years, 176 were built for use in that city alone.[6]

1914

1914 would be a year of going backwards, and a time to recognize that the golden years of 1909 to 1912 were phenomena, things of the past in more than a chronological sense, and that the world, indeed, would never be the same.

Who would have thought that Fairview-type car 274 would be the last streetcar ever built by the car shops when it poked its vestibule out into the sunshine of June 14, 1913?

Henry Ewert, *The Story of the B.C. Electric Railway Company*

- The First World War breaks out on August 4; the first troop train leaves Vancouver on August 21.
- The population of greater Vancouver is 175,000, comprising 42 per cent of the total population of the Lower Mainland. The city itself has almost 98,000 residents.[12]
- Eighty per cent of Vancouverites are of British origin.
- B.C. Electric has 232 streetcars in daily service.
- Frank Stillman Barnard (later Sir), one of B.C. Electric's founders, becomes B.C. lieutenant-governor.
- The third, and final, C.P.R. station opens in Vancouver.
- The Panama Canal opens on August 15, shortening the distance from Vancouver to London, England, from 14,292 to 8,700 miles (23,000 to 14,000 kilometres). This creates exciting new potential for global freight trade from both Vancouver and New Westminster.

Despite New York's backing, this had-for-a-fad streetcar did not catch on anywhere in North America. Instead, it spawned political concerns in Vancouver. W.G. Murrin, soon to become general superintendent of B.C. Electric's railway department, warned his superiors in a November 1912 letter that delayed introduction of the stepless car to Vancouver could prevent the company from gaining public recognition as an innovator; credit would go, instead, to a top provincial politician. In his words: ". . . a very serious tactical error has been made in allowing so great a delay. It might have been used as a very strong argument with the Attorney General that we were doing everything possible to keep ahead of the times, while now the Attorney General may claim the credit of having forced us to adopt lower stepped cars."[7]

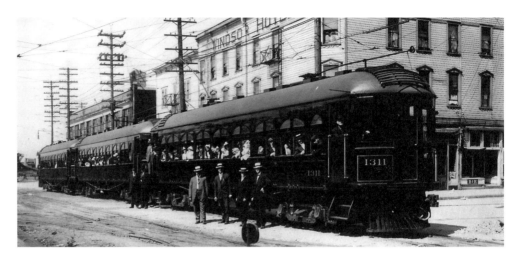

BOUND FOR GLORY – Three deluxe, recently completed interurban cars – named Connaught cars to honour the visit of the Duke and Duchess of Connaught – prepare to leave Front Street in New Westminster for Dominion Day festivities on the morning of July 1, 1914. The cars, 1311, 1310 and 1309, marked the end of an era. They were the last interurbans built by B.C. Electric's New Westminster shops; almost 200 interurbans and streetcars were constructed there between 1903 and 1914.

The train is bound for Chilliwack, a splendid 64-mile (102.7-kilometre) run. It has just pulled through B.C. Electric's New Westminster depot, the two-storey brick building in the background.

This train could easily attain a speed of 56 miles per hour (90 kilometres per hour). Each car was equipped with a toilet and water cooler. Notice the absence of bars or grillwork over the windows. The motorman's air whistle appears laterally above the windshield, before which he sits on a high stool. B.C. Electric officials pose outside the cars. From left: superintendents W. H. Elson, E. Sterling; company officials Webb and Spring.

PHOTO SOURCE: CMBC: IS-10-3

Transit Uniforms: "Gave a man an air of authority"

The motormen and conductors always wore blue serge suits. I remember Dad used to press them every Sunday morning. He did it himself because we weren't very wealthy people, and there were four kids. Dad used to use vinegar and water to take the shine off – you know how blue serge shines."

Carol Fraser, daughter of Godfrey James Payton,
a popular B.C. Electric motorman [13]

S plendid uniforms and a strict code of conduct promoted the image of early Vancouver's transit conductors and motormen as proud public servants with high status in the community. William Middleton writes in *The Time of the Trolley*: "A job in the street railway service was a highly prized one. A handsome blue uniform with brass buttons gave a man an air of authority, and the work was considered vastly superior to occupations that required manual labor." [14]

But human nature being what it is, not all transit employees adhered to rules regarding uniforms, which sometimes prompted a letter of complaint from a B.C. Electric official. The following, written by the company's manager of transportation on January 20, 1914, is typical: "I am advised that Conductor 298, on Run 4, Fairview line, is wearing a very badly delapidated [sic] uniform; the pockets are torn, and in the back there is a patch on his coat, and his general appearance is very bad . . . he is certainly no credit to the service appearing in a suit of clothes such as he appeared in on the 19th instant." [15]

Some transit employees charged that bearing a company number on their hat was akin to animal branding or identification of criminals. A 1913 letter from union representatives to general manager R.H. Sperling states: ". . . the idea of being numbered,

OPEN TO THE PEOPLE – Before the days of police escorts and secured vehicles, Vancouver's observation car 124 made the perfect transport for an official visitor. In this case, Canada's former prime minister Sir Wilfrid Laurier, his entourage and hosting dignitaries ride the decorated car in 1914. The city's special occasions always demanded streetcars and the observation car proved a valuable adjunct to the fleet. This view looks south on Granville Street from just north of Hastings, near Cordova. Note the Bank of Vancouver at the northeast corner of Granville and Hastings.

CLOTHES MAKE THE MAN – A streetcar motorman, clad in an overcoat and company-issued cap and uniform, poses at a time clock in this circa-1913 photo; this marked the first year that these clocks were installed. It was a motorman's responsibility to report his vehicle's on-time performance at the terminus of a streetcar line. The clock, a sophisticated instrument of its time, was kept locked, accessible only to B.C. Electric operating staff.

PHOTO SOURCE: CVA: L9N 1189.3

taged [sic], branded, or whatever you like to call it, is abhorrent. . . . the only thing it does for the public is to give them a leaver [sic] on a man's good temper (sometimes upsetting it) by following the company's lead and letting a man know that he is not named, but numbered, the same as a criminal." [16] Even so, it's unlikely that motorman No. 1, D. McLean, ever complained about his designation.

Some employees admired their new uniforms so much that if they left the company within a year, they took their outfits with them. Company correspondence indicates concern about the cost of the uniforms; it was hoped that in April 1914, a suit for motormen and conductors could be made for $18 or less, the same cost as an inspector's uniform. [17] Each inspector received two uniforms; one was free, and the employee paid half the cost of the other.

At first, Vancouver's transit uniforms were made of "Scotch cloth" because Canadian-manufactured fabric in 1906 proved of "poor material." [18] But in less than a decade, transit workers decried the use of foreign material for their uniforms. A Calgary official warned Sperling in March 1915 correspondence that "agitation" in his city advocated the local manufacture of street railway uniforms. [19] Perhaps fearing union unrest in Vancouver, Sperling wrote to the same official three days later that his company had entered contracts with two Vancouver tailoring firms who agreed that all related labour would be done within the city and solely by union workers. [20]

Meanwhile, it was expected that the wearers of these uniforms would serve as public symbols of exemplary behaviour. They were forbidden to smoke, drink or swear on the job. As early as 1892, a published list of "discipline and rules" for such workers appeared in the U.S., highlighting on-the-job regulations, such as: "A driver must not spit tobacco juice so that the wind will carry it on to the passengers." [21]

FROM HORSELESS TO HORSES – Vancouver's first streetcars were originally slated as horse-drawn vehicles. This one, pictured here as a city parade float on June 12, 1914, receives horse-power of another kind. Although advertised in this photo as "Vancouver's first street car," its identity is still in dispute.

PHOTO SOURCE: CVA: L9N 1009

THE REAL THING? — Despite its sign, this early vehicle, which sits atop a crude truck, remains unconfirmed as Vancouver's first streetcar; no streetcar with this appearance ever operated in the city or its region. It's possible that transit officials scrambled to find an aged streetcar after a request to display one of the city's first vehicles. Perhaps they brought in the vehicle from another region, such as Washington or Oregon.

As a parade float, it rides past B.C. Electric's head office at Hastings and Carrall. Some sources date this photo at 1915, but a knowledgeable source, *The B.C. Electric Employees' Magazine*, identifies it as May 19, 1920.

PHOTO SOURCE: CMBC: SC-10-15

A MYSTERY MACHINE – This photo, taken in 1914 or 1915, shows one of Vancouver's first streetcars, converted to an open-sided work car at the Carrall Street yards. It could well be contentious car 10, stripped to its barest form. Vancouver archivist Major Matthews and master mechanic George Dickie, an expert on B.C. Electric's rolling stock, insisted that this vehicle operated as car 10 in Vancouver. But another expert, William Rines, B.C. Electric's former supervisor of railway maintenance, believed that this streetcar operated as car 10 only in Victoria. Its origins remain a mystery.

PHOTO SOURCE: CMBC: SC-10-14

A CLASS OPERATION – This beautiful head office and interurban depot, photographed here in 1914, was one of the finest of its type in Canada. Designed by architects Somervell and Putnam and constructed for $420,000, it symbolized the power of the B.C. Electric Railway Company. Always known as "the Carrall Street station," it opened on August 6, 1912.

This view looks south from Hastings Street with Carrall Street to the left. The two interurban cars shown here, built in St. Louis, Missouri in 1913, were among 28 numbered 1217–1244; a restored 1231 runs along False Creek in Vancouver today. The last interurban train left this depot on July 16, 1954, signalling the closure of the station.

PHOTO SOURCE: CMBC: IS-10-6

The Competition

Automobiles: "devil-wagons" provide new rides

At the wheel of an open-air Ford, a jaunty woman with feathered cap and swirling scarf is pictured in the March 15, 1913, edition of *The Province* (see page 194). Behind her stretches a large banner headline AUTOMOBILE NEWS. The appearance of this dashing logo in a Vancouver newspaper, with its special section for a target audience, reflects the new presence of the car in daily life.

By this time, public transit vehicles were old hat, the source of commuter complaints, although brand-new streetcars kept arriving on city streets until 1914. In contrast, automobiles were the sexy new transportation toy, a symbol of status and greater freedom.

The B.C. car market flourished between 1911 and 1913. During this time, the province imported almost 5,000 new automobiles, half of them for the Lower Mainland. Most of the

THE PRICE OF SUCCESS – This electrical eyesore, which dominates a lane entrance west of Main Street at Pender in 1914, symbolizes Vancouver's progress in this era. Electricity affected the daily lives of residents, who came to depend on its benefits, and powered the city's street railway system. The mass of wires contrasts with the understated, decorative light standard that stands to the right.

PHOTO SOURCE: CVA: L9N 1241

new owners were executives and entrepreneurs who had benefited from the recent economic boom. One Vancouver resident, Ralph Shaw, recollects when licence plate numbers first topped 1,000. "Just think of there being more than 1,000 cars in British Columbia. The marvel of it all."

The first automobile ran on Vancouver streets on September 26, 1899, powered by steam. Industrialist John Hendry bought the city's first gasoline-powered car in 1904, the same year that Frank and Fred Begg started Vancouver's first car dealership. By 1912, there was one automobile for every 116 people in B.C. (Almost 400,000 people lived in B.C. in 1911.) By 1914, the province had 6,688 automobiles, compared to 263 in 1908.[22]

With many cars on Vancouver streets, accidents between automobiles and streetcars increased. By 1912–13, such incidents were reported regularly and it wasn't always the car driver's fault. In one case, in September 1913, the brakes of a Robson streetcar failed at Pender and Granville and it hit the automobile of sugar magnate B. T. Rogers. No injuries resulted, but the car's rear wheels were heavily damaged.

Automobiles were not universally loved. Early streetcar men called them "devil-wagons" and scoffed at their unreliability and frequent mechanical breakdowns.

ACCIDENTS WILL HAPPEN – A new air-controlled fender, with instructions for the motorman visible in his operator's compartment, adorns streetcar 284 at Prior Street car barn, off Main Street, in 1914. The protruding half of the fender would clamp up to the other, helping to keep people or animals out of harm's reach. The local media and the public lobbied heavily for the installation of fenders on the city's early streetcars to prevent pedestrian-related mishaps due to falls or collisions.

The large handle visible above the car's number was used to open the front exit door. This streetcar was built in Philadelphia in 1913. Adjacent vehicle F. 1 was B.C. Electric's only wrecking car at the time, dispatched with a work crew to any derailment or accident.

PHOTO SOURCE: CVA: L9N 1209.1

Transit employees had reason to act smug; streetcars had operated in Vancouver for 14 years before the first gas-powered car appeared in the city in 1904. A modern observer dismisses the city's first cars: "Grotesque looking monstrosities with big brass headlights, canvas tops, as often as not they stalled on a hill with either mechanical trouble or a flat tire. What were they to compete with well-established streetcar lines?"[23]

Motor buses: new options discussed

By 1913, the motor bus began to emerge as an alternative to the streetcar. Vancouver's city council hit B.C. Electric's street railway service with a direct challenge when it proposed an amendment to the city charter; the change would give the city power to run its own motor buses or give exclusive franchises to a private company for such a venture. B.C. Electric's George Kidd, who would become president in 1914, and the company's board first discussed the possibility of operating its own motor buses in 1912.

Bus transportation on a mass scale appeared an untested and dubious proposition, but as bus tires and bodies improved, the newfangled vehicles gained popularity. B.C. Electric ultimately joined the trend and started its own motor bus business after the end of the First World War.

Taxis: started in 1910

Henry Hooper started Vancouver's first incorporated taxi cab company in May 1913, after serving as chauffeur for the city's first gas-powered automobile, owned by John Hendry. Hooper operated his cab company on Hastings Street between Granville and Howe.

In Vancouver's early years, taxis refused to pick up Chinese passengers, prompting the Chinese to start two of their own taxi companies to service their community.

DAPPER AND DASHING – A crew poses with some fashionable hangers-on before a looming locomotive in 1914. The locomotive is one of a set of three, 990–992 (originally 911–913), purchased from Dick-Kerr Company, the British electrical giant, for B.C. Electric's freight business. All three survived well into the 1950s.

This view looks to the east on the north side of False Creek. The Granville Street station appears to the left; it was the downtown Vancouver terminus for B.C. Electric's Vancouver-Marpole-Steveston and Marpole–New Westminster interurban operations from 1905 to 1914.

Just behind the photographer is the trestle across False Creek, which the locomotive will cross to take its freight through Kerrisdale to Marpole and perhaps beyond.

PHOTO SOURCE: CMBC: IF-10-1

ANYTHING GOES – Anyone with an automobile could get into the jitney game during the First World War years. In this 1915 view southward along Granville Street from Davie Street, two jitneys hurtle towards Vancouver's downtown core while a streetcar stands in the distance. The jitneys bear the signage Fairview Belt Line, "borrowed" from the name of B.C. Electric's most-travelled streetcar line.

B.C. Electric had made huge investments in vehicles and infrastructure by this time, as shown in the outstanding track work visible here, and the company helped legislate the demise of competing jitneys in 1918.

Although jitneys brazenly stole waiting transit passengers, they created credibility for the notion of transit vehicles on rubber tires – an innovation still to come.

Jitneys: wild rides posed major threat

The biggest threat to Vancouver's streetcar service, which resulted in vastly reduced ridership and ultimately a transit workers' strike, came from the jitneys. These Fords, and some touring cars, vied aggressively with streetcars for their five-cent fares. ("Jitney" is a Yiddish word for a small coin or five-cent piece. The term first appeared, applied to these cars, in Los Angeles.)

Private drivers followed streetcar lines and lured passengers away; they overstuffed their jitneys, cramming the passengers onto benches. More than a half-dozen people usually piled in, sometimes grabbing on to retrofitted handlebars and even, according to former Mount Pleasant resident Ralph Shaw, "standing on the mud guards."

Jitneys zoomed along main streets, usually just a few minutes ahead of a streetcar to nab waiting passengers. Some even displayed the same destination signs as those used by streetcars. Vancouver's streetcars could not compete with these freewheeling competitors, who were often unemployed family men or returned servicemen desperate for income. Public vehicles were stuck with the limitations of their tracks, and forced to comply with a charter that limited speed and frequency of service. A streetcar took 42 minutes to cover the Fairview belt line, while a jitney bolted through in less than a half-hour. Moreover, a jitney owner had almost no overhead, since his vehicle required no right-of-way and no accident insurance.

More than 100 jitneys were operating in Vancouver by mid-January 1915; by the end of the month, that number jumped to more than 250, resulting in an average loss of $2,000 a day for B.C. Electric.[24] Public transit ridership declined dramatically after jitneys appeared, dropping by more than 17 million passengers between 1914 and 1915. In the same year, the company's revenues fell by more than $1.3 million.[25]

B.C. Electric responded with reduced fares to entice passengers back to public transit. (In Victoria, after a massive publicity campaign, the company introduced orange Tango Tickets, eight for 25 cents, on May 3, 1915. The origin of the tickets' name is unknown.) Ten days later, B.C. Electric reduced fares on the interurban line between Vancouver and New Westminster to compete with the jitneys on Kingsway. The company lobbied for support from both the municipal and provincial governments to regulate the jitneys; meanwhile, editorials sympathetic to B.C. Electric's difficulties appeared in *The Daily Province* and the *Victoria Daily Colonist*.

However, the company gained little sympathy from Vancouver's mayor L.D. Taylor, who scoffed that the "present management of the B.C. Electric Railway have only themselves to blame for their present plight, and like the rest of us must be prepared to meet business competition."[26] By December 1915, the company had received no nod of support for jitney regulation from any level of government.

The ever-increasing competition from private transport and resulting financial losses prompted a massive strike by transit workers several years later. This city-wide action redefined public transit as a unique and special service worthy of preserving. City residents could no longer view public transportation as just another means of travel; it was recognized as an established part of Vancouver's history and growth, never to be taken for granted again.

At Close Quarters: No chaperone required

Before cars, Vancouver's early streetcars and trams were a socially acceptable way for young men and women to meet. Those who might otherwise have remained strangers as they walked or cycled past each other could now chat at close quarters for the length of the ride. Best of all: no chaperone was required. A streetcar could carry young couples to Kitsilano Beach or English Bay for a sunset stroll. An interurban could whisk them away to a private country locale, away from prying eyes, or take them lakeside for a romantic picnic.

Transit staff weren't oblivious to their vehicles' often too-cozy conditions of intimacy. On a crowded streetcar, a conductor had to squeeze and push past standees, sometimes leaving room for close encounters of the unexpected kind. On a regular route, conductors soon knew their daily passengers on a first-name basis and some would find a girlfriend or wife among their favourite female patrons.

After disembarking, young couples could meet at streetcar stops and shelters while a transit schedule could help a young woman tell her watchful parents when she'd be back home at night. Even a stop at a transit terminus could make a memorable outing in itself. Vancouver resident Gladys Sutcliffe recalls of later decades: "Beside the streetcar terminus [in Kitsilano] stood a fish and chips stall which served the most delicious fresh-made-while-you-waited fish and chips this side of England. How toasty brown they were! What flavour!"[27]

Streetcars, in particular, made dating – and shopping – a snap as they offered easy access to downtown Vancouver and its panoply of commercial activity. One could, for example, have tea on the rooftop panoramic terrace of the luxurious Vancouver Hotel after buying dry goods at the well-stocked Charles Woodward's store or Hudson's Bay Company. The main post office and bank at Hastings and Granville were mere steps away from a streetcar stop.

Streetcars Deliver Bundles to Newsies: "We'd shout 'Extra, extra' with the war news"

ONCE A NEWSIE – Retired Vancouverite Ralph Shaw.

PHOTO CREDIT: HEATHER CONN

Long before today's media-saturated world, Vancouverites relied solely on newspapers to learn of current events during the First World War. (Vancouver's first radio station didn't begin broadcasting until 1922.) Downtown delivery boys, or "newsies," shouted out the headlines on street corners. (Newsies, usually 10- to 13-year-olds, occasionally went on to greater glory. Ralph Shaw, a retired MacMillan Bloedel executive in Vancouver, began as a newsie, as did author Jack London.) The young entrepreneurs waited each day for the streetcar to deliver their bundle of papers, which the conductor tossed to them from the front of the vehicle.

Shaw, now 97, recalls his days as a Vancouver newsie when the war broke out:

I remember the news of the big battles. The papers put out "Extras." They'd be delivered by the streetcars at 10 o'clock at night. We'd get them in our arm and

EXTRA, EXTRA, READ ALL ABOUT IT – A young newsie poses on Granville Street south of Hastings, circa 1910. These boys and their hollered headlines served as vital news sources during the First World War.

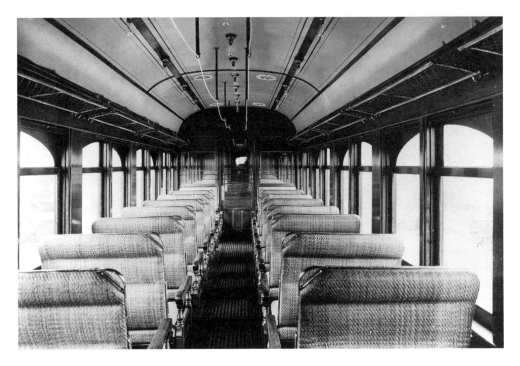

INSIDE A CONNAUGHT CAR – When B.C. Electric's car-building shop in New Westminster completed its construction program in 1914, it had made 147 large streetcars, numerous loco-motives, smaller single-truck streetcars, freight cars, work cars and 30 interurban coaches.

The last interurban cars built were numbers 1309, 1310 and 1311, dubbed Connaught cars; the interior of one of these, in a rare photo, is shown here in 1914. These beautiful cars were built for service on the company's Vancouver-to-Chilliwack operation. All three offered daily pas-senger service for the next 50 years.

THE END OF THE LINE – A streetcar has arrived at its south Vancouver terminus on Main Street. In this northward view, work has just begun to extend the streetcar line south across Marine Drive (River Road then) to connect with B.C. Electric's five-year-old Marpole–New Westminster interurban line. This was an extremely useful transfer point for South Vancouver residents. Service would commence on the new extension on December 7, 1914.

PHOTO SOURCE: CVA: STR P. 313 N. 276

Bomb scare:
a joke or German invasion?

Two Vancouver transit employees, both practical jokers, found an easy target for a prank in 1914. The start of the First World War had many civilians fearful of spy activity or a possible German attack and the two street railway workers decided to have a little fun.

They knew that the night-shift floorman at B.C. Electric's Main Street substation often dozed off after eating a large meal on the job. On their way to work through Chinatown, the pair bought a Chinese basket-bomb firecracker and hid it under the floorman's chair when he was half asleep.

After the two men lit the fuse and scampered to safety, a terrible blast rocked the night stillness. When they investigated, the floorman had disappeared, but he emerged soon enough, wild-eyed, convinced that German spies had placed the bomb in the station. He had two police officers in tow, leaving the two guilty parties to explain their part in the supposed sabotage.[30]

go running along the street shouting "Extra, Extra" with the war news and casualty list. We'd make 20 cents or a dollar…the mark-up on the papers.

I used to pick up my papers at 10th Avenue and Main Street, where the streetcars loaded and unloaded them. The streetcars were coming regularly but the [papers] weren't off the press when they were supposed to be. It was supposed to be 4:30 in the afternoon for the evening paper but sometimes it would be 9:30 at night. Late production. The early papers were The World, *which was taken over by* The Vancouver Sun. *Then the* News-Herald *started [about 1932]. Those were the early newspapers.* The Province *was being published then.*

Vancouver's Japanese community had its own newsies, who received bundles of the Japanese-language newspaper *Tairiku Nippo* from streetcars. Every afternoon, about a dozen Japanese Canadian boys waited for their papers outside the newspaper office. "Those first off the press were packaged for Steveston to be raced to catch the three o'clock interurban train," recalls one source. "Another batch was similarly dispatched to the New Westminster and Fraser Valley areas. Helpful conductors with periodic liquid inducements would drop them off at the proper stops to be picked up for home delivery. Only then did the boys get their allotment. With gunny sacks slung over their shoulders, they pedaled to their respective routes in Vancouver, all in time for evening perusal."[28] The rest of more than 3,000 subscribers received their *Tairiku Nippo*, an eight-page newspaper founded in 1907, by mail.

In Burnaby, when young newsie Charlie Brown took on a *Province* paper route, the papers came from New Westminster on the streetcar; the vehicle ran as far as the

1915

- Close to 200 jitneys seduce riders away from streetcars at the beginning of the year.

- The half-mile (.8-kilometre) Georgia-Harris Viaduct, worth $.5 million, opens on July 1; although double-tracked for streetcars, these vehicles never operate on it.

- The Ohmer fare register system goes into effect on interurbans on December 6 to make fare collection more efficient, but the mechanized system never catches on.

- One hundred and fifty-two streetcars operate in Vancouver during rush hour. This is a major drop in service from previous years.

- The first shutdown of public transit in Vancouver occurs November 1 with the closing of a one-car shuttle operation on Commercial Drive between Powell and Venables due to lack of passengers; it's a signal of the changing times and the end of the golden years of public transit.

- The Vancouver Millionaires win the Stanley Cup in the Vancouver Arena, off Denman Street.

- A depression hits Vancouver.

- Ridership in 1915 is 40,599,623 throughout B.C. Electric's system, almost 14 million below the previous year's figures. Freight hauled is down almost 100,000 tons to 258,029 tons.

Burnaby–New Westminster border at 10th Avenue and 6th Street. Occasionally, some-one would forget to load the papers onto the streetcar and the boys would have to wait until a bundle arrived. "Wish I had a dollar for every hour I sat waiting for those papers," said Brown, who served about 15 or 20 customers over a large area.[29]

Back then, streetcars didn't provide the speediest service. It was often quicker to walk from New Westminster home to Burnaby than to ride the streetcar, according to Brown. B.C. Electric extended streetcar service into Burnaby up 6th Street and along the former interurban right of way (Edmonds Street) to connect with the interurban. Locals dubbed this single-line streetcar route The Siberian Railway, presumably for its relatively isolated course. (In the summer, this line operated an open-sided car, to keep passengers more comfortable in the daytime heat.)

PRIME SHOPPING DISTRICT – Streetcars still rule in this 1915 view of Hastings Street, west from Carrall Street. B.C. Electric's imposing head office and interurban depot stands to the left. By this time, Hastings has supplanted Cordova Street as Vancouver's major shopping and business area. Almost 90 years later, this scene is easy to identify as many of these buildings are still standing.

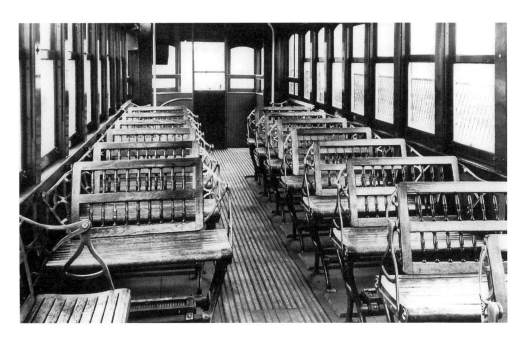

DON'T GET TOO COMFY – This photo, c. 1915, offers a rare peak inside a typical streetcar; few such interior views exist anywhere.

"I have fond memories of the woven wicker seats in the streetcars," recalled Jeannie Wong of southeast Vancouver. "During the summer, the seats would leave impressions on your legs. The backs of the seats would reverse so that when the streetcars changed directions, you could still be facing the right way." [31]

The walkover seats, despite their craftsmanship and easily repositioned backs, are clearly not designed for long-term lounging. Similarly, standees have nothing to hold onto, while the wooden-slat floors offer ample room for movement in the event of a sudden stop. The windowsills feature dark-wood finish above and green paint below.

PHOTO SOURCE: CMBC: SC-10-11

RARE, ON-SITE REPAIR – A maintenance man changes a trolley wheel on car 292 at the northwest corner of Main and Prior streets, the site of one of B.C. Electric's streetcar barns, in 1915. Such a change happened only rarely; a trolley wheel and its assembly were virtually foolproof and not prone to damage. This car was built by J.G. Brill of Philadelphia in 1913.

PHOTO SOURCE: CMBC: SC-10-18

NOTES

1   Ewert, *The Perfect Little Streetcar System*, p. 28.

2   Ewert, *The Story of the B.C. Electric Railway Company*, p. 119.

3   Roy, "The British Columbia Electric Railway Company, 1897–1928; A British Company in British Columbia," p. 79.

4   Browne, "Happier days on the trams," *The Sun*, April 8, 1978, p. 6.

5   William H. Rines Collection, property of Henry Ewert Collection.

6   Middleton, *The Time of the Trolley*, p. 116.

7   W. G. Murrin to B.C. Electric secretary in London, M. Irwin, in a Nov. 21, 1912, letter, Box 178, folder 1.

8   Report of the Department of Railways of the Province of British Columbia, from 1911 to December 31st, 1916, p. D 41.

9   McNamara, *Marpole – heritage of 100 years*, Vancouver, B.C., p. 20.

10   McGeachie, *Bygones of Burnaby*, p. 82

11   Interview with the late Ted Gardner, Feb. 4, 2002.

12   Taylor, *The Automobile Saga of British Columbia,* p. 82.

13   BC Hydro Power Pioneers, *Gaslights to Gigawatts*, p. 27.

14   Middleton, *The Time of the Trolley*, p. 362.

15   Jan. 20, 1914 letter from acting manager of transportation to James Hilton, B.C. Electric Railway Company, general manager's correspondence, Box 4.

16   Note attached to February 1913 letter, BCER, general manager's correspondence, Box 4.

17   April 1914 Letter from accountant E.H. Adams to George Kidd, comptroller, BCER, general manager's correspondence, Box 4.

18   April 18, 1906 letter from Sperling to B.H. Binder, BCER secretary in London, BCER, general manager's correspondence, Box 4.

19   March 22, 1915, letter from A.G. Graves, Calgary commissioner, to Sperling, BCER, general manager's correspondence, Box 4.

20   March 25, 1915 letter from Sperling to A.G. Graves, BCER, general manager's correspondence, Box 4.

21   Fairchild, *Street Railways – Their Construction Operation and Maintenance*, (1892), 1991.

22   Taylor, *The Automobile Saga*, p. 82.

23   Hall, "Devil Wagons and Trolley Cars," *Westworld*, Nov/Dec 1978, p. 40.

24   Kidd to Urwin, January 16, 1915, Box 62A-1163; Kidd to Urwin, January 28, 1915, Box 62A-1163.

25   Roy, "The British Columbia Electric Railway Company, 1897–1928," p. 205.

26   Roy, "Electric Railway," p. 213.

27   Linds, *Making History*, Kitsilano binder, p. 221.

28   Takata, *Nikkei Legacy – The Story of Japanese Canadians from Settlement to Today*, p. 34.

29   McGeachie, *Bygones of Burnaby*, p. 36.

30   *The Family Post*, May 15, 1950, p. 2.

31   *Collected Memories*, p. 35.

From Sleek to Obsolete to Repeat Performances

Gone . . . are the carmine-colored two-train street cars that could load huge crowds quickly. They had automatic doors and ran out to Joyce Road and to other far-flung areas. They were the sleekest mode of transportation Vancouver ever had on its streets.

Tom Browne, "Happier days on the trams,"
***The Vancouver Sun*, April 8, 1978**

Vancouver's glory years of rail-based public transit, so elegantly embodied by its interurbans and streetcars, were over after 1915. B.C. Electric had made huge investments in vehicles and infrastructure by this time, yet saw more of its business stolen by the thriving jitneys, to the tune of $350,000 a year. To try to maintain its customers and lure others back, the transit system grew more responsive; it created public timetables for the first time, increased vehicle running times, provided shuttle lines into downtown Vancouver and added extra streetcars at rush hour. As a public relations gesture in June 1916, it introduced a free informational leaflet, available on streetcars and interurbans, which still remains today: *The Buzzer*.

On the labour side, an eight-day strike for higher wages in June 1917 put almost all B.C. Electric conductors, motormen and car barn staff out of work. The following year, employees struck again for nine days over wage issues. In such unsettled times, the right to a fair salary grew increasingly vital. With strong lobbying from B.C. Electric, the city of Vancouver banned jitneys in 1918.

In the decades to follow, streetcars and interurbans continued to serve hundreds of thousands of Vancouverites each year, but the vehicles could not keep pace with buses and automobiles. Streetcars were dismissed as obsolete and were burned to oblivion on a regular basis between 1948 and 1955. Work crews methodically ripped up their tracks to make way for highways.

The city's last streetcar ran on April 24, 1955, and the last interurban on February 28, 1958. However, one of the city's long-disappeared interurban lines still left its mark almost a century after its inception. A large portion of its east-west route formed a blueprint for the path of SkyTrain, the advanced light rapid transit line that opened in Vancouver on December 11, 1985. (SkyTrain blends conventional rapid transit – subways – with light rapid transit and automated "people mover" systems; it operates driverless trains on an elevated dual guideway.)

Today, the lovely old public vehicles of Vancouver's early transit days are reappearing. Restored versions of interurbans 1207 and 1231 now operate as the city's Downtown Historical Railway, thanks to the efforts of dedicated volunteers and substantial city and provincial government funding. Efforts are underway by other local historical organizations to restore interurbans 1220 and 1223.

Such resurgence of history promotes public transportation at a time when cyclists, transit advocates and environmentalists seek to curtail Vancouver's car traffic and related pollution. Today, as in Vancouver's glory days, public transit improves our quality of life. May we keep the best of history with us.

INTERURBANS RESTORED — Cars 1207 and 1231, rescued from oblivion and thoroughly restored, operate B.C. Electric's old South Shore freight railway line, Vancouver's Downtown Historic Railway along the southern edges of False Creek.

PHOTO CREDIT: DIANNA EWERT

Bibliography

Books, Articles, Government Publications and Theses

Adachi, Ken. *The Enemy that Never Was*. Toronto, Ont.: McClelland and Stewart Limited, 1976.

Anderson, Kay J. *Vancouver's Chinatown – Racial Discourse in Canada, 1875–1980*. Montreal, Que.: McGill-Queen's University Press, 1991.

BC Hydro Power Pioneers. *Gaslights to Gigawatts – A Human History of BC Hydro and its Predecessors*. Vancouver, B.C.: Hurricane Press, 1998.

Burkinshaw, Robert K. *False Creek: History, Images, and Research Sources*. City of Vancouver Archives, Occasional Paper No. 2, 1984.

Burnes, John Rodger. *North Vancouver: 1891–1907*. North Vancouver, B.C.: Carson Graham Secondary School, 1971.

Collected Memories – A Guide to the Community Markers of South East Vancouver. Vancouver, B.C.: The Discovery Project for South East Vancouver, 1997.

Davis, Chuck. ed. *The Vancouver Book*. Vancouver, B.C.: Evergreen Press, 1976.

Ewert, Henry. *The Perfect Little Streetcar System*. North Vancouver, B.C.: North Vancouver Museum and Archives Commission, 2001.

Ewert, Henry. *The Story of the B.C. Electric Railway Company*. North Vancouver, B.C.: Whitecap Books Ltd., 1986.

Fairchild, C.B. *Street Railways – Their Construction Operation and Maintenance* (a photoreproduced version of the original edition of 1892). Edmonton, Alberta: Havelock House, 1991.

Hall, Frederick. "Devil Wagons and Trolley Cars," *Westworld*, Nov/Dec 1978.

Hamilton, Reuben. *Mount Pleasant Early Days: Memories of Reuben Hamilton, Pioneer; 1890*. Vancouver, B.C., City of Vancouver Archives, 1957.

Ito, Roy. *Stories of My People – a Japanese Canadian Journal*. Hamilton, Ont.: S-20 and Nisei Veterans Association, 1994.

Keller, Betty. *On the Shady Side – Vancouver 1886–1914*. Ganges, B.C.: Horsdal & Schubert, 1986.

Kelly, Brian and Daniel Francis. *Transit in British Columbia – The First Hundred Years*. Madeira Park, B.C.: Harbour Publishing Co. Ltd., 1990.

Kloppenborg, Anne, ed. *Vancouver's First Century: A City Album, 1860–1985*. rev. ed. Vancouver, B.C.: Douglas & McIntyre, 1988.

Knight, Rolf. *Along the No. 20 Line – Reminiscences of the Vancouver Waterfront*. Vancouver, B.C.: New Star Books Ltd., 1980.

Kobayashi, Audrey. *Memories of Our Past – a brief history and walking tour of Powell Street*. Vancouver, B.C.: NRC Publishing, 1992.

Light, Lois. "The Candid Camera Streetcar." *Westworld*, September 1981.

McDonald, Robert A. J. *Making Vancouver: Class, Status, and Social Boundaries, 18631913*. Vancouver, B.C.: UBC Press, 1996.

McDonald, Robert A. J. and Jean Barman, eds. *Vancouver Past: Essays in Social History*. Vancouver, B.C.: UBC Press, 1986.

McGeachie, Pixie. *Bygones of Burnaby: an Anecdotal History*. Burnaby, B.C.: Century Park Museum Association, 1976.

McNamara, Peg. *Marpole – heritage of 100 years*. Vancouver, B.C.: Marpole-Oakridge Area Council, 1975.

Middleton, William D. *The Time of the Trolley*. Milwaukee, Wisconsin: Kalmbach Publishing Co., 1961.

Morley, Alan. *Vancouver – From Milltown to Metropolis*. Vancouver, B.C.: Mitchell Press, 1961.

Nicol, Eric. *Vancouver*. Toronto, Ontario: Doubleday Canada, Limited, 1970.

Nielsen, Barbara. *Collingwood Pioneers: Memories of a Vancouver District*. Vancouver, B.C.: Collingwood Pioneers, 1991.

Reid, Glen and Alan Lysell, eds. *The Days Before Yesterday in Cedar Cottage*. Vancouver, B.C.: Gladstone Secondary School, 1968.

Riedman, Sarah, *Clang! Clang! The Story of Trolleys*. New York: Rand McNally & Company, 1964.

Rines, William H. Collection, property of Henry Ewert Collection, North Vancouver.

Roy, Patricia E. "The British Columbia Electric Railway Company, 1897–1928; A British Company in British Columbia." PhD thesis, The University of British Columbia, 1970.

Roy, Patricia E. *Vancouver: An Illustrated History*. Toronto, Ont.: James Lorimer and Company, 1980.

Roy, Patricia E. *A White Man's Province*. Vancouver, B.C.: University of British Columbia Press, 1989.

Scullion, Bob and Fred Thirkell. "Pedalling Photog Peddled Pictures to Passengers," *Vancouver Sun*, Aug. 5, 1995.

Sladen, Douglas. *On the Cars and Off*. London, Eng.: Ward, Lock and Bowden Ltd., 1895.

Stacey, Duncan and Susan Stacey. *Salmonopolis – The Steveston Story*. Madeira Park, B.C.: Harbour Publishing, 1994.

Takata, Toyo. *Nikkei Legacy – The Story of Japanese Canadians from Settlement to Today*. Toronto, Ont.: NC Press Ltd., 1983.

Taylor, G. W. *The Automobile Saga of British Columbia, 1864–1914*. Victoria, B.C.: Morriss Publishing, 1984.

Vancouver, The Golden Years 1900–1910. Vancouver, BC: The Vancouver Museum and Planetarium Association, 1971.

Yee, Paul. *Saltwater City: An Illustrated History of the Chinese in Vancouver*. Vancouver, B.C.: Douglas & McIntyre, 1988.

Interviews

Ted Gardner, Sechelt, B.C., February 4, 2002, by Heather Conn

Jim Wong-Chu, Vancouver, B.C., January 14, 2002 by Heather Conn

Ralph Shaw, Vancouver, B.C., June 12, 2001, by Heather Conn

Newspapers and Journals

The B.C. Electric Employees' Magazine

The B.C.E. Family Post (also Intercom), William H. Rines Collection, property of Henry Ewert Collection

B.C. Saturday Sunset

The Buzzer

Canadian Journal of History of Sports, May 1988, p. 52–59

The Columbian

The Vancouver Sun (also *The Sun*)

The Vancouver Daily News-Advertiser (also *The Weekly News-Advertiser*)

The Province (also *The Daily Province* and *The Vancouver Daily Province*)

Vancouver Historical Society newsletter

Vancouver World (also *The Daily World* and *The Vancouver Daily World*)

Miscellaneous

B.C. Electric Railway Company Ltd. Papers including Letter Books, General, and Petitions, University of B.C., Special Collections.

Report of the Department of Railways of the Province of British Columbia, from 1911 to December 31st, 1916, Victoria, B.C.: William H. Cullin, King's Printer, 1917.

Photographic Sources

BC Hydro, Information Services, Special Collections

Burnaby Historical Society (Burnaby Community Archives)

Burnaby Village Museum

City of Richmond Museum and Archives

City of Vancouver Archives

Coast Mountain Bus Company, Photo Archives

Henry Ewert Collection

Japanese Canadian National Museum

Library of Congress, Prints and Photographs Division, Washington, DC

North Vancouver Museum and Archives

University of B.C., Main Library, Special Collections

Vancouver Public Library, Main Branch, Special Collections

William H. Rines Collection, property of Henry Ewert Collection

Photo Credit Codes

BC Hydro	BC Hydro Information Services, Special Collections
BHS	Burnaby Historical Society (Burnaby Community Archives)
BVM	Burnaby Village Museum
CMBC	Coast Mountain Bus Company, Photo Archives
CVA	City of Vancouver Archives
HE	Henry Ewert Collection, North Vancouver
LC	Library of Congress, Prints and Photographs Division
NVMA	North Vancouver Museum and Archives
RA	City of Richmond Museum and Archives
VPL	Vancouver Public Library, Special Collections

Appendix A

Some Rolling Stock Facts and Figures

Page of Photo

17   Interurban car "Steveston" was built by B.C. Electric in 1905, and renumbered 1207 in 1912 when it was rebuilt for multiple-unit operation. It was in service on the last day of interurban operation, February 28, 1958, and operates, refurbished, today on the Downtown Historic Railway.

18   Built by B.C. Electric in 1907 as interurban car "Sumas," it was wrecked in 1909 in "the Lakeview disaster" and rebuilt for multiple-unit operation as car 1216. In 1913 it was rebuilt as a mail-carrying passenger coach numbered 1501, and soon sent to Victoria to operate on the new Saanich interurban line.

22   Streetcar 12, built by John Stephenson Company, was one of the original six cars ordered for service on Vancouver's new streetcar line. Built in 1890, it was powered by two 30-horsepower General Electric motors and had a body length, not including vestibules, of 16 feet.

28   For streetcar 15, the information is identical to that of car 12 above.

32, 35, 45, 47, 56, 57   Westminster and Vancouver Tramway streetcar 2, very soon to be renumbered 7, was built by an Ontario firm, Patterson & Corbin, in 1891. As was the case with Vancouver's early streetcars, car 7 was powered by two 30-horsepower General Electric motors. W. & V. T. purchased seven 35-foot vestibuled interurban cars, numbered 10, 12–17, from Philadelphia car builder J.G. Brill in 1891 and 1892. All 10 of these vehicles welcomed their passengers with two upholstered longitudinal seats, and all 10, renumbered, would continue service with B.C. Electric upon its formation in 1897.

33   For streetcar 10, the information is identical to that of car 12 above, with the exception of its different window count in the same body length.

36, 113   For streetcars 10, 11, 13, and 14, the information is identical to that of car 12 above. Though cars 11 and 13 arrived, as ordered, as unmotorized trailers, they were quickly given motors, as this photo shows by their motorman's controls.

48   Double-trucked open freight car 4 was powered by four 50-horsepower General Electric motors; it was 33 feet in length.

53, 113   Streetcar 25 was built by Canadian General Electric in 1898. With one of its sides open, the other still closed, it was the first official streetcar in operation in North Vancouver, one of four streetcars that inaugurated service there. Severely damaged in a wreck in early 1907, car 25 was scrapped.

54, 74   Streetcar 21 was built by Canadian General Electric in 1897. As car 25 above, it seated 32 riders in a body, exclusive of vestibules, 21.5 feet in length.

66   Streetcar 24 was built by John Stephenson Company, car 27 by the Canadian General Electric Company. Each of these single-trucked streetcars was powered by two General Electric motors.

70   Streetcar 19 was rebuilt into a flat car with motors, numbered S-60, in 1905, and scrapped in 1912.

77   As well as streetcar 32, streetcars 24 and 36 also finished their careers in North Vancouver; they were former Westminster and Vancouver Tramway interurbans 14 and 16, respectively.

78   Thirty feet in overall length, streetcar 26 was built by Ottawa Car Company.

81   The streetcar in this photo is one of the three W. & V.T. cars, 6, 7, or 8, and still in that company's paint job, more than four years after B. C. Electric's advent.

82   Interurban car "Surrey" was renumbered 1204 in 1913 when it was rebuilt for multiple-unit operation. With 36 seats in its "parlour" and 20 in its "smoker," car 1204 would remain in service until its scrapping in November 1953.

85, 104   Interurban car "Richmond" was renumbered 1205 in 1912 when it was rebuilt for multiple-unit operation. Interurbans of this "name" class were powered by four 75-horsepower General Electric motors, and weighed more than 71,000 pounds.

85   Streetcar 71, double-trucked and powered by four 40-horsepower Westinghouse motors, was constructed in May 1906.

97   Streetcar 72 would be in daily Vancouver streetcar service until its scrapping in late March 1952. As other cars in this series, it weighed approximately 44,000 pounds and seated 42 riders.

111   Built by Ottawa Car Company in 1899, streetcar 31 seated 42 riders and officially offered standing space for a further 24. Later enclosed, this car would offer service until its scrapping in April 1926.

120   Completed in late 1905, streetcar 75 would serve Vancouver until its scrapping in March 1949.

121   Locomotive 900 would operate on B.C. Electric's Ruskin–Stave Falls line from 1923 until 1944, and be scrapped in 1948. It was powered by four 75-horsepower General Electric motors. Later in 900's career, it was renumbered 950.

122   Forty-foot closed freight car 107 was powered by four 50-horsepower General Electric motors. As express car 1801, it was used at Vancouver's Kitsilano shops as a mobile tools-and-supplies stock car from December 1925 until its scrapping in March 1946.

123   Built by B.C. Electric in 1905, express car 1802 operated on B.C. Electric's Ruskin–Stave Falls line from November 1922 until the line's shutdown in December 1944, after which 1802 was scrapped.

128   Streetcar 151 was one of a set of 10 (150–159) built in 1908 by John Stephenson Company. Car 151 was sent in May 1911 to North Vancouver for service there, ending its career in March 1947, one month before the end of streetcar service in North Vancouver. It subsequently became part of a short-lived motel complex near Ruskin.

131   Locomotive 503, earlier numbered 101, was built by B.C. Electric in 1899. This was the company's first locomotive.

133   Locomotive 952 was ultimately rebuilt into a snow plough and renumbered S-103. As such, this vehicle resides today in a railway museum at Snoqualmie Falls, Washington.

135, 136, 137, 189   Observation streetcar 124 weighed 35,200 pounds and offered seating for 50 passengers.

141   Streetcar 62 contained seating for 24 riders, 12 along each side of the car; it was one of a set of identical cars, 60 and 62.

142   Please see page 18 reference above.

147   In June 1930 sprinkler S-50's water tank was removed and weed-killing apparatus installed; with this new configuration came a new number, X-53.

147   Please see page 77 reference above. Cars 32, 34, and 36 were scrapped in June 1914.

149   Streetcar 178 was scrapped in May 1953.

152   Built by Canadian General Electric in 1897, streetcar 23 would soon after this photo have its vestibules enclosed and a more modern fender attached to each end of the car. To reverse direction, the motorman simply walked the trolley pole, by its attached rope, to the opposite end of the car, returning the pole's roller to contact with the trolley wire.

152   Streetcar 172, built by B.C. Electric in 1910, was scrapped in October 1951.

153, 195   Locomotives 990 and 991 arrived for service in 1909, 992 in 1910. Each was powered by four 160-horsepower motors. The original cost of each was $16,500. Locomotive 991 was scrapped in May 1951, the other two locomotives in December 1957.

154   As interurban car 1400, it was one of three "combines," passenger-carrying vehicles fitted up with a special express/baggage section, 1400, 1401, and 1402.

158   Streetcar 223 was scrapped in March 1950.

165 Interurban car 1301 was scrapped in November 1952, car 1401 in September 1951, and baggage-express car 1700 in November 1950. Each had four 125-horsepower motors.

166 Interurban car 1203 was the first of the series of "name" interurban cars built by B.C. Electric in its New Westminster facilities. Originally named "Delta," car 1203 was scrapped in February 1953.

167 After the cessation of streetcar service in New Westminster on December 5, 1938, cars 100 and 102 transferred to Vancouver for further service. Car 100 was scrapped in August 1949, 102 in July 1949.

176 Car 305 was rebuilt into a single-ended car in October 1945, but scrapped in November 1949. This car seated 44 riders and weighed 48,600 pounds.

179 Streetcar 133 was scrapped in October 1951.

183 Streetcar 500 was double ended and weighed 39,000 pounds.

188, 199 Interurban car 1311 was completed on May 1, 1914, the last interurban car built, or purchased, by B.C. Electric. Cars 1309 and 1310 had been built a few months earlier. Each of the cars weighed 81,820 pounds and seated 42 in the "parlour" and 20 in the "smoker." Each of these cars was slightly more than 55 feet in length, five feet longer than the "name"/1200-series cars. Cars 1309 and 1310 were scrapped in October 1954; car 1311 was saved but succumbed to vandals in a few years.

194 Streetcar 284 was built by Brill in 1913 and scrapped in February 1950. F-1 was built by B.C. Electric in 1911; it was scrapped in 1921 and its wrecking material transferred to a more modern wrecking car.

203 Streetcar 292 was scrapped in October 1952.

206 Please see page 17 reference above in regard to interurban car 1207. Interurban car 1231 is one of a series of 28 cars, numbered 1217–1244, purchased from the builder, the St. Louis Car Company, by B.C. Electric in 1913. Refurbished, it operates with car 1207 today on Vancouver's Downtown Historic Railway.

Appendix B

Streetcar Service in Greater Vancouver, 1890 to 1915
(Burnaby = B, New Westminster = NW, North Vancouver = NV)

Whenever possible, the date is that of the first day of regular streetcar service. When information is lacking or controversy exists, no precise date is provided. All information is derived from B.C. Electric's own records. To avoid confusion, present-day street names are used throughout.

YEAR	DATE	STREET	BETWEEN
1890	June 27	Cambie Street	Cordova and Hastings streets
	June 27	Carrall Street	Cordova and Powell streets
	June 27	Cordova Street	Cambie and Carrall streets
	June 27	Granville Street	Hastings and Drake streets
	June 27	Hastings Street	Cambie and Granville streets
	June 27	Main Street	Powell Street and 2nd Avenue
	June 27	Powell Street	Campbell Avenue and Main Street
1891	October	Columbia Street (NW)	Leopold Place and 6th Street
	October	*Edmonds Street (B)	Kingsway and 6th Street
	October	1st Street (NW)	Park Row and 3rd Avenue
	October	4th Avenue (NW)	Pine and 6th streets
	October	Leopold Place (NW)	Columbia Street and Royal Avenue
	October	Park Row (NW)	1st Street and Royal Avenue
	October	Pine Street (NW)	3rd and 4th avenues
	October	Royal Avenue (NW)	Leopold Place and Park Row
	October	*6th Street (B, NW)	Edmonds Street and 4th Avenue
	October	3rd Avenue (NW)	1st and Pine streets
	October 8	*Campbell Avenue	Hastings and Venables streets
	October 8	*Commercial Drive	18th Avenue and Venables Street
	October 8	*Hastings Street	Campbell Avenue and Carrall Street
	October 8	*Venables Street	Campbell Avenue and Commercial Drive
	October 22	Broadway	Granville and Main streets
	October 22	Granville Street	Broadway and Drake streets
	October 22	Main Street	Broadway and 2nd Avenue

1892   No new streetcar service begun.

1893	May 9	*Columbia Street (NW)	6th and 12th streets
	May 9	*Kingsway/12th Street (B, NW)	Columbia and Edmonds streets
1894	No new streetcar service begun.		
1895		Alberni Street	Chilco and Denman streets
		Chilco Street	Alberni and Georgia streets
		Denman Street	Alberni and Robson streets
		Hastings Street	Cambie and Carrall streets
		Robson Street	Denman and Granville streets
1896	No new streetcar service begun.		
1897		Denman Street	Alberni and Georgia streets
		Georgia Street	Chilco and Pender streets
		Pender Street	Georgia and Granville streets
1898	No new streetcar service begun.		
1899		Denman Street	Davie and Robson streets
1900	May 20	Davie Street	Denman and Granville streets
	September	Columbia Street (NW)	Hospital Street and Leopold Place
1901	No new streetcar service begun.		
1902		Main Street	Broadway and 16th Avenue
		Powell Street	Campbell Avenue and Semlin Drive
1903	No new streetcar service begun.		
1904	September 16	Main Street	16th and 33rd avenues
	September 16	33rd Avenue	Fraser and Main streets
		Davie Street	Granville and Richards streets
		Granville Street	Pacific Street and the V. & L.I. Railway
1905	July 4	"Kitsilano line"	Granville Street and Kitsilano Beach
1906		Frances Street	Victoria and Vernon drives
		Georgia Street	Main Street and Vernon Drive
		Vernon Drive	Frances and Georgia streets
	September 3	Lonsdale Avenue (NV)	21st Street and the ferry wharf
1907	January 18	1st Street (NV)	Lonsdale and St. Davids avenues
	January 18	4th Street (NV)	Queensbury and St. Davids avenues
	January 18	Queensbury Avenue (NV)	4th Street and Keith Road
	January 18	St. Davids Avenue (NV)	1st and 4th streets
	January 25	1st Street (NV)	Lonsdale and Mahon avenues
	January 25	Keith Road (NV)	Forbes and Mahon avenues

1907	January 25	Mahon Avenue (NV)	1st Street and Keith Road
	February 14	Grand Boulevard (NV)	Keith Road and 19th Street
	July	Keith Road (NV)	Forbes Avenue and Marine Drive
	July	Marine Drive (NV)	Keith Road and Mackay Avenue
		Broadway	Main and Fraser streets
		Robson Street	Granville and Richards streets
		Columbia Street (NW)	Braid and Hospital streets
1908	June 29	Lonsdale Avenue (NV)	21st and 25th streets
1909	May 13	Cordova Street	Cambie and Granville streets
	May 13	Granville Street	Cordova and Hastings streets
	September 6	a new Granville Bridge	4th Avenue and Pacific Street
	October 23	4th Avenue	Alma and Granville streets
	November 6	Hastings Street	Boundary Road and Campbell Avenue
	December 18	Dundas Street	Semlin and Templeton drives
	December 18	Eton Street	Nanaimo Street and Templeton Drive
	December 18	Templeton Drive	Dundas and Eton streets
		Kingsway	Broadway and Victoria Drive
		Victoria Drive	41st Avenue and Kingsway
	December 23	Fraser Street	Kingsway and 25th Avenue
		Fraser Street	25th and 49th avenues
1910	May 14	Eton Street	Kaslo and Renfrew streets
	May 14	Kaslo Street	Eton and McGill streets
	May 14	McGill Street	Nanaimo and Renfrew streets
	May 14	Main Street	33rd and 50th avenues
	May 14	Nanaimo Street	Eton and McGill streets
	May 14	Renfrew Street	Eton and McGill streets
	May 14	Grand Boulevard (NV)	19th and 20th streets
	May 14	Lynn Valley Road (NV)	Hoskins Road and Sutherland Avenue
	May 14	Sutherland Avenue (NV)	Lynn Valley Road and 20th Street
	May 14	20th Street (NV)	Grand Boulevard and Sutherland Avenue
	May 29	Lynn Valley Road (NV)	Dempsey and Hoskins roads
	October 11	Richards Street	Hastings and Robson streets
		Cambie Street	Hastings and Robson streets
		Robson Street	Cambie and Richards streets
	December 2	Broadway	Granville and Maple streets
		Broadway	Maple and Trafalgar streets
1911	January 13	Broadway	Commercial Drive and Fraser Street
	February 25	Alma Street	4th and 10th avenues
	February 25	10th Avenue	Alma and Sasamat streets
	February 25	Sasamat Street	4th and 10th avenues
	March 14	Fraser Street	49th and 59th avenues
	May 1	Fell Avenue (NV)	Marine Drive and 20th Street
	May 1	Mackay Avenue (NV)	20th and 22nd streets
	May 1	20th Street (NV)	Fell and Mackay avenues
	May 1	22nd Street (NV)	Mackay Avenue and Bowser Avenue and School Street

1911	July 17	Granville Street	Broadway and 16th Avenue
	September	Main Street	50th and 63rd avenues
	October 7	15th Avenue	Commercial Drive and Findlay Street
	October 7	Findlay Street	Commercial Drive and 15th Avenue
	October 7	Kingsway	Earles Street and Victoria Drive
	October 10	Granville Street	16th and 25th avenues
	November 16	Commercial Drive	Powell and Venables streets
1912	May 3	Kingsway	Broadway and Main Street
	May 20	Oak Street	Broadway and 16th Avenue
	June 6	Main Street	Marine Drive and 63rd Avenue
	June 10	Pacific Street	Granville and Richards streets
	June 10	Richards Street	Pacific and Robson streets
	June 10	Brunette Avenue (NW)	Columbia Street and Fraser Mills line
	August 25	Nanaimo Street	Broadway and Hastings Street
	September 9	King Edward Avenue	Granville and Oak streets
	September 9	Oak Street	King Edward and 16th avenues
	September 19	41st Avenue	Dunbar Street and West Boulevard
	October 14	Cambie Bridge & Street	Broadway and Robson Street
	October 14	16th Avenue	Main and Oak streets
	November 14	4th Avenue	Drummond and Sasamat streets
	December 2	Begbie Street (NW)	Columbia and Front streets
	December 2	Carnarvon Street (NW)	8th and 6th streets
	December 2	8th Street (NW)	Carnarvon and Columbia streets
	December 2	6th Street (NW)	Carnarvon Street and 4th Avenue
	December 9	Lonsdale Avenue (NV)	25th Street and Windsor Road
1913	January 19	Marine Drive	Oak and Hudson streets
	January 19	Oak Street	King Edward Avenue and Marine Drive
	June 2	Crown Street	16th and 10th avenues
	June 2	Dunbar Street	41st and 16th avenues
	June 2	16th Avenue	Crown and Dunbar streets
	June 2	Victoria Drive	54th and 41st avenues
	June 10	Fraser Street	59th Avenue and Marine Drive
		41st Avenue	Main Street and West Boulevard (no service ever)
	September 29	Kingsway	Earles and Joyce streets
	December 22	Hastings Street (B)	Boundary Road and Ellesmere Avenue
1914	December 7	Main Street	Marine Drive and the Marpole interurban line

1915   No new streetcar service begun.

* Initially, only interurban service, rather than streetcar service, was operated on these streets, including 6th Street between 6th Avenue and Edmonds, which meant very few stopping places.

By 1915, B.C. Electric was operating streetcars on 72 miles (116.25 km) of streets in Greater Vancouver.

Appendix C

Interurban Service in Greater Vancouver, 1890 to 1915

1891   October 8

Regular terminus-to-terminus passenger service began on the 14.25-mile (22.53-km) Central Park line, Vancouver to New Westminster, from the corner of Carrall and Hastings streets, along Hastings, Campbell Avenue, Venables Street, and Commercial Drive to 18th Avenue. From that point, Cedar Cottage, the route followed a 6.15-mile (9.9-km) private right-of-way to Edmonds Street and Kingsway, whence it accessed downtown New Westminster via Edmonds, 6th Street, 4th Avenue, Pine Street, 3rd Avenue, 1st Street, Park Row, Royal Avenue, Leopold Place, and Columbia Street. On May 9, 1893, a new line was opened between Edmonds and the depot on Columbia Street via Kingsway/12th Street, shortening the Vancouver-New Westminster run to 12.15 miles (19.55 km). On December 2, 1912, the Highland Park cut-off, 3.6 miles (5.79 km) between Highland Park and 12th Street Junction, was inaugurated for interurban traffic; this new line took the interurbans off Burnaby's and New Westminster's streets, speeding up schedule time, and finalizing the Central Park line at 12.5 miles (20.12 km).

1905   July 4

Regular passenger service began on the 14.55-mile (23.42-km) Vancouver-Marpole-Steveston line from its Vancouver station off Granville Street, two blocks south of Pacific Street. (Built as the C.P.R.-owned Vancouver and Lulu Island Railway and opened for service on July 1, 1902 as a steam railway, it had been leased, and electrified, by B.C. Electric.) On May 10, 1914, the Granville Street station was replaced by a new depot off the west side of Granville Bridge at 3rd Avenue.

1909   November 15

Recently constructed by C.P.R.'s V. & L. I. Railway, and leased and electrified by B.C. Electric, the 10-mile (16.09-km) Marpole-to-New Westminster line inaugurated passenger service, meeting the Central Park line's route at 12th Street Junction, half a mile (.8 km) before New Westminster's depot.

1910   July 1

Regular passenger service began on the 20.5-mile (33-km) New Westminster-to-Jardine stretch of the Chilliwack line.

1910   October 4

Regular passenger service began on the 63.8-mile (102.67-km) line from New West-minster to Chilliwack.

1911   June 12

Regular passenger service began on the 14.7-mile (23.66-km) Burnaby Lake line, a third interurban connection between Vancouver and New Westminster. Trains followed the Central Park line's route to Commercial Drive near 6th Avenue, whence they swung eastward onto a 9.7-mile (15.61-km) private right-of-way to Sapperton. From that point, they used the Sapperton streetcar line's track on Columbia Street to the New Westminster depot.

1912   June 10

Regular passenger service began on the 3.5-mile (5.63-km) Fraser Mills line ("Millside Sub-Division"). Trains operated from New Westminster's depot on the Sapperton streetcar line, turning from Columbia Street onto Brunette Avenue on a newly-constructed two miles (3.22 km) of track, of which the final .8 mile (1.29 km) was on a private right-of-way.

1912   September 16

Regular passenger service began on the 2.14-mile (3.44-km) Queensborough line from New Westminster's depot. Streetcars were used until December 7, 1913 when the Fraser Mills and Queensborough lines commenced operating as a single interurban line, 5.64 miles (9.08 km) in length.

No new interurban lines would be built in 1913, 1914 or 1915. Excluding streetcar line trackage, B.C. Electric was operating 111.19 route miles (178.94 km) of passenger interurban service in Greater Vancouver by 1915.

Appendix D

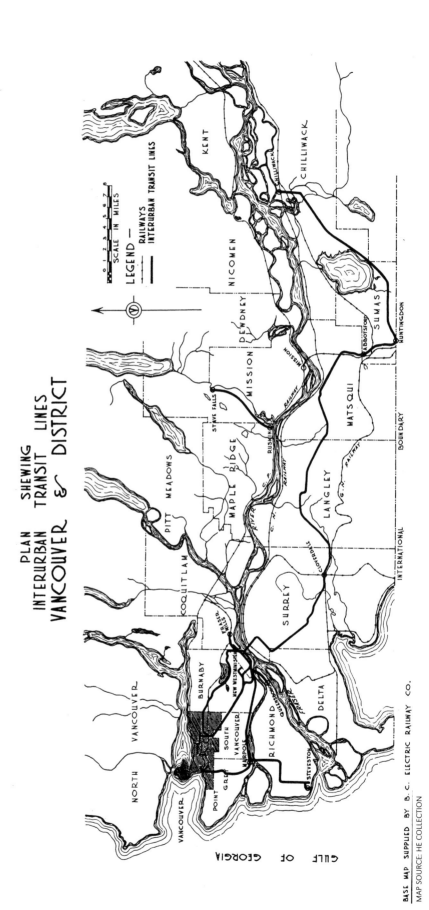

PLAN SHEWING INTERURBAN TRANSIT LINES VANCOUVER & DISTRICT

BASE MAP SUPPLIED BY B. C. ELECTRIC RAILWAY CO.

MAP SOURCE: HE COLLECTION

Index